on
vegetables

**modern recipes for
the home kitchen**

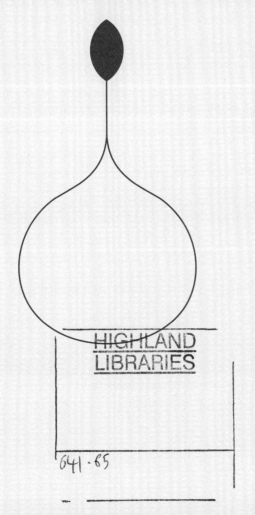

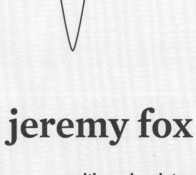

jeremy fox

**with noah galuten
foreword by david chang
photographs by rick poon**

Φ

foreword

It is not an understatement to say that Jeremy Fox makes the best tasting vegetables on the planet. Though not a vegetarian, he happens to be naturally gifted with handling produce, and his passion for seed-to-stalk, nose-to-tail vegetable cooking is undoubted. I've eaten great vegetable dishes all over the world, but no one has changed my views about produce more than Jeremy has.

The first meal of his I had was at Ubuntu, the vegetarian restaurant in Napa, California, where he was cooking vegetable dishes like I'd never seen. His peas, white chocolate, and macadamia exemplify how delicious a dish can be when suspended in the right time and place. That meal cemented, in my mind, an opinion I still hold today: Jeremy is one of the greatest chefs America has ever produced.

At Ubuntu, groundbreaking food came at a professional and personal cost. His well-deserved success took him away from the kitchen, and spiraled him into something much darker. I could relate to the burdens he endured during those years, but I never envied them. Chefs get into cooking for a multitude of reasons. Somewhere on that list—usually, high at the top—we do it so we can immerse ourselves in the kitchen. We put what's on the plate before anything else and choose to put life on hold. The irony though, is that as a chef rises to fame, he or she is often effectively pulled away from what they want to do most: cook.

Jeremy tells that story in this book, but he also tells his inspiring story of moving past that. He has come out on top at Rustic Canyon—wiser, more self-assured, and ultimately happier with the food that he's cooking. These days, he isn't cooking at the expense of his own life, his cooking is vital, and supports life. Rustic Canyon is among the best expressions of refined, local, market-driven cooking that exists today. Jeremy's beautiful dishes are, at the end of the day, just delicious food that you want to eat. His menu showcases the best that California has to offer and is a beautiful expression of the dialogues Jeremy has with farmers and products he works with every day.

On Vegetables covers all that ground and more. It's for both home cooks and chefs alike: it encapsulates Jeremy's hard-earned culinary insight and sense of humor; it reminds us of pleasures of being in the kitchen, and the life-giving power of food. It gives us a glimpse into the mind of a one-of-a-kind chef we're extraordinarily fortunate to have working today.

david chang

the whole plant

Pretty much every great chef in the world believes in what we call "nose-to-tail cooking." The idea is simple: If you're going to kill something, you damn well better not waste any of it. Well, we humans are supposed to be sentient beings, so we should probably all share in some kind of ethical responsibility in how we handle the creatures that we consume. Why kill a chicken if you only want the boneless, skinless breast? If you're hungry, and you want bacon, you've essentially decided that a pig deserves to die. So shouldn't we also be burdened with the task of using every last part of said piggy—hoof, snout, liver, kidney, and all? I, of course, say yes.

Okay, so why am I talking about dead pigs in a book about plants?

Well, what if cooking responsibly isn't just about honoring things with heartbeats? What if it's about more than that? I really hate throwing things away. Discarding edible food is incredibly wasteful. We have droughts, hunger, and rapidly depleting fossil fuels. But also—and I can't stress this enough—throwing away food embarrasses me. It makes me feel like a hack chef just going through the motions. I don't want to just cook nose-to-tail; I want to go seed-to-stalk, too. I want to cook the whole damn plant.

At my restaurant, Rustic Canyon, we don't throw away pea pods. We don't throw away parsley stems. We don't even throw away fava pods. Beet trimmings? Let's cook them into a beet gazpacho. Even the smallest scraps can be used as components of a larger dish. Carrot tops, fennel fronds, beet greens—use them all.

When you go to a farmers' market and they ask if you want the tops and greens trimmed from all of your vegetables, tell them no. In fact, tell them you'll also take all the tops and greens that everyone else left behind.

At this juncture you may be wondering if all of these scraps, shells, peels, and roots could possibly make the food taste better. In fact, you may even be wondering if it makes the food taste worse. But that, actually, is missing the point. Using everything should be the standard. It should be a challenge we put on ourselves not to be wasteful. So this is not the simplest approach to cooking, nor the easiest to standardize because of the varying factors of yield, but it might be the most functional. It requires you to cook thoughtfully, even frequently. Hopefully this book will inspire you to let each meal have a narrative, a through-line into whatever it is that you cook next. The tops from yesterday's carrots can be tomorrow night's pesto. Last night's roasted beets lead to tonight's braised greens.

So yes, it tastes good—hopefully very good. I work tirelessly and obsessively (I'm kind of a maniac) to make sure my food tastes great. But flavor is not the true purpose—it's just one of the desired results. The ultimate goal is to look at the plant as a whole, from top to bottom, and to learn how to cook better, smarter, and cheaper. I want to unlock flavors that have been undiscovered after the past half century of people assuming that certain bits are food and other bits are just garbage. This is by no means a full and comprehensive collection of everything one can possibly do with every part of the plant, but it's a start.

but first ...

Yes, this is a book about vegetables. Yes, this is a vegetarian cookbook. But I also don't want you to get the wrong impression. Vegetarian food does not need to suggest any connotations. It does not have to be "granola." The only requirement is that it contains no meat. That's it, plain and simple. While I greatly enjoy the healthful, vegetal pleasures of, say, Purple Haze Carrots with Yogurt and Sumac (page 99), I am also a man who will shake with excitement over thick-cut homemade bread slathered with butter, swiped with béchamel and mayo, stuffed full of three different cheeses, and then pressed together until the cheese melts and oozes out of the crispy, fatty, golden-brown bread. So yeah—sometimes you just need one of these.

... a grilled cheese sandwich

You should make the béchamel ahead of time, as you want it to be cold before putting it in the grilled cheese sandwich. As for the sandwich itself, you can substitute other cheeses if you like—any good melting cheese will do—though I'm especially fond of this combination.

serves 4

béchamel sauce
1 tablespoon (15 g) unsalted butter
1 tablespoon all-purpose
  (plain) flour
¼ teaspoon kosher salt
½ cup (120 ml) whole (full-fat) milk

grilled cheese
¼ cup (60 ml) béchamel sauce
  (above)
8 slices Pain de Mie (page 285),
  ¾ to 1 inch (2 to 2.5 cm) thick
2 tablespoons finely grated
  Parmigiano-Reggiano cheese
6 ounces (170 g) raclette cheese,
  thinly sliced
4 ounces (115 g) provolone piccante
  cheese, coarsely shredded
2 tablespoons Mayonnaise
  (page 268)
4 ounces (115 g) unsalted butter,
  at room temperature

make the béchamel sauce
In a small saucepan, melt the butter over medium heat, but don't let it brown. Whisk in the flour—don't let it brown either—and once it is incorporated, add the salt, then slowly whisk in the milk, a little at a time to form a paste. Once you have added about half of the milk, pour in the rest and continue whisking over medium heat, until the béchamel can easily coat the back of a spoon, 8 to 10 minutes.

Remove from the heat, taste for seasoning, and refrigerate, covered, until completely cool.

make the grilled cheese
Preheat the oven to 300°F (150°C/Gas 2).

Spread the cooled béchamel on one side of each of 4 slices of the bread. Sprinkle the Parmigiano over the béchamel and then start layering the remaining cheeses.

Spread the mayonnaise on the remaining bread slices and place them, mayo side down, on top of the cheese (like you're making a sandwich!).

Next up, you'll be grilling these sandwiches. Depending on how many pans you want to use, or how large your griddle is, you will probably need to cook these in batches.

Set the pan or griddle over medium heat. Butter one side of the sandwich and lay the sandwich, butter side down, onto the hot surface. Toast the sandwich, adding additional butter if needed. Meanwhile, butter the other side of the sandwich while it is in the pan. Once the first side is golden brown, flip it over and crisp the other side. You can also start to press the sandwich down with a spatula while it cooks.

This should be a slow process, as the goal is to have a crispy, gooey sandwich. If the bread is fully toasted but the cheese is not melted, finish it off in the oven.

I like to let the sandwich rest for 3 to 4 minutes before slicing, so that the cheese has a chance to set. Otherwise, the cheese may run all over your plate. This is not a bad thing; it just might be more of a fork-and-knife situation, rather than just being able to pick it up and eat it with your hands. Regardless, whenever it's done to your liking, cut it in half and eat it.

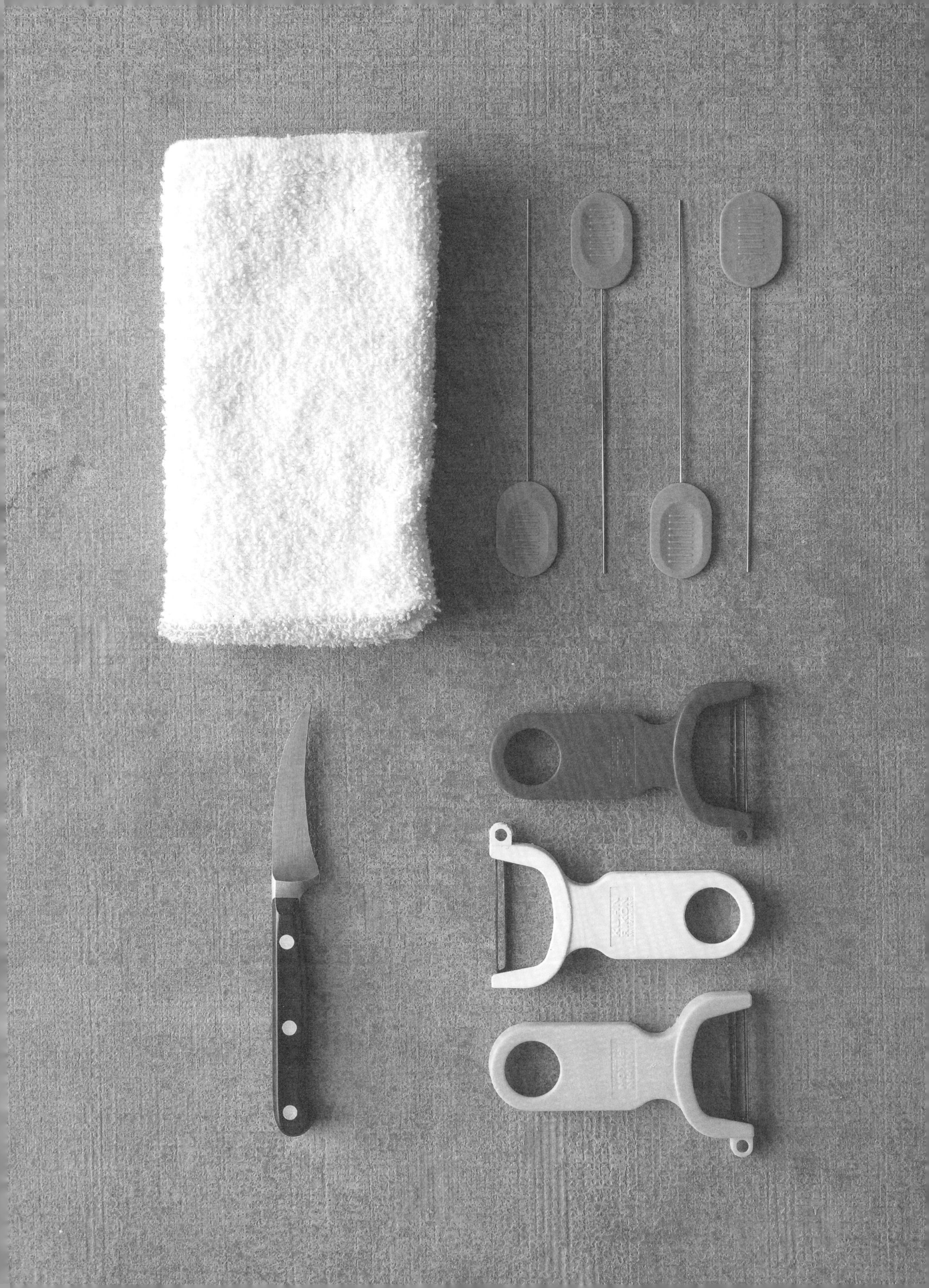

i am not a
vegetarian

To clarify: If you're looking for "10 Easy Weeknight Dinners for Vegetarians," this book will not be of much use to you. This is not a book about how to survive on a vegetarian diet. Why not?

Well for starters, I am not a vegetarian.

This is not a book about vegetarians: It is a book about vegetables. Or to be more specific, plants. In much of the world, there is often a mentality of either liking meat *or* vegetables.

I still eat steak. I cook pig trotters on a regular basis. I obsess over the many things to do with the head of a humanely raised hog. But I also believe that a carrot deserves the same attention. Yes, you can sprinkle salt over a ripe avocado and it will taste wonderful. But what else can you do? Plants, I dare say, deserve your full attention.

However, not all plants are created equal. I believe strongly in eating what grows around you, which is part of why I moved to California: I wanted to go where more things grow. I've had the absolute pleasure to work with, and get to know, some unbelievably kind and talented farmers, whose ingredients are the real stars of my cooking. That's why you'll find some of those amazing farmers profiled later on in this book.

If you've already started skimming through this book, you may have noticed that it is organized in the way that I think about cooking. What is growing locally right now? What do I have on hand? How can I stock my larder so that it makes me even *more* excited to cook?

So this is not a book intended to give you a full menu for your dinner party, or to show you how to throw together a vegetarian family brunch. This book, quite simply, is about cooking plants: to expose people to all the different things one can do with a vegetable. Maybe the Porcini Mushrooms en Papillote, Fondue of the Peels & Egg (page 166) would be a great dish to serve beside a grilled rib-eye. Perhaps you'll like making Radishes, Goat Cheese, Nori & Mustard (page 223) as an appetizer for your friends. It's really up to you.

The important thing to know is that when you find yourself cooking through this book, don't get too worried if you can't find the exact things that I use in my recipes. That is how I cook the things that I find in my surroundings. If your surroundings are different, you are going to want to adjust and adapt to those as needed. This is not a bad thing. Ultimately, I want this book to inspire you to change the way you think about vegetables, and to have the confidence to expand your horizons. I hope that this is not just a place you go to for a recipe—I want this to be a gateway to a whole new way for you to view cooking.

things i like

Squeeze Bottles

They are a convenient way to dispense liquids—whether it's olive oil, a condiment like Mayonnaise (page 268) or Black Olive Caramel (page 265)—with a lot of control over portioning. Squeeze bottles are not expensive, so you may as well have some around.

A Mortar and Pestle

Great for processing smaller amounts that wouldn't even work in a food processor: garlic paste, breadcrumbs, and especially nuts, since it won't turn them into a paste. You get to work with your hands and it's nice to feel like you're doing something primitive sometimes. You also have more control than you do with a food processor.

Flat Vegetable Peelers (Star Peelers/Y Peelers)

I prefer this type of vegetable peeler over the sideways ones because it gives me more control. If it gets dull, buy a new one. Don't be afraid to buy cheap ones and keep replacing them.

A Bird's Beak Knife

I use this more than any other tool in my kitchen. It's a fairly inexpensive knife—you can get cheap ones at the counter of your kitchen supply store. It's great for everything from trimming baby radish leaves, and getting the dirt off of carrots to peeling asparagus and coring tomatoes.

A Good Hat

I like to keep hair out of my food, but I like to look good, too. So if you can do both, that's pretty great. I still wear a hat in the kitchen, though most executive chefs don't anymore. But to me, there's no level of success that means your hair can't fall onto the food. Bandanas work too, but I'm unable to pull that look off.

Coffee Grinder

Great for small quantities of spices. I actually find that coffee grinders work better than specialized spice grinders. Keep a separate one for spices rather than coffee.

Cake Testers

A metal cake tester isn't just for cakes; it also works great for beets, potatoes, and other root vegetables, as well as meats, fish, and bread. It's basically great for testing interior temperature and doneness on everything. You can base your judgment on either resistance, or feeling the tester temperature with your finger after you insert it into the food.

A Kitchen Timer

Maybe you already have this on your phone, but *setting* timers is important. There have been a lot of times when I said "I don't need a timer, I'll remember," and that doesn't always work.

Forks

Great for mashing things like berries and avocados. Some people crush with spoons, but the rounded end doesn't work as well. I've seen people mash these things with a whisk too, but I think forks have more control, and don't get as much food stuck in them.

Sharpies

How else are you going to label your blue tape?

Blue Tape

This is commonly known as blue painter's tape. It's good to label and date your ingredients, especially things in your larder. Always cut the tape with scissors, don't tear it, or else bad things happen—namely, chefs like me yell at you.

A Digital Scale

Weight is more precise than volume. Some recipes are more exact than others, and that's when a scale is essential. Accuracy in bread making is especially important, and grams are more precise than ounces since they're smaller units of measure.

Sharp Scissors

How else are you gonna cut that tape? Also good for snipping fresh herbs.

Deli Cups

In restaurants we just called them "delis." Delis were something completely new to me when I moved from Atlanta, Georgia to San Francisco, California in 2001. We used to store things in old goat cheese and fruit puree containers—anything we could get our hands on. But once I discovered delis, everything changed. They are durable, airtight, reusable, and basically my favorite universal storage container. They're great for sauces, nuts, purees, stocks— honestly, everything. You may not be able to find them everywhere, but you can find them online or at pretty much any restaurant supply store.

Clean Folded Towels

This is a big part of setting up an organized workspace. Towels are for everything from handling hot pans and pulling dishes from the oven to wiping up spills. In a professional kitchen it becomes an essential appendage. Keeping them clean and folded is one of those self-discipline things. It's important to take all of the necessary steps to ensure success. If I see a cook with a crumpled towel on his station, that's usually an indication that he's ignoring a lot of other parts of his job as well.

adulthood, accolades & anxiety

There was a time when everybody told me I was a really big deal. The *New York Times* said that my restaurant Ubuntu was the second-best restaurant in the country. *Food & Wine* called me one of the best new chefs of 2008. I was told that I was the first chef ever to receive a Michelin star for a modern vegetarian restaurant, though I've never done the research to fact-check it. The hallways of Ubuntu were lined with press photos of me holding vegetables, and framed articles about the glory of this Napa, California, restaurant with a yoga studio attached, and its brilliant, game-changing chef.

I was that chef. I was also miserable.

Ubuntu was showered with accolades, but failing as a business. I was doing public appearances about clean, wholesome living, all while not really eating or sleeping. I was also taking a terrifying number of prescription drugs.

At this time I should probably inform you that the food in this book is not necessarily the food that I got well known for. When I was cooking at Ubuntu I was driven by anxiety and depression—it was dragging me forward while also running me into the ground. When it was bad, it infected everything. Solutions became inconceivable and all I could think to do was just put my head down and work. By the time I remembered to look up, it was usually too late.

At Ubuntu the plates were gorgeous, complicated, hypernatural displays, like edible terrariums. It felt as though the flowers on top of the dishes were like levitating bodhisattvas. The food, precise and exact, was the polar opposite of my mental state, which was scattered and foggy. It was unhealthy and unsustainable.

How I got to that dangerous place, how I came out of it, and how I finally learned to unite my food and my brain—is my story as a chef. Unlike at Ubuntu, the food in this book comes from a place of stability and clarity. It is the best food I've ever made.

I bounced around a lot as a kid. I was born in Cleveland, Ohio, but when I was in the middle of fourth grade, my mom went into rehab and I moved in with my dad and stepmom. By seventh grade I was living in a suburb of Philadelphia. Then my mom showed up for my sister's high school graduation, and she and my dad rekindled their whatever, so after that we all lived together in Atlanta, Georgia. Then they split up again and I went back with my dad for ninth grade. Then he got remarried and I moved back in with my mom. I ate a lot of fast food growing up. The only home-cooked meals were things like pork tenderloin stuffed with garlic cloves and cooked forever. My dad would roast brisket sometimes, but for just long enough to be cooked through and not even slightly tender. My first experience cooking was adding toppings to frozen pizza. On rare occasions I would actually go out to eat. The Cheesecake Factory was, at least back in high school, the height of luxury to me. Restaurants felt important, even then—they were places that could bring people joy, even if they had a hard time finding joy elsewhere.

But it was the Stanley Tucci movie *Big Night* that really got me interested in cooking for a living. It made the restaurant industry seem like a club I wanted to be a part of. I went to college for about a year and a half but hated college life, so I dropped out. Thanks to *Big Night*, the restaurant business seemed very artsy to me. I finally went to culinary school in Charleston, South Carolina, but it was not at all like it was in the movies. I got down on myself almost immediately. Everybody there was younger than me and had already worked in restaurants for a couple of years. So I worked full-time in one kitchen and worked as an unpaid intern at another, all while going to culinary school. By then I had been diagnosed with attention deficit disorder, which explained why I never felt capable of learning anything in school. To pass my classes I had to just ignore my teachers and teach myself everything directly from the book.

At one point I was working around a hundred hours a week, and because of the ADD I had started taking stimulants. At that point I needed it just to stay awake at night and get through work. But the drugs made me even more nervous than I already was. My energy got inefficient and scattered. I was napping in restaurant booths during my break just to try to survive.

The workload in restaurant kitchens was difficult and the hard work felt appropriate—but then, punishment always sounds appropriate when you have low self-esteem. I started out making seven bucks an hour as a line cook and there was a lot of mental and physical abuse that came along with it. The chef would throw plates at me, or have me hold out my

hand and whack it as hard as he could. I remember having put up a side of calamari sauce and then feeling the ramekin hit me in the back of the head because there was a drip coming down the side. In his defense, I never did put up a dirty ramekin again. I also hold zero animosity toward the guy. Quite the opposite, in fact.

In retrospect, I think that I climbed the culinary ladder relatively quickly. I became sous-chef, and then chef de cuisine at a fairly hip place called Mumbo Jumbo. Suddenly I'm twenty-four years old, making thirty-five thousand dollars a year, and fully embracing the kitchen culture that I had romanticized. Meanwhile, I was also searching for something that could drown out my anxiety. It was like there was a constant hole in my chest and I kept searching for something external to fill it. Eventually I found an issue of *Saveur* magazine about California and I immediately fell in love. I thought, "Well hey! Maybe that's what I've been missing this whole time! Maybe California is the solution to all my problems!"

I landed in the Bay Area two days before 9/11 and was making even less money than before. Thirty thousand dollars is basically nothing in Northern California. But once again I just put my head down and figured that working hard and ignoring my problems would solve everything. Of course, the anxiety was as bad as ever. I worked for a chef who was under a lot of pressure to open his new restaurant. We had an ungodly workload and the vast majority of it fell on me. I didn't handle it as well as I should have, so once the surprisingly positive review came in, I felt I'd done my part. I left, I went to Rubicon and then Charles Nob Hill before taking a job running the kitchen for a resort hotel in Aspen, Colorado. I thought that maybe I could elevate this type of food into something new, but I was unhappy almost immediately. The place was too corporate; I couldn't get the ingredients I wanted; and I didn't want to cook breakfast food, or room service, or banquet food. So, big surprise: I hated my job and thought it was everyone else's fault. At this point I had put myself in the unfortunate position of hating myself *and* everybody else. "I'm an artist," I told the general manager. "Let me do what I do." In truth, I was being a cocky asshole. My attitude got so bad that they finally had to bring in a task-force chef to replace me. Then I moved back to Northern California where I had no choice but to live with my girlfriend at her parents' house. Basically, I was lost.

And then I found Chef David Kinch. I had been a huge fan of his and had even tried to get him to hire me in the past. His new restaurant, the highly anticipated Manresa, was close to where I was staying, so I just showed up and begged him to let me *stage* (work for free). Right when I started, I knew it was the best kitchen I had ever seen: It was calm, focused, and wholly devoid of chaos or machismo. Quality trumped quantity. I loved it there and wanted very badly for it to be my home. Then one day a cook didn't show up to work, so they gave me his job.

My ego was so destroyed at this point that I craved grunt work. I used to love cleaning the walk-in. I knew that no matter what, I would work cleaner and smarter than everybody else. I realized that in my previous restaurants I had been more focused on the title of "chef" than on what the job really meant. At Manresa that all changed. I learned about substance instead of swagger. I went from hotel chef to kitchen bitch boy, but cared more about this job than any I'd ever had. I was so anxious about doing well that I started showing up hours before my shift and working for free. I was taking everything in, paying attention to all the stations. The other cooks would haze me and I didn't care. I just took it, kept my mouth shut, and got back to work.

Not much later, they had to cut back on staff. They were switching from being open seven days a week to just five. "I've got to let three of you go," Kinch told us, "but I haven't made my decision yet." Basically, he was saying that he'd decide who was getting fired during that night's dinner service. Well I had a horrible service and I was also the newest hire, so I was convinced that I was done. At the end of the night I was cleaning the walk-in and Kinch walked up to me, put his hand on my shoulder, and said, "Don't worry, you're safe." I think I probably cried. Looking back I can see why he kept me—I cared more about the restaurant than I did about myself at that point.

So I began to rise in the kitchen ranks yet again. I obsessed over ingredients and devoted my down time to practicing charcuterie and terrines. We grew our own vegetables and I began to learn about planting, harvesting, and cooking seasonally. I studied process and technique, slowly building my confidence back up and getting promoted along the way. By the end of my time there, almost five years later, I was chef de cuisine. It was the most stable and safe job I'd ever had.

At that point people had begun reaching out to me about head chef positions. But I was happy then, and creatively fulfilled at work, so I decided to be patient and wait for the right opportunity to come along. That's when someone introduced me to Sandy Lawrence, who was opening a vegetarian restaurant attached to a yoga studio. She was looking for a chef, and the plan was for the restaurant to grow as much of its own products as it possibly could—tying the kitchen completely to the garden. We would plant, grow, and pick our own produce, just like at Manresa, but with an even bigger focus on the vegetables themselves. It was beautiful there, and the idea of a simpler life really appealed to me. There were really no great vegetarian restaurants at the time (at least through my decidedly carnivorous lens) and, in my mind, I was finding my own place of peace. I would grow plants, make food, and live this idyllic, perfect life. It seemed like a pretty good plan.

So we opened Ubuntu. I was terrified of screwing this whole thing up, of embarrassing David Kinch, of the world finding out that I was a no-talent hack. But there was nobody telling me what to do, so I just started creating. I had no choice but to find new and exciting ways to use the truly wonderful produce that was coming out of our garden.

We weren't busy from day one, but we were executing well right away, which was impressive for a 120-seat restaurant with a tiny kitchen and almost no refrigeration whatsoever. The garden was the heart of the restaurant—what gets picked in the morning goes on the plate that same night. It wasn't long before Michael Bauer of the *San Francisco Chronicle* came in to review us. I probably plated most of his dishes myself, so I knew that if he was going to hate it, I would have nobody to blame but myself. Then the review came out and we received three-and-a-half stars, which was basically unheard of for a new restaurant. It may have been the most gushing review I had ever read. In fact, it was so positive that I disagreed with it. The attention alone made me anxious. I didn't even think that what I was doing was that good, or innovative. I was just working with what we had. I was waiting for everyone else to realize what I already felt about myself. It's funny looking back, because if he had given us fewer stars I would have considered myself a failure. Instead he gave us three-and-a-half and I felt like a fake.

adulthood, accolades & anxiety

After the review came out we got pretty busy. But Napa is a strange place, and ten years ago there weren't a ton of restaurants in the downtown area. During tourist season there are a lot of wealthy gourmands looking to indulge, but once the season ends, it's a city of seventy-five thousand residents who don't really want to eat fancy vegetables on a cold and rainy winter day. When the season came to a close we went from packed houses to only serving fifteen to twenty people a night. Another good review would roll in and it would help for a few weeks before it came back down to being slow again.

In fact, we were especially dead on the night when *New York Times* restaurant critic Frank Bruni came in. I didn't even realize it was him until after the fact. I even gave him directions back to his hotel after dinner. Not long after his visit, the *New York Times* called to confirm some facts, and I was fairly convinced that they were going thousands of miles out of their way to point out that a restaurant that nobody had ever heard of sucks. As it turns out, I was wrong. Remember when I said that the *New York Times* named Ubuntu the second-best restaurant in the country? Well this is when it happened. I was stunned, to say the least. Overnight we became busier than we could handle. Then, thanks to our success, the health department showed up. We had limited refrigeration and our farm was not certified by the state agriculture department. Technically, we were not allowed to serve vegetables that we had grown in our own garden. The health department gave us an "F". We had to spend close to $150,000 just to get everything up to code. But we did it, and got perfect scores every time from then on.

Then came more accolades. I was named *Chronicle's* Rising Star Chef, Dana Cowin named me as *Food & Wine* Best New Chef. Eventually, we earned a Michelin star. At first it was vindication for me—the external praise and accolades that I figured would finally solve all of my problems, both emotional and financial. The press would make us busy and I would be fulfilled. But the season ended, and once again we slowed to a crawl. Ubuntu was one of the most talked about restaurants in the country. We should have been booked up months in advance. We would be busy on weekends, and then dead on a Wednesday. In the winter we were doing only twenty to thirty covers a night. I remember that on one Oscar Sunday we had zero reservations. Literally zero. So we just closed up and went home.

Meanwhile, the seemingly endless array of press and publicity continued. There were speaking engagements and meetings with PR companies. Just over a year in, I was already taking anxiety pills. I was so stressed out by the attention and all of the flying to events. It started with a few pills to get me through the flights. Then the anxiety got worse. The pressure of public speaking and becoming a "food celebrity" was too much for me to handle. I saw a specialist who just gave me the kitchen sink: stimulants for my ADD, tranquilizers and sleep aids to help me at night, and antidepressants for my overall mood. I had used different stimulants in the past and taken way too much— way above my prescription. But I thought maybe I was better at controlling myself this time around. I should have been better at reigning myself in. At the time I felt like I needed the drugs to get me through. The idea of putting on a happy face and meeting with a PR company gave me a crippling stress. I followed the prescriptions at first, but then I would have to meet with editors at elite food magazines, so I took extra stimulants because they perked me up and made me more talkative. It was hard to stop taking the drugs because, frankly, they worked. I was supposed to be representing this health-forward restaurant and lifestyle, and I was going to In-N-Out after work, scarfing down cheeseburgers and anti-anxiety pills.

I was going down a dark path, but I sort of just put my head down and let the pills do their job. I knew that people I cared about liked my food. Jean-Georges Vongerichten came in, ate with his hands, asking for another helping of the peas with white chocolate. David Chang and Thomas Keller ate there as well. René Redzepi called it his favorite meal of the year. That's when I realized that we were going to be influential but not successful—that at best we were going to be the band that inspired The Beatles, but a band whose name nobody would ever remember.

The critical acclaim had lead to an inevitable backlash, the drugs were taking over, and I was becoming toxic again. I turned inward, and that's when things tend to go badly for me. My personal life had started spilling over into the kitchen. I was supposed to be this stoic leader, but I was showing big, deep cracks. My chest felt like it was either going to explode or collapse. I can't imagine that I was a good boss, or even mildly enjoyable to be around.

Everything had finally boiled over, so I sat down with Sandy, our owner, and she acknowledged that this thing wasn't working anymore. I don't think I wanted to leave—I just wanted this awful feeling to go away. She offered me my "dining allowance" of eight thousand dollars—the restaurant equivalent of your dad handing you a wad of sweaty bills before he kicks you out of the house for good.

How had everything gone so bad so quickly? Once again I was angry, bitter, and lost. I went to Los Angeles to cook a series of dinners at a restaurant called Animal and thought it would be a good idea to go totally off my meds, cold turkey. I was a wreck. I had no focus, no time management, and what essentially amounted to the worst version of ADD I'd ever had. I was a "dry drunk," but with pills instead of booze. By the end of the week they had basically kicked me out of the kitchen and just had me going into the dining room to shake hands and say hi. To be honest, I wasn't even sure I wanted to cook anymore. A turnip looked like a stranger. The *Los Angeles Times* was even running a "Jeremy Fox Watch." I became the food tabloid version of the Kardashians. I was still off the meds, but it didn't feel all that different. Everything was foggy.

Yet, I also needed money, so I took a job running a new restaurant in Oakland. I was broke, both financially and emotionally. I had no ideas or vision. I was an empty keg —all foam and no beer. I didn't last long.

I got offered a job as creative director of a rotisserie and wine place. I was still feeling awful, so I thought things would get better if I started taking the drugs again. They didn't. I accepted the job but didn't even have the energy to put forth much effort. The food was okay but I wasn't. Nothing felt right, and—surprise, surprise—I clashed with the owner. Everything was somebody else's fault and never my own. I think that if I was healthy I could have fixed a lot of these subpar situations. But I wasn't healthy. I was far from it. I was chasing jobs again, focusing on money over everything else and was out the door after three months.

Right around this time, in 2010, is when I actually signed the contract for this very cookbook. But my brain was too scattered and unprepared by what was going on at the time. I was physically and mentally incapable of creating something that I was willing to put out into the world. I

pocketed the advance anyway, but was still so broke that my car was impounded. I took some consulting jobs in Los Angeles and had to ask for the money up front just to get my car out of hock. I had become a chef terrified of cooking. I even considered moving back to Atlanta to live with my mother.

Then I met the woman who would become my wife. I had become sort of known at Ubuntu for these lavender almonds and she was a buyer, so I thought maybe I could start selling the almonds to make ends meet. Rachael was so far out of my league that I knew I had to get my life together if I wanted a shot with her. It got me much more serious about treating my drug reliance.

Rachael and I fell in love very quickly. I'm not going to lie— waking up next to her made self-motivation a whole lot easier.

To make some extra money, I cooked a series of pop-up dinners that I ultimately thought were pretty unremarkable. There was one positive that came out of it though: Two of our guests during the dinner series were Josh and Zoe Loeb. Their restaurant Rustic Canyon was in need of a chef, and they had reached out to me about the position. I deliberated for a while, still unsure if I was ready. Eventually, we talked, and for the first time in my professional life I laid everything out on the line. I told Josh and Zoe about all of my problems, my addictions, and my anxieties, and took responsibility for my failures. After much debate on my part as well as a lot of encouragement from Rachael, we agreed to terms. So in January of 2013, I started my newest chapter as a chef. Just like when I showed up at Manresa, I arrived humbled and hungry. I inched forward.

But real change takes time. I'd like to be able to say that it was like the movies—I hit rock bottom, I met my future wife, and suddenly my issues just vanished into thin air. The truth is that emotional evolution is a very gradual process. The hope is that as you get older, you begin learning to recognize the signs before it's too late—emotional awareness is much more useful in the moment than in hindsight. It was not long into my time at Rustic Canyon that the nasty feeling in my chest started taking over again. I was frustrated and I couldn't pinpoint why. I was volatile and I could feel myself going down that dark road. Finally, I took a step back, and basically gave myself a time out. I acknowledged to myself that things weren't as bad as my brain was telling me, and that everyone around me was on my side. It was me that was against me. With this realization, the tension dropped. Somehow I managed to catch it in time, and gradually I felt better. I started to relax and build a peaceful and productive place of work—both in my kitchen and inside my own head. Things started to become clear and each month was better than the one that preceded it.

As this calmer and more collected version of myself emerged, I was eventually able to sit down and start writing this cookbook—finally honoring the contract that I had signed five years earlier. When my mindset improved, everything else did too. My personal happiness was directly tied to my professional happiness and also, it turns out, my creativity.

I got rid of the overcomplicated plating of my Ubuntu days: No more tweezers and tiny flower garnishes. No more fifteen- to twenty-hour days for my kitchen staff. I wanted to create sustainable success. When I left Ubuntu, the food looked like plants growing out of soil. Now at Rustic Canyon the food looks like itself, but tastes like a better version of itself. I want people to know what they're eating. I want them to be able to eat it without instructions. There is nothing on the plate purely for aesthetic reasons. Should a garnish look nice? Of course. But it's also supposed to taste good. I think that food from a happy kitchen tastes better than food from an unhappy one. Peace tastes better than anxiety. This is the sort of cooking I care about now. Diners, it turns out, agree with me.

In 2013 Rustic Canyon had its busiest year to date; then 2014 beat it. So did 2015. Our menu continues to evolve, the staff is staying on, and I'm doing for Rustic Canyon what I never could at Ubuntu: running a successful restaurant. The business is working and I'm no longer pushing people to the brink and then breaking them. For the first time since Manresa, I feel like I'm truly fulfilling the requirements of my job. Ubuntu was all about Jeremy Fox. Rustic Canyon is about the restaurant, the farmers, and the team. I like this way. I like this food.

WINDROSE FARM

WE GROW WHAT WE SELL!
IN PASO ROBLES, CA
windrosefarm.org
805·239·3757

WE DO

- ROTATE CROPS
- COMPOST
- INTERPLANT
- LISTEN TO THE SEASONS

WE DON'T
USE
- PESTICIDES
- FUNGICIDES
- HERBICIDES
- CHEMICAL FERTILIZERS

After 20 years of being certified organic, the official standards no longer reflect how we choose to grow.

We cultivate with emphasis on holistic development of the relationship between soil, plants and animals.

We treat our farm as one single, self-sustaining organism.
WE WELCOME YOUR QUESTIONS.

weiser family farms

alex weiser

At my restaurant, Weiser potatoes are literally the only ones we ever use. The flavor of them is the pure essence of potato and their product is unbelievably consistent.

The farm started up in 1977 when Sid Weiser, a chemistry teacher at Garfield High School in East L.A., decided to live out his dream of owning a farm. So he uprooted his family—including his thirteen-year-old son, Alex—and moved two hours north to Tehachapi, California. "It was great," Alex told me. "I went from living in the city to having an ATV and driving around in the country. My job was to check for irrigation leaks."

When they first bought the land, all they grew were apples. "We lost a lot of money on apples and realized we had to do other things." When they found out that the land had a history of growing potatoes, they added it to their repertoire.

Okay, fine. But why are their potatoes so much better than everyone else's?

"We have a great climate," Weiser shared. "We're a mountain valley, and we can have three crops a year that are fresh. In Idaho, it's frozen ground most of the year, whereas we can grow up and down the hill and get spring, fall, and winter crops all within thirty miles. We get frost too, which makes for better flavor. We get more *terroir*. A lot of our competitors grow along the coast—where you do get temperate climates—but they don't have the depth of flavor you get from hot days and cold nights."

Then in 1981, California started allowing farmers to sell directly to market, and all of a sudden farmers' markets were opening throughout the state. "I wanted to go to college," Alex told me, "so my dad said, 'Great. Go to farmers markets and pay for your college.'" Alex and his friends started showing up at these brand new markets and selling the family wares. It worked. "After years of my dad not liking the conventional business of farming, I was coming back from the market and telling him that people were excited and they loved the product."

Some of those customers were acclaimed California chefs. "People like Nancy Silverton and Mark Peel were buying our products and then telling us to grow things. 'Hey, they grow *this* in Italy, why don't *you* try to grow it?'" Chefs, farmers, and home cooks were communicating with each other at the ground level and everybody was benefiting from it. "So eventually we realized that Santa Monica didn't want 'number twos' anymore. They wanted 'number ones.' So now I can grow purple potatoes and fingerlings instead of just whites. Heirloom tomatoes started showing up. So I saw that all happen. That was all happening over thirty-five years."

All right, so they grow some of the best potatoes in the world. But I also go crazy for their carrots, Broccoli di Cicco, Spigarello, sunchokes, radishes, and melons. "I mean, there are only, like, four spots on the planet where you have a Mediterranean climate," Alex said, "and one of them is Southern California."

It's the perfect storm of passion, information, and location all coming together in the best way possible.

"It's not like a lot of farming today, which is built around business," Alex said. "For those guys, it's about volume and schedule. They know that they can charge eighteen dollars a box for melons in May, so they grow more in May. They grow based on price, not flavor."

Alex's method works. The flavor is incredible. But it also means a lot to me that Weiser really is a family farm. "First it was my dad and my mom and I," Alex said. "Now it's my sister, brother, nieces, nephews. It's a Jewish farming family, which is pretty rare I think."

But I think my favorite thing about Alex Weiser is that you can tell how much he loves his job. He loves interacting with people, being a representative of farmers markets and raising the quality and awareness around locally grown produce. There's no ego—he just loves it. "We take care of the soil and it takes care of us."

I've had the pleasure of cooking two dinners at Alex's farm and they meant a lot to me. That dialogue between chef and farmer is critical to both of us. "We have the best palates in the city giving us their feedback," he said. "People wonder why we're growing certain things, and it's because we have the information on the street of what chefs want and what will sell. It's such a pleasure to farm for people who notice the subtle changes in a vegetable. It blows me away. It inspires me."

coleman family farm

romeo coleman

Romeo Coleman is a no-nonsense farmer. He's also a big guy—he could easily pick me up and curl me with one arm. Maybe if I ask nicely, he might. He also happens to be one of the nicest guys on the planet.

Coleman Family Farm is famous for their lettuces, but I also really love their celtuce, fenugreek leaves, lemon verbena, and Mexican sour gherkins. I feel like every time I go there's something new that I haven't seen before, and then the following week— it's gone. He won my heart because he was the only person who would cut down his borage leaves for me.

Romeo grew up on the family farm, which his father, Bill Coleman, started in 1963. "My dad had an interest in farming, and he started farming with some Filipino people in Santa Barbara," he told me. Bill worked a full-time job and farmed on weekends, saving up enough money to get a six-acre farm in Carpinteria, California. He tried to sell his produce at the big central market in town, but was told that he was too small. "So he got together with some guys and they helped start the Santa Barbara Farmers Market. He was one of the original farmers there."

His father is still the driving force behind a lot of their experimentation. "My dad being something of a horticulturist," Romeo went on, "and liking all sorts of different plants, he's able to experiment. Then I can see what does well and what doesn't, and what I can sell and make money off of. So that's a factor in what we grow." The Coleman family put together a really wide and impressive variety of herbs. "Anise hyssop is a kind of herb my dad

started growing and people liked it, so now we grow more."

But what has it been like to take over the family business? For people who've seen Romeo at the Santa Monica Farmers Market since he was little, the changeover seemed inevitable. "It's not something I've always wanted to do," he told me, "but it's something I *eventually* wanted to do, if that makes sense. When I was a kid, I had no idea. But I went to Cal Poly [California Polytechnic State University] and studied agriculture, and then came back and wanted to grow the farm and expand it to be a little bit bigger. Being able to have a livelihood and support a family is something I love doing."

The Coleman family has expanded from the original six acres with another twelve that Romeo is renting. The climate is ideal for growing lettuce during all four seasons, but the rest of their stuff is pretty extraordinary, too. "It's a coastal place," Romeo says of the farms. "My parents' place and my place, they're both south-facing slopes that get sun year round—even in the winter when the sun dips down. We're just close enough and far enough away to get ocean influence, but it's more moderate. We don't get too much frost, and don't have it for very long. There's always a breeze, so that keeps the temperature moderate. That in turn helps keep the lettuce from getting too cold. It gets a lot of sun, it cools off at night—it's perfect."

But in California, that climate has been changing pretty drastically over the last few years. Temperatures are spiking and water is running low. "This year in particular, we had two weeks in January

when it was almost at ninety degrees here, which is just ridiculous." The average January high temperature in Carpinteria is in the mid-seventies. The biggest problem, though, is the bagrada bug, which showed up in Carpinteria around 2010. "There's no proof, but when [the infestation] starts at L.A. County near the airport, you assume it came in on a plane." The bagrada bug thrives in warmer temperatures, so as summers are getting hotter, the bug has been taking down things like kale, broccoli, turnips, radishes, and the like.

Then there's "the water situation," as Romeo referred to it. "There are a lot of people working on it and thinking about it, but when it comes down to it, our reservoir system in California can't hold enough water for all the people here. It was built during the FDR days, and how many people were living in California then? Not as many as there are now. And the population doesn't seem to be decreasing. So that's a huge open question that everyone is trying to solve."

With Romeo being a father now, these long-term questions have to mean even more. I asked him if he hoped that his kids might take over for him one day, like he did for his dad. "No," he answered flatly. "My kids are gonna do what they want to do. If it happens to be this, I'll support them. If it's tightrope walking across the Grand Canyon, I'll support them, too."

For the good of humanity at large, I certainly hope that somebody takes over for him when it's all said and done. That is some damn fine lettuce.

windrose farm

barbara spencer

Barbara Spencer is one of those people with whom everyone, I think, wishes they could spend more time. If you spend even twenty minutes at her stall at the farmers market, it is inevitable that three or four people will walk up to her, give her a hug, and walk away happier than when they showed up.

Barbara's personality comes through in her produce, too—beautiful blades of minutina tied up in biodegradable twine ("I hate twisty ties."), heirloom winter squash laid out on colorful blankets, and garden pots filled with baby lettuces or delicate pea tendrils. She has an obsession with details, and a passion to keep pushing herself to continue to evolve.

"I know there are people who never experience that sensation of having something that you would do full-time, even if you never got paid," she told me. "If you never had to work, you'd do it anyway. I've gotten it twice."

Barbara was a professional cellist for most of her life. Then, in her mid-forties, she thought it would be a good idea to retire into manual labor. She met her eventual husband, Bill, and the two fell in love with a property up in Paso Robles, California. Barbara had no farming, or even gardening, experience.

It started with some uniquely great water. In wine country, the water is usually limestone based, but theirs is granite. "That's part of the *terroir*. The *terroir* is everything. It's the water, it's the soil—which is affected by the water—and whatever the rock and mineral compounds are that the water is traveling through. We're in a frost

pocket, which is why we can grow apples—English and French apple trees seem to think it's just great."

It's been a process of constant learning for the two—striving for perfection, followed by the calm that comes from knowing that perfection is impossible.

A key point in their farm's history came about when a nursery in Pasadena was throwing out tomato plants and gave her Cherokee Purples and Green Zebras. "Everything that we've done heirloom-wise comes from the fact that somebody gave me his garbage pile of tomato plants." In her mind, it was the genesis of everything they would go on to do. After tomatoes, Barbara and Bill tried lettuce. "Oh my god," she said. "That's what happens when you grow greens? That's what lettuce looks like?"

They visited farmers markets to see what was being made available. But rather than just grow the things that were proven to be big sellers, Barbara wanted to find things that nobody else was growing.

The quality and exceptionality of heirloom varietals feed off her passion and curiosity. "We explain it to people by saying that it's like a pie. A tomato, a squash, an apple: It's really a pie, and there are only so many ingredients in there. When you do your business graph—your pie chart—only so much is flavor and so much is shelf life," she says. "When they do hybridization, they had to throw something out.

Not that Celebrity or Early Girl tomatoes are terrible, but some original part of them is gone now. Maybe it's just the color, but the

flavor is fine. If you want onions that bounce off walls, something has to go away, because there's only so much space in the pie of what it is, a squash—be it a pea, a flower, an apple. And luckily, we can sell at places where it doesn't matter. We can go back and grab the one that everything started with."

I asked her what I've asked every farmer: do you see yourself stopping? "I see myself slowing down. Bill is assisting with that. He made it very clear—I'm slowing down. But no, I don't think I could ever really stop."

Instead, she's focused on her next farm fantasy—reworking the fields into something even more sustainable. "We read *Acres U.S.A.* magazine and they're always talking about building your soil, carbon sequestration, all the new systems of how you really want to cover all your ground for capturing carbon and things like that." She imagines a farm that is built like a prairie or a forest, in which there is no bare ground. "How do I create a system where there are herbs under the trees and then intermediates of these other perennial edibles and greens so that everything is covered? Then the soil stays in, the roots stay in and the life of the soil is the highest possible."

"So, quitting? No. But I'd love for the farm to just . . . go on forever."

It's a complicated thing to try to achieve. In fact, the most ideal version of it may well be unattainable. But striving for it is the fun part. "You're only as good as your last dinner. You're only as good as your last session, or your last solo. There's no sitting back."

thao farms

kong thao

Some people are just obsessives, and it doesn't matter if what they're working on is a passion project or just a job. I genuinely like every single thing that Kong Thao brings to the farmers market, though I'm particularly fond of all of their brassicas—they are absolutely gorgeous. The most stunning part to me, though, is that everything he brings to the market is always so pristine and crisp.

"That comes from my dad," Kong tells me. "He's the most meticulous person about everything. He wants everything to look consistent. He wants everything to be precise."

His father, Vang Thao, is fifty-six. "As a kid, everything that went on the truck, he'd make us wash it first. He'd make us change the water. Now his main job is to drive the tractor. He does all of that and . . . his [crop] rows . . . " I'm pretty sure I can hear him shaking his head from the other end of the phone. "He drives the straightest line."

Kong's parents, Vang Thao and Khoua Her, started their farm twenty-seven years ago. They moved from Laos to Thailand before eventually settling in California's Central Valley. "In Laos, they lived pretty much in the jungle, so they grew their own food and raised their own animals," he said. "When they came to the States there was no work, so they started farming."

Ten children later, Thao's is a full-fledged family operation that grows over three hundred produce varieties across twenty-one farmed acres. Kong and his brother run the markets and the business side, while his mom "does everything else. She is the backbone of the farm. Everything starts and ends with her." Her ability to find and save seeds is a big part of how they are able to grow things that you just can't find anywhere else.

"It's always been trial and error for us. I didn't go to college to be a farmer. Our specialty is Asian produce, since that's what my parents knew how to grow. Because of that, Torrance has always been our big market. But in Santa Monica it's a different clientele, so we started doing things that people in Santa Monica would want to use. Every year we get better and better."

As the farm has grown and customers have gotten more knowledgeable, the family's passion for variety and quality has grown with it. "What's cool," he said, "is that ginger is relatively new for us—six or seven years. But over the years, we started trying new methods and now we're at a point where our ginger is doing really well." With farming, cooking, and really everything in the world, it's not about having a magic touch—it's about putting in the hard work and caring about the result. "Wherever you go," Kong told me, "you adapt to what grows better there. So right now, I'm ready to plant guava trees. I've got like 120 of those, but we got hit with frost, so I have to build structures. I have to build a climate for them so they don't get hit by frost. You start investing in it."

More than anything else, I think I love Thao's because their obsessiveness matches up really well with my own. There's no substitute for caring way, way too much about everything. "I think we're trying to get better every year," Kong went on. "New things, different things, stuff we've never done before. The restaurant scene has really grown over the last few years. Now we have more demand from very specific people and we want to grow more specific things—different things that we don't see anywhere else."

So do obsessives ever retire? "I don't think my parents ever want to retire," he answered. "But they may want to slow it down. My brother and I just want to buy my dad a new tractor. That way he can just plow his field."

Ah, yes, retirement—or in other words, a brand new tractor.

rancho gordo

steve sando

Steve Sando is a man who, through his company, Rancho Gordo, in California's Napa Valley, has devoted a large chunk of his life to obsessively producing and promoting the native ingredients of North America.

"I have no agricultural background at all and my whole focus has always been as a frustrated home cook," he told me. "I remember hearing someone was making balsamic vinegar in Napa and thinking, 'Wait, you're making vinegar from Modena, but we aren't growing beans that are indigenous?'"

Now is probably a good time to tell you that Steve Sando is really into beans. He is a champion for tremendously flavorful and diverse heirloom varietals. I go pretty crazy for his yellow eye beans, and they were the inspiration for one of my favorite things I ever made at Manresa (Rustic Yellow Eye Bean Stew, Torn Bread on page 72). But the road to convincing people to sell his beans was not easy.

"I think the problem with beans is that people either think of them as depression era food or health food," he said. Initially, the Napa Farmers Market wouldn't even let him sell beans there, so he had to go to the Yountville Farmers Market "which was mostly for tourists." Luckily, Yountville also happens to be the location of Thomas Keller's world-renowned restaurant, The French Laundry, and when Keller noticed Steve's beans, everything started to change. Once the chefs realized how good these beans tasted, that was all that really mattered.

Rancho Gordo heirloom beans taste way better than the canned ones you find at the supermarket. They have a purer, stronger flavor, with no commercial additives or genetic changes. "We refer to [canned beans] as commodity beans," Steve said. "They're grown for the convenience of the grower and canner with a higher and consistent yield per acre. They are an incredibly cheap, green protein. I think they're kind of boring, but we do need them. Heirlooms are much worse for the yield, but the payoff is in flavor and texture."

A big part of what Steve does now involves trying to get more people to grow these native beans of the New World. But it's not easy. "To make beans work, I'm told, you need to do a certain scale or you're not going to do anything." Older bean farmers can be set in their ways, and are often scared off by the smaller yields. "We tell them we can charge more and actually make them more money, but they still won't do it." So what about newer farmers? "Young, idealistic farmers are a nightmare, too. They just leave the fields in the middle of the year because it's too hard."

Who does that leave?

"You need something between a crusty old fart and an ideologue," he says. "It's hard because you read about sustainable and farm-to-table. Everybody is a policy wonk, but nobody is doing the work. It's not easy to do. Are you gonna be there to pay the bills if it doesn't work out? It's really easy to have an opinion. It's frustrating."

While a lot of his work involves flipping through seed catalogues, Steve has also been traveling to Mexico, searching for new ingredients and trying to grow them in California. But a lot of them just don't grow up here. That's what led him to The Rancho Gordo-Xoxoc Project: two companies working together to keep small farmers growing their indigenous Mexican crops. If those farmers stop growing, the crops could very well disappear for good. "Down there, the farmers are told to get rid of the heirloom beans, and then there's this fat gringo coming down to tell them to have a leap of faith and keep growing them."

As Rancho Gordo evolved, Steve began selling more than just beans—he added grains, chilies, corn, seeds, herbs, spices, and more. "To go from my living room to home garden to this business in fifteen years is kind of amazing," he told me. "But I want to emphasize that there was no master plan. I think it was the right person at the right time with the right product."

I'm inclined to agree.

freshpoint

karen beverlin

Karen is not a farmer. I'm actually not even sure if she has houseplants. But at the Wednesday Santa Monica Farmers Market—one of the best farmers markets in the world—she is an important person. Home cooks may not know who she is, but for most of the chefs who care about great farmers market produce, she is an essential part of the equation.

Most simply put, Karen's job—which was basically invented for her at FreshPoint—is to facilitate getting produce from farms and farmers markets directly to restaurants across Los Angeles. But on the whole, the job is multi-faceted. Sometimes it's about filling orders, making sure they get on the trucks and then make it to the restaurants on time. Other times she's out there stumping for some great new thing that a farmer is growing and nobody knows about yet.

"When I'm super excited about something and no one agrees with me, it's really sad," she told me. "But getting feedback from the chefs I most closely work with is huge. I learn so much and it changes how I view things, drastically."

For me, it's incredibly important to be at the market as often as possible, talking with farmers and seeing what's available and what's coming up soon. A lot of chefs don't ever go to the market though, and it's up to Karen to ensure that that they're getting the right product for their restaurants.

"There's no one that I work with, either as a farmer or a chef, who isn't honest and true. If we accidentally deliver extra stuff because something

happened on a truck, we always get a call to tell us that they got something extra. They don't have to but they always do. And if a farmer's invoice is missing something, I add it, because we need to pay them for it."

"If I had my druthers," she continues, "asparagus would be eaten only between March and June and we wouldn't be hurting Peru's water table, and their ability to get safe drinking water for their own people, and everything would be seasonal. But it's not."

In California, the farmers markets have been critical for sustaining family farms. "It gives them a way to sell small quantities of many items so that they could be sustainable and use the methods that they want to use. They get feedback from chefs and tweak what they do—and enjoy it while they're doing it. That's huge and that's purely because of farmers markets," she went on. "Today we picked up from twenty-seven different farmers. That would take us forever to pick up, with multiple trucks out to make those pickups, which is also prohibitively expensive."

Another topic that came up with Karen, as it's been coming up with all of the farmers I've been talking to, is drought and climate change. "We talk about it all the time," she told me. "About how challenging it is because seasons are shorter or longer. Farmers are following the same planting schedule and then a ninety-degree January wipes stuff out. It has been really hard in terms of consistency of menu. This has been the most challenging year for availability that I have ever seen."

These small farmers are actually better for conserving water in the state as well. "One of the problems with big, huge growers is they're driven by market," she said. "So the broccoli market goes up, everybody plants broccoli, and 120 days from then, the broccoli market tanks because everybody was chasing the market. The thing about small farmers is they plant what works for their area. So they don't want to spend extra money on water—they want to put on as little water as possible. So in most cases, they're planting crops that are perfect for that microclimate."

Karen exhales deeply, simultaneously passionate and frustrated, but still with a smile on her face. Taking two different businesses—farms and restaurants—she is finding a way to make them benefit and sustain one another in the best way possible, all while doing it with an unflinchingly positive attitude.

the plants

storage, purchasing & a few basic preparations

This will not be a comprehensive list of every plant in the world. That would be a very long and very different book. Instead, I'm just going to highlight a few of the plants that I love, and what it is that I love about them. But I also want to explain just a little bit about what to look for when you're shopping for these ingredients, and then how to store them once you get them home. I would certainly recommend reading this section before you get into the recipes.

Why?

Glad you asked. Most of the recipes in this book are really just about highlighting great products. Something as basic as the Tomato Raw Bar (page 240) will be decidedly un-delicious if you buy bad tomatoes. Similarly, if you buy a great tomato and then leave it in the fridge for three days, the tomato raw bar will also not taste very good. The goal is to buy great ingredients and then to treat them with respect.

I also want to dig into some basic preparations for a few of these plants. More guidelines than rules, these are a basic explanation of how to poach a potato, roast a beet, or shuck some peas—just basic cooking principles. To know how to cook is far more important than to follow a recipe.

amaranth

You'll find amaranth seeds in health food stores, in the grain section. Gluten free, amaranth is used in much the same way as quinoa, though I prefer the texture of quinoa.

I've always been drawn to the greens of the amaranth plant because they are gorgeous, but it wasn't until later that I found ways to cook with them. The leaves taste vegetal and remind me of spinach. The young leaves are tender, and as they get older they're more typically used in Asian stir-fries. Some amaranth varietals are purely decorative, so plant them in your yard and be happy.

what to look for
You want sturdy leaves that are not wilted. I like to look for high concentrations of the reddish-pink color.

storage
Any leafy green, when you get home from the market, will start to wilt. Wash it right away in cold water to refresh it. Store it in a big resealable plastic bag with a dry paper towel on the bottom and a damp one on top. Make sure to keep it airtight. If the leaves are looking frail, mist them with a spray bottle filled with water.

artichokes

Artichokes can be a laborious ingredient for home cooking, between the mess of removing the leaves and having to put them in acidulated water to keep them from oxidizing. Artichokes are the crawfish of the earth—you have to work to get the meat out. I tend to like them whole-roasted or steamed, or halved and put on the grill and served with melted butter or aioli.

what to look for
Be careful of an artichoke that is turning black or brown on the stem or leaf area, as it could be starting to rot from the inside. I find that tightly coned leaves indicate a better product.

storage
Keep them dry and in the refrigerator; as if they get wet, they'll start molding. They don't need to be stored in an airtight container or bag, but I wouldn't hold them for longer than a few days or the stems will soften up.

asparagus

In order to appreciate asparagus, use it only when in season. I think that getting it shipped in from the opposite hemisphere means it's going to taste like jet fumes. People don't think about that. It's a vegetable. You ever notice how funky your clothes smell after you get off a plane? Well imagine what air travel does to a porous plant that's going to wind up inside of your mouth.

what to look for
You want crisp—not soft or bendy—stalks. The tips should not be mushy and verdant, and the tiny leaves at the tip should be strong looking.

storage
Store in a standing up container with the stalks sitting in water, or they'll start drying and wrinkling at the top near the spear. Cover with a damp cloth towel, which will keep the tips moist as well.

how to peel and blanch asparagus
Not all asparagus should get peeled, so use your judgment: If the asparagus is thinner than your pinky, you can probably leave it alone.

I also like to manicure some of the leaves that are just below the tip of the asparagus. With a bird's beak knife (you should really get a bird's beak knife; see page 12), carefully cut off those little leaves that are on the stalk. Using the knife, cut a thin line around the circumference of the asparagus, about 1½ inches (4 cm) below the tip. This will run all the way around the stalk, and function as the stopping point for your vegetable peeler once you are peeling the stalk.

Snap off the tough base end. It should break off naturally, so just let it break however it breaks. Since we're cleaning the rest of the asparagus so carefully, I like to leave the stalk feeling a bit more rustic and handmade. I think that contrast is really nice.

With a vegetable peeler, peel the asparagus from the bottom of the stem straight up to the thin line that you've already cut. The result should be gorgeous, pristine asparagus that is ready for blanching.

Using kitchen twine, tie the asparagus into bundles of 8, tying it just tightly enough that the asparagus are secure, but not so tight that the twine digs into them. The twine should run from just below the tips all the way down to the base— but with space in between for the asparagus to breathe a bit.

Bring a pot of heavily salted water to a boil. It should have enough water so that you won't lose your boil once you add the asparagus.

Meanwhile, prepare an ice bath. At the restaurant, I fill a deep hotel pan with ice water and then set a smaller perforated one over it. That way the water stays cold but the asparagus won't ever touch the ice. There's no scientific backing to this, but for whatever reason I really prefer it when the ice doesn't "burn" the asparagus through direct contact. You can simulate this with a strainer and a large bowl if you'd like, or just plunge it directly into ice water. Your call.

Place the asparagus in the boiling water. If the pot loses its boil, cover the pot with a lid to get back up to temperature. You're looking for a gentle boil; I don't think anything really benefits from a violent boil. The asparagus will cook, depending on the thickness of the stalks, anywhere from 2 to 5 minutes. You'll want to be able to gently squeeze the base and know it's neither raw, nor too soft. If you're not sure, take it out, slice off a piece of the base and taste it.

Once ready, drain the asparagus and transfer to the ice bath. Remove the twine and agitate the stalks, allowing any little bits of excess asparagus debris to fall off. Let the asparagus cool completely, but don't leave them in any longer than they need to be. Lay the stalks on towels to dry.

beans

Beans are a workhorse ingredient that you should keep on hand. I didn't eat a lot of beans growing up, but gained a new respect for them when I first visited the Rancho Gordo (page 32) stall at the Ferry Plaza Farmers Market in San Francisco. Steve Sando's beans made me really appreciate how different, how varied, and how delicious beans can be.

what to look for
Make sure there aren't a lot of broken beans—the beans won't be perfect, but excessive amounts of broken or crushed beans suggests a certain lack of care on the part of the processor.

storage
Store them in a cool, dry place in an airtight container.

how to cook beans
Fully submerge the beans in water and soak for at least 4 hours and preferably overnight, in a container large enough for them to increase in volume without overflowing. Drain the beans and discard the soaking water.

Start the beans in a pot with a 3:1 cold water to bean ratio. Toss in one or both halves of an onion, a carrot, and a celery

stalk. You can also throw in 1 or 2 bay leaves (dried is fine, but I prefer fresh). Hold off on seasoning just yet. Bring the pot to a boil, skimming off any gray scum that comes to the surface. Reduce the heat so the liquid is at a bare simmer and cook the beans, uncovered, for a couple of hours. I like my beans cooked more than most—until they are totally creamy. The slower and more evenly you cook the beans, the more consistent the texture will be. You could even cook the beans below a simmer—just so the water is hot enough to break them down.

Once the beans are cooked, salt them until the liquid itself tastes good.

I like to pull the pot off the heat, drizzle in some olive oil, and crack in some fresh black pepper. Let the beans cool in their own liquid—I find that they tend to dry out without it, and lose some of the color, taste, and appearance—and store the beans in the liquid as well.

Now taste the broth again: I always want the broth to be good enough to eat on its own, but then again, I'm a broth guy, so I can eat just the broth with sliced scallions and olive oil and be perfectly happy.

Cooked beans, stored in their liquid, will keep refrigerated for up to 1 week.

beets (beetroot)

I could have an endless number of beet recipes in this book. They're some of my favorite vegetables to cook. The versatility is really appealing to me: Beets are cheap, their greens are delicious, the juice is incredibly useful (see Beet Molasses, page 266), and you can do a ton with all the beet by-products.

what to look for
You want firm beets with healthy greens. As with any root vegetable, be wary of beets with amputated stems, as they may well be trying to hide something from you. Healthy greens and stems are the best indicators of a healthy root vegetable—like the gills of a fish.

storage
First, separate the beets from the greens and store them separately (as they are separate ingredients, you want to store them as such). Wash and dry the beets; then store, covered, in the refrigerator, but not too long as they go soft when they dry out. As with any root vegetable, if you see that they're getting soft, cook them and then refrigerate them so they will last longer.

Store the beet greens as you would any other greens, see Amaranth (page 38).

how to roast beets
Preheat the oven to 375°F (190°C/Gas 5). Wash the beets under cool, running water and pat dry. Lightly coat them with olive oil and a good pinch of kosher salt.

Place the beets in a baking dish with just enough water to cover the bottom of the dish and bake until there is no resistance when the beets are pierced with a cake tester, 45 minutes to 1 hour. For whatever reason, I've found that small beets take about as long to cook as large ones.

Once the beets are finished cooking, remove them from the oven and let them cool down enough so that you can handle them. Using gloves or a towel (fair warning—red beets will stain the towel), peel off the outer skin. You now have roasted beets.

borage

Borage is a fuzzy herb with pretty, mild-tasting flowers that mostly just get used for garnish. Nobody seems to want the leaves, which is a shame, so I usually make a special request for farmers to harvest them for me. The greens actually have a lot of chlorophyll, so even if you cook them down or braise them, they will retain a lot of their brightness. You can also stuff and steam the leaves, or juice them for, say, a borage granita.

I don't recommend eating the greens raw, as they are fuzzy little bastards.

what to look for
You want bright, strong leaves with minimal discoloration. Borage tends to be something that a lot of farmers might grow on the perimeter of their farms to attract bugs and bees so that they don't hit the actual crop, so you may well find lots of holes in the greens. That's not necessarily a bad thing, but you may not want *all* of the leaves to have tons of holes.

storage
See Amaranth (page 38).

broccoli

Broccoli is one of those vegetables that I liked only raw as a kid. Back then I only knew vegetables as raw or canned.

The first time I had good, fresh broccoli cooked with olive oil, chili flakes, and garlic, I realized how great broccoli could be. In the fall and early winter, broccoli is a lot sweeter. Then, as the season turns colder, it becomes hardier and more vegetal tasting.

what to look for
Whether it's Broccoli di Cicco or Calabrese (the most common broccoli with those big heads), the florets should be alive. They shouldn't be brittle and just fall apart into a million pieces. Keep an eye out for aphids as well, which tend to like to hide in broccoli. If you see a few, that's something you can rinse off, but if there are a lot, don't buy the broccoli. No one wants to eat an infested vegetable.

storage
Broccoli gets rubbery if left uncovered in the refrigerator; you can store it loose in a bag.

how to blanch broccoli
If you're working with whole Calabrese broccoli, cut it into florets about 1 inch (2.5 cm) wide. If the florets are bigger than that, I like break them up by cutting halfway through the base of the stem, and then peeling the floret apart the rest of the way with my fingers. This way, you wind up with smaller, torn florets, rather than something with hard, unnatural edges that look like they were cut by a machine.

If you are using broccolini, cut it down into 2 to 3 pieces so that some of the pieces will be stems with the florets attached and others will just be stems.

If using Broccoli di Cicco or flowering broccoli, just check to see how woody the stem is. That part is inedible, so cut it off.

Meanwhile, should you plan to cook a lot of broccoli for a big crowd, you can blanch it a day in advance and refrigerate it until needed.

To blanch broccoli, follow the same method as for Asparagus (page 38), but cook the broccoli for 1 to 2 minutes, then transfer to the ice water bath. Let it cool down, then dry it.

carrots

This is another extremely versatile vegetable. You can eat it raw, juice it for pasta dough, make a pesto out of the tops, even dehydrate the pulp and mix it into a crumble (page 290).

For the most part I have stopped peeling carrots as long as they are grown properly and cleaned well. If you are roasting them and don't peel them, they form a really nice skin, almost like a meat skin on a roasted animal. Hell, if you've got a really big one, you can even present it to dinner guests before carving it up.

what to look for
Carrots should not be rubbery. If they are—move along. Personally, I look for the weirdly shaped carrots; I call those misfit carrots. I always considered myself a misfit, and not like everyone else. So when I see carrots that most people are picking over because they aren't what they thought carrots should be, those are the ones I scoop up. I like giving misfits a chance.

storage
Carrots can be washed and dried before being stored. Remove the greens and store them separately. Carrots can be stored loose in a bag; if they are left totally uncovered in the refrigerator they will get a bit rubbery. Their crispness is one of their best attributes.

how to roast carrots
I like oven-roasting carrots rather than pan-roasting on the stovetop, as I find they cook more evenly. Preheat the oven to 350°F (180°C/Gas 4). If the carrots have their greens still attached, trim them off for another use (like Salsa Verde, page 269, or Pesto, page 270), but keep about an inch of the stem still attached.

Wash your carrots thoroughly, but don't peel them. Using the tip of your bird's beak knife, scrape off any dirt that is hidden in the little circular indentation at the stem.

Dry the carrots and toss them with just enough olive oil to coat. Season with salt and spread them evenly on a baking sheet or ovenproof sauté pan (depending on quantity), making sure that they aren't stacked or overcrowded.

Roast the carrots, rotating the pan about halfway through, until they take on a good bit of color. Depending on the size of the carrots, this could take anywhere from 10 to 30 minutes. I like it when they've just started to wrinkle and caramelize. A soft carrot doesn't bother me. Once cooked, season to taste with salt.

cauliflower

One of our signature dishes at Ubuntu was Cauliflower in a Cast-Iron Pot (page 106). It would come off as this rich, decadent dish but it was really just cauliflower. People flipped out.

what to look for
If it's white cauliflower, you want it to be as white as possible. Discoloration (of any color cauliflower) is an indication of its time out of the ground. Also, like with broccoli, you want to avoid it if it's rubbery or has an aphid infestation.

storage
see Broccoli (page 40).

how to core cauliflower
This is my trick for coring cauliflower so that you get big, whole florets without making a giant mess of cauliflower crumbs. This works with broccoli as well, but not quite as perfectly as it does with cauliflower.

Place the whole cauliflower stem-side up on a cutting (chopping) board. Take a knife and cut out the core like you would with a tomato, cutting in a cone-shaped motion around the stem and into the heart of the cauliflower. If done properly, the cauliflower florets should just fall to the side around the core.

If you then want to make the florets into smaller pieces that don't look like they've been cut at funny angles, cut partway through the stem of the floret, then use your fingers to tear it apart the rest of the way. The result will be a small, pretty, rustic-looking floret.

corn

Corn is another vegetable that is versatile and fun to explore. Thanks to its natural starch content, if you juice the kernels and cook the juice on the stove, it thickens up like a creamy puree, which you can use to replace the butter in polenta or grits.

You can even dehydrate the pulp and it will form into sheets that you break apart like honeycomb. Dehydrated corn pulp crunchies tossed with chili, lime, and sugar is damn delicious.

what to look for
Peek inside the husks and make sure the cob looks okay. You don't want any gaps in between the kernels.

storage
Clean the corn right away and use it pretty quickly. Husk it,

much easier when the corn is fully dry—just rub it down with a towel to get it off.

crosnes

Crosnes look (unfortunately) like maggots. Sometimes crosnes are called Japanese or Chinese artichokes. I don't love them raw, but they're great pickled. Taste and texture wise, crosnes remind me of water chestnuts. They are fairly delicate and shouldn't be cooked for too long.

what to look for

Look for crisp—not rubbery—crosnes. Crosnes are not particularly common, but I will occasionally find them at farmers markets in the late winter or early spring. Alex Weiser (page 24) happens to grow some excellent ones.

storage

Store crosnes in the refrigerator and don't let them dry out, or they will lose their crispness. They are laborious to clean, as they grow on a stem underground and can snap easily. Once washed, store them in a bag or container with a dry paper towel on the bottom and a damp one on top.

cucumber

I enjoy a crunchy dill pickle—or occasionally the light, clean flavors of a raw cucumber with simple condiments like lemon juice and olive oil. I am not especially interested in cooking them in ways beyond pickling though.

what to look for

Cucumbers should be firm—not rubbery. Avoid gashes or nicks in your cucumbers, as they tend to bruise the flesh.

storage

Wash, dry, and store, covered, in the refrigerator. Use cucumbers quickly as they tend to soften up.

eggplant (aubergine)

Obviously, eggplant Parmesan is awesome. But in order for me to really enjoy eggplant, I need to cut it, salt it, and drain it—otherwise it hurts my mouth. I also really love it out of the smoker; or roasted and prepared as baba ghanoush, a Middle Eastern eggplant spread.

what to look for

Eggplants come in myriad shapes, sizes, and colors. The important thing is you want the skin to be taut and glossy. Avoid brown spots.

storage

Refrigerate and use within a couple days; keep dry and covered.

fava beans

Pretty much any time you read about fava beans, they are being double-shucked. Favas grow in large pods and each individual bean within the pod has a thick skin enclosing it. So typically, with favas, a cook would remove the beans from the large pod and then shuck the beans again, peeling the exo-skin off each.

But is this necessary? Not always.

I've really started getting into the anatomy of favas. At the beginning of the season the pods will be really soft and tender—you don't always have to shuck them. They are actually great roasted whole, as in the Whole Roasted Young Favas with Their Pesto & Pistachio (page 133).

Meanwhile, when they do get double-shucked people throw away those pods and skins, but I think that's a huge waste. There are actually ways to use them. For instance, I like to make a fava bean pesto using the cooked beans themselves, blanched fava skins and the roasted, chopped pods—take a look at the fava bean pesto that is made in Whole Roasted Young Favas with Their Pesto & Pistachio.

You can also take the fava beans without double-shucking them, and braise them down in a sofrito.

Some people swear that the huge pods have noxious gasses and are poisonous, but I've never found this to be the case.

what to look for

You want to look for green pods without any discoloration.

storage

Keep favas covered, in the refrigerator. Should you desire, you can shuck them raw and then store until a later date.

which favas to shuck and which to leave whole

Early in the season you can pick out the small, young pods. They have a bit of delicate fuzz and you can easily pierce the wall of the pod with your nail. These are young enough to not need shucking and can just be roasted and eaten whole. Usually, the pods are anywhere from 2 to 5 inches (5 to 12 cm) long.

Once the pod starts feeling a lot more leathery, like car upholstery, those are going to have to be double-shucked. If you really want to, you could leave them whole and braise them for a very long time, and that works fairly well. But in most cases when you are using older favas, you are going to want to double-shuck them.

fennel

I got pretty interested in learning how to use all the different parts of the fennel plant—exploring the varied textures of the stalks and getting way too excited about all the weird nooks and crannies. Where the stalks start to branch out from the bulb, toward the middle, the plant gets a little woody. This part needs to be chopped up and cooked down—stewed or braised. But then the very top of the plant has this skinny twig that, if you dehydrate it, has a pleasant, delicate crispness to it. The fronds, meanwhile, can be treated like herbs and used in things like Salsa Verde (page 269).

Meanwhile, the bulb is pretty versatile. You can shave it raw or slow-cook it until it gets tender and spreadable but still holds its shape. You can even juice the bulb, but I should warn you that the juice gets pretty intense.

what to look for

You want the fronds to be vibrant and not too wet. If the fronds are yellowing, the fennel is old. Avoid bruises, nicks, discoloration, or browning of the bulb.

storage

Fennel is much easier to store if you wash, dry, and break it down. I like to store each component separately: Pick the fronds, chop the stalks, and leave the bulb whole.

shaved fennel with olive oil and lemon

This is a great way to highlight just how delicious a great bulb of fennel can taste when it is served raw. First, trim off any outer layer that is especially ugly or rough looking. Halve the bulb, slicing straight down through the core, and remove the core from each half just like as you would a head of cabbage. Using a mandoline (or really impressive knife skills), thinly shave the fennel. The slices should be thin, but not so thin as would cause them to lose their crunch. Season to taste with olive oil, lemon juice, and salt.

figs

Thanks to their rich and decadent taste and texture, figs are quite possibly the foie gras of the fruit world, though less controversial. I like them lightly grilled, with a little salt, Parmesan, olive oil, and arugula (rocket).

If you find yourself with super ripe figs, don't even bother cutting them. Just squeeze the meat directly onto some grilled bread and season it with olive oil, salt, and pepper.

what to look for

You want the figs to be ripe—they should feel almost like a rare steak or the fleshy meat below the inside of your thumb. While figs can be soft, they should not mushy. Pick or purchase them when you want to eat them—and then eat them quickly.

storage

Do not refrigerate. Store figs at room temperature. Again, you want to eat these very soon after purchasing.

garlic

You will notice that I use a lot of garlic in my cooking. But you'll also notice that I almost always remove the garlic germ. I find that when you remove the germ, you can actually use more garlic without the aggressive bite. It's much easier to create balanced flavors this way.

what to look for

You want tightly packed bulbs. Loose garlic bulbs are usually a bad sign. If the bulbs are sprouting green shoots, the garlic has gotten old.

storage

Store garlic at room temperature.

how to remove garlic germ

Garlic germ is fairly simple to remove. Once you've peeled the garlic and trimmed off the root end, you can usually see where the germ goes down the center. Using a bird's beak knife, slice through that center lengthwise, then use the tip of the knife to pluck the germ from one or both sides.

green garlic

I love green garlic. Back when I was living in Atlanta, Georgia, in 2000, I would call restaurants in California and get their menus faxed to me. I would see green garlic on all of these menus and I didn't know what it was. In my mind, it was literally just garlic cloves that were green. But then when I moved to California I was really excited to find it.

Green garlic is the young, immature garlic before the individual cloves have fully formed. It's got a great garlic flavor without the bite. You can use the whole thing—bulb and green tops. I love to pickle it, use it to make green garlic butter, and fold it into scrambled eggs. I'll even take the tougher tops and purée them with parsley stems and grapeseed oil—it makes a great marinade for a steak.

what to look for
You want garlic tops that are not too discolored. The stalks should be straight all the way down—not a rounded bulb (when the flavor gets more intense).

storage
Leave it whole, covered in the fridge.

kiwi

I love the sweet-tart combination of good, juicy kiwi, and while it taste good on its own, I actually find that kiwi takes on savory elements quite well. It is delicious paired with goat cheese. I'm not crazy about the skins though, and it's one of the few things I throw away. I always thought kiwi was a tropical fruit, but it turns out that it's pretty common in farmers' markets throughout Southern California.

what to look for
Kiwi should be neither especially soft nor hard.

storage
Store at room temperature and use within a few days.

kohlrabi

Kohlrabi tastes similar to turnips, but sweeter and without all of the bite. I like to crush lightly poached kohlrabi, or slice it thinly and bake it slowly between silicone baking mats. The leaves can be braised, and the stalks can be beer-battered and fried.

Kohlrabi is also great raw. Cut it into batons and serve it with a yogurt sauce, or shave it into a salad with apples, celery, goat cheese, and walnuts.

what to look for
Look for fairly big bulbs, with slight fuzz, but mostly smooth, almost like a grape. Don't bother with the tiny ones; they're cute, but are a waste of time, because it's all skin and fibrousness without much flesh. Pick bulbs with uniform color and avoid splotches and indentations in the stem. Ideally, try to buy kohlrabi whole with the greens attached, as the greens tend to dry out quickly when precut.

storage
See Beets (page 40).

raw kohlrabi batons with yogurt sauce
The most important step in working with kohlrabi is how you trim it. Cut off the stem and the root. Peel the outer fibrous layer until all you have is one smooth surface.

Cut the kohlrabi into 2-inch (5 cm) batons.

To make the yogurt sauce, if you have homemade Labneh (page 281), use that. Otherwise, look for thick and tart store-bought yogurt—Greek yogurt should work well. Season the yogurt with olive oil, lemon juice, salt, and add some finely grated lemon zest. If you find your sauce too thick, thin it out with a little water. All that's left to do is dip and eat.

lima beans (butter beans)

Lima beans are my favorite beans and I always look forward to lima bean season in the late summer. Such a wonderfully creamy bean, it manages to hold its shape even when completely cooked.

what to look for
The pods should look healthy, without much browning. It's okay if the pod is starting to dry and tarnish, but you don't want a mushy brown. Basically, these guidelines apply to any shell beans.

Limas should be stored, covered, in the refrigerator.

melons

I didn't used to like melons on their own, but as I've gotten older, I've really started to appreciate them. Melon and prosciutto is a classic combination, and one that I happen to like a lot. But cooked melon can also be great. One of my favorite dishes in the summer is Cool Melon & Coconut Milk Curry (page 153).

what to look for
A melon should have a slight give when you press it—a mild tenderness. Smelling helps, too: As cantaloupe ripens, it grows more fragrant.

storage
Once a melon is at your desired ripeness, eat it. Refrigerate melons if you have to, but as with tomatoes, their flavor holds much better without such exposure to cold air.

mushrooms

King trumpets—widely available across the United States (and beyond) are my workhorse mushrooms. I love them in crispy applications, such as making them into Mushroom Bacon (page 292) or chips. I use button and cremini (chestnut) mushrooms for stocks, purées, and conservas (page 305). Morels, matsutakes, and porcini are wonderful, though they have a fairly short season. I personally don't like the flavor of dried mushrooms and only like to use fresh.

what to look for
Avoid any fresh mushrooms that are too dry.

storage
Keep mushrooms in a paper bag in the refrigerator. Porcini age quickly, while cremini and king trumpets are a little more resilient. Do not rinse mushrooms until the day you plan to use them. Dry them thoroughly before cooking.

okra

I have a soft spot for okra; I don't mind the slime that turns a lot of people off. During my teenage years in Atlanta, Georgia, I ate a lot of okra: fried, in gumbo, or braised all day with salt pork. Young okra pods are delicious when shaved raw.

what to look for
If they are large and overgrown, the pods are too tough to eat, but the seeds can be removed and eaten. If you want to eat them whole, look for small, tender okra pods.

storage
Wash okra on the day you plan to use it. Store covered in the refrigerator until use.

roasted young okra with sea salt
Heat a cast-iron pan over medium-high heat with a touch of peanut (groundnut) oil (you can use other oils, but I like peanut as an homage to Southern cooking). Using 1- to 2-inch (2.5 to 5 cm) okra pods, toss the okra in, and sear them until the pods get some color, then roll them in the pan. You barely need to cook okra when it's young—you don't want it to turn to mush. Once just tender, toss the okra with some sea salt and transfer to a plate. Finish with a squeeze of lemon.

onions

I remember being sent to my room because my grandmother made stuffing with onions and I couldn't bear to eat them. I had decided in my eight-year-old brain that they were awful. But now, as an adult, I love onions—they are a staple in my kitchen. Even if you can't taste or see the onions in your food, a lot of great dishes are created with them. Sometimes, onions act as a neutral thickener, like in the Cold Melon & Coconut Milk Curry (page 153), or the Smoked Split Pea Shell & Carrot Soup (page 200), where it provides structure and body—the skeleton if you will.

You want large white onions for Caramelized Onion Stock (page 310). Spring onions are great for roasting. Take advantage of the differences between types of onions. If you need a lot of finely diced onions, for example, you probably aren't going to want to use tiny cipollini.

what to look for

Avoid onions with bruises or soft spots. If you're buying onions with the tops attached, the tops should be slightly firm.

storage

Remove tops and store those in the refrigerator. Keep the onions in a cool, dry place. Do not cover or they will start to mold. Also, while onions and potatoes like to be stored in similar conditions, do not store them together, as each releases a gas that will attempt to destroy the other.

peas

Peas are the bell ringing in spring. The difference between great and average peas is so profound to me. My grandfather used to grow peas in his little garden in the suburbs of Philadelphia. I loved them raw, right out of the pod, but hated them cooked. I used to pick peas and carrots out of my fried rice and would wind up with a pile of peas and carrots on the side of the plate.

Nowadays, I don't use raw peas often, but instead prefer to blanch them just to remove the raw flavor, so that they have a bit of softness, but still I want them to pop like caviar.

what to look for

Healthy looking pods are good. Avoid really large peas, as they tend to be starchy. If you do wind up with big peas, they taste best when cooked until soft and then mashed or puréed.

storage

Peas should be covered and refrigerated.

how to shell peas

I find that the stems and the string (which runs around the seam of a pea pod) are far more bitter than the pods themselves. So when I shell peas, I try to peel off the whole stem and all of the string in one full motion. You don't have to do it that way, but here's the thing: As chefs and cooks, sometimes we have to do these monotonous tasks for hours on end, so I try to give myself little challenges to make it more fun. Getting the whole thing off in one fell swoop is satisfying—like trying to peel an orange and keep the entire peel in one piece.

Take your bird's beak knife and cut through the stem, then carefully peel all the way down the seam (where that string is),

down to the bottom, then around the tip and back up the other side. If you manage to pull it off, the pod will separate into two distinct pieces and you can easily pop out all of the peas.

Don't forget to save the pods for things like Pea Shell Stock (page 311).

peppers

Pretty much any roasted pepper will give you a smoky component when added to a dish, and Quick-Pickled Peppers (page 307) are one of the greatest things on the planet. I will, occasionally, use seeded jalapeños, though personally I'm not into using much hot pepper in my own food.

what to look for

Look for firm, wrinkle-free peppers.

storage

Store them covered in the refrigerator.

potatoes

Potatoes are probably the most versatile vegetables in this book where they are turned into fries, gratins, chips; simmered, mashed, pounded, and fried like tostones; or used as a thickener in soups.

what to look for

You want potatoes that are not soft and don't have a ton of blemishes or "eyes."

storage

Store in a cool, dark place as you would an onion, but not *with* onions, as onions and potatoes hate each other during storage, and can cause each other to turn much faster.

how to poach potatoes

Scrub the dirt off of your potatoes and place them in a pot of cold, moderately salted water with a couple of bay leaves (fresh ones if you've got them). You want to avoid overpowering the flavor of the potatoes, so even a big pot shouldn't have any more than, say, 3 leaves. Bring the pot up to a gentle simmer (the potatoes will break up if the water is at a rolling boil).

Depending on the size of your potatoes, cooking them could take anywhere from 15 to 45 minutes. When in doubt, insert a cake tester into the potato—it should meet no resistance and slide right through.

Drain the potatoes in a colander. If you have used huge, heavy potatoes, you may want to pull them out with a slotted spoon so that they don't crush one other.

After that, you could peel them if you wanted to make a velvety-smooth purée (as with the King Trumpet Mushrooms, Potato Purée, Puntarelle, & Bordelaise, page 163); mash them; toss them with some olive oil and rosemary and then roast them in the oven; or pound them flat and fry them in a sauté pan—among other ideas.

radishes

Radishes are some of my favorite vegetables. In Napa, we grew ten to twelve different varietals and picked them all really small with the greens still attached.

I love radishes raw with softened butter—a classic French preparation. I also do a twist on that with the Radishes, Goat Cheese, Nori & Mustard (page 223).

Certain varietals, like black radish (the most intense) and daikon are excellent cooked, like Daikon Braised In Orange Juice (page 129).

Radishes with thick, tough skin, such as watermelon radish, should be peeled, but any small tender ones (or even black radishes) should be left unpeeled.

what to look for
Look for nice radish greens, which are not yellowing or wilted. You want a crispy, fresh radish.

storage
Store them covered, in the refrigerator. Unless you plan to serve the radishes with the greens attached, store the greens and root separately, as you would beets and their greens (page 40).

summer squash

I prefer summer squash—especially zucchini (courgette)—to its winter cousins. I like gold zucchini a lot too, and Costata Romanesco (which nets you those beautiful squash blossoms). Tromboncino is another great squash varietal, named after a trombone.

I got in the habit of picking zucchini when they were very small, peeling part of them like one might asparagus and then serving it like crudo. Then I would remove the stamen from the flower and either gently pickle it, or serve it raw like fish roe.

what to look for
You want a firm squash. Watch out for nicks, blemishes, and discoloration. The stem, where the vegetable attaches to the plant, should be somewhat green and vibrant. If flowers are attached, they should not be too wilted. The stem base will turn pale when the squash gets older.

storage
Cover squash and refrigerate.

sunchokes (jerusalem artichokes)

This may very well be my favorite plant to cook. When I worked in Charleston, South Carolina, under Mike Lata, he let me come up with a special one day. I wasn't even a sous-chef—basically a kid just doing grunt prep work during the day. Mike told me to make something with sunchokes and I had absolutely no clue what I was doing. I think I made a sunchoke-fennel mash with scallops. It was more or less okay, but it got me started obsessing over this small, knobby ingredient.

I eventually noticed that everybody was always peeling sunchokes, then simmering and puréeing them. I discovered that when you pan-roast sunchokes in the skin, they get this crunchy exterior but the inside stays creamy and sweet, like candy. Now I never peel them and I'm much happier.

what to look for
Sunchokes of any size actually work well, but avoid any parts that are mushy or rotting. You also want to avoid any with dark spots, or with too much of a stem, as it tends to be fibrous.

storage
Unless you are using them the same day that you bought them, store sunchokes covered, in the refrigerator. You will notice that the narrow points will start to dry out quickly.

how to roast sunchokes

Preheat the oven to 400°F (200°C/Gas 6). Line a baking sheet with parchment paper. Thoroughly wash the sunchokes, taking care to remove all of the dirt. Dry them well (you can just leave them on a baking sheet for a bit if you want) and cut off any exposed, oxidized red bits and tiny fibrous hairs. Coat the sunchokes with salt and oil (grapeseed or olive oil would both work great) and spread them on the lined baking sheet. Roast the sunchokes in the oven until soft, golden brown, and caramelized, 25 to 35 minutes.

tomatoes

Tomatoes are another ingredient that I began to look at differently after growing it at Ubuntu. We grew all different varietals, and our patrons would get really excited to be able to try as many as they could. To highlight the pure flavor of the tomatoes we would serve them as a Tomato Raw Bar (page 240).

But like carrots, corn, and beets, the tomato is an ingredient that is massively versatile. Raw, blackened, juiced, roasted, blanched, stewed, dried—there are so many wonderful variations.

what to look for

Avoid too-soft or bruised tomatoes. Heirloom tomatoes will sometimes have those hard canyons in them, so be wary of those, as they are not fun to eat and you will have to cut around the hard spots.

storage

Tomatoes are best when never refrigerated, but if they're close to turning bad, you should move them to the refrigerator.

very, very basic tomato preparation

Cut open a tomato, sprinkle it with salt, and eat it. See how basic that was?

green (unripe) tomatoes

Green tomatoes are simply tomatoes harvested while they are still green and firm. Popular in the South, they are delicious breaded and fried, and served with a dipping sauce.

what to look for

The tomatoes should be firm, not too pale—medium to dark green.

storage

Unlike ripe tomatoes, these should be kept in the refrigerator.

recipes

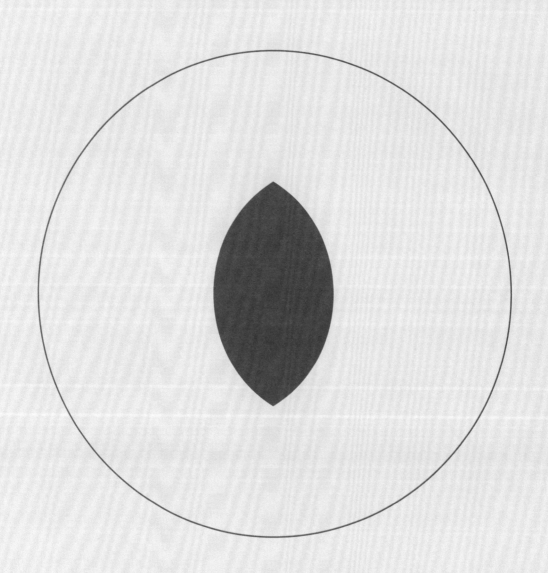

does southern california have seasons?

The short answer is: yes. The long answer is slightly more complicated.

Fall is strange here—as seasons go, I think fall has the least definition to it. Most of the ingredients from summer are still hanging around, and winter ingredients start showing up early. It's like purgatory, but a really great purgatory filled with beautiful broccoli, mushrooms, citrus, avocados, persimmons, squash, and lima beans. Okay, so maybe it's actually the opposite of purgatory.

The flavors change a little. Food grows earthier and the color of the ingredients—even the finished dishes—fades and becomes more dull and muted. Spring is green, summer is a rainbow, and fall brings you more into the earth tones of the plant color palette.

In some ways, fall can be whatever you want it to be. I can eat nutty, fruity, refreshing salads, like Baby Kiwi & Burrata (page 141), or dishes like Lima Bean & Sorrel Cacio e Pepe (page 71). While not as showy as spring or summer, fall might be an even better reflection of what is great about cooking, shopping, and eating in Southern California.

I must say, though, that even in winter, the farmers markets here are pretty bright places. I can still find radishes, arugula (rocket), brassicas, small squashes—even tomatoes. This is very different from how I remember the Atlanta markets of fifteen years ago, where one mostly saw things like hardy greens, potatoes, rutabagas (swedes), turnips, and cabbage.

There are also ingredients that had been available for months that start to change come winter. Broccoli is around in the fall, but by the winter it starts to bolt—with more pronounced stems, which I actually find a lot more fun to cook with.

Since California winters are so different than the ones back East, I really like to embrace that difference. Fennel is confited and enlivened with kumquat (page 137); caramelized sunchokes get the tart boost of grapefruit (page 234). There's beauty in that contrast—of bright sun beating down on a sometimes-chilly winter morning.

And then there's spring—which, more than any other season, is the one I look forward to every year. When I lived on the East Coast, spring's arrival was such an abrupt change—starting with peas arriving and the vanishing of root vegetables. The weather clears and bright green things begin to pop up: asparagus, favas, spring onions, green garlic.

If winter is the doldrums (a term I always loved from reading *The Phantom Tollbooth*, a popular children's book), then spring brings light back into the world. Ingredients are crisper. You begin to use less butter and cream, less roasting and caramelizing—cooking becomes lighter.

Whereas winter vegetables don't have as much useable waste, in the spring I start to look for creative ways to use asparagus peels, pea and pods, and the like.

But it's the pure brightness of spring that I really love. You're blanching and then shocking things to keep them vibrantly green and flavorful; taking a red fruit and cooking it down the way you would a short rib in winter; using hyperseasonal green garlic to lift up country gravy. Even French Onion Soup (page 180) is brighter, lighter, and more of the moment.

And, of course, there's summer. Patterns that started with spring grow more pronounced: less fat, less butter and cream. Summer products are so good, you want to do as little to them as possible. Roast some eggplants (aubergines) and set on a plate. Grill some corn, lightly dress it, and eat it.

While a great tomato is delicious with nothing but a sprinkle of salt, I also love scoring it, roasting it, and cooking it down into its deepest self.

Summer also might be the most interactive shopping season of the year. It's about knocking on melons to check for ripeness; and pressing your fingers against a peach to tell how much give there is, while trying not to bruise it and annoy the hell out of the farmer. It's about bright and oddly shaped tomatoes of all different hues and sizes, plump blackberries, and juicy stone fruit.

Ultimately, though, this season takes me back to spending summers with my grandparents in the suburbs of Philadelphia, Pennsylvania. My grandmother and my aunts would go to certain farms for the best peaches, corn, or plums. They were opinionated about which ones had the best produce on any given week, and I think part of that still sticks in my head when I wander the markets in the summer.

I don't have a pastry background and I've always regretted how in my past kitchen jobs I never spent any time working in the pastry section. But I've always had an affinity for desserts that were made by savory chefs. And though my lack of technical pastry knowledge may show up in some of these recipes, the results, I think, are some unique and delicious desserts interwoven with the savory recipes.

So yes: There are seasons in Southern California. But they bend and spread and bleed into each other like no place I've ever lived before. As such, no matter where you are, I encourage you to cook with what you find around you. Work with whatever ingredients manage to pop up in your surrounding area. Try to embrace the spirit of this book and its recipes, rather than worry about finding the exact products that grow around me.

baby artichoke fritto
with black garlic aioli

serves 6 to 8

3 lemons
24 baby artichokes
2 quarts (about 2 liters) Vegetable Stock
   (page 312)
kosher salt
½ cup (120 ml) Aioli (page 265)
2 tablespoons Black Garlic Purée
   (page 295)
2 cups (475 ml) extra-virgin olive oil
2 cups (475 ml) grapeseed oil
2 to 3 tablespoons rice flour
Black Garlic (page 295), for garnish

Fried artichokes taste great dipped into regular aioli, but I love the addition of black garlic, which works beautifully here. Keep in mind that once the artichokes are braised, they can be held at room temperature until you're ready to fry—but once they're fried, serve them right away.

directions

Fill a bowl with 4 cups (950 ml) of ice water. Halve 2 of the lemons and squeeze their juice into the ice water; drop the empty lemon halves in.

Use a bird's beak knife to trim away any large outer leaves from the artichoke and then gently trim off the outermost layer of the stem. Cut off the tip of the artichoke, creating a flat top, and place each trimmed artichoke into the acidulated ice water to prevent discoloration.

Meanwhile, in a large pot, bring the vegetable stock to a simmer over medium-high heat. Reduce the heat to medium-low and season to taste with salt.

Add the artichokes to the pot. Cut out a round of parchment paper that will fit snugly inside of the pot (a cartouche). Lay the cartouche over the artichokes and cook at just below a simmer until barely tender, about 45 minutes.

Remove the pot from the heat and let the artichokes cool to room temperature in the broth. Remove them from the broth and using the tip of a teaspoon, scoop out any inedible fuzz from the cavity. Dry the artichokes on towels until they're completely dry before you fry them (if not, they might splatter and/or cause the oil to overflow when they're fried).

Meanwhile, in a small bowl, stir together the aioli and black garlic purée until combined.

In a Dutch oven or deep, heavy pot, heat the olive and grapeseed oils over medium-high heat until the oil registers 350°F (180°C) on a deep-frying thermometer.

Meanwhile, lightly dredge the artichokes in the rice flour, shaking off the excess.

Working in batches, carefully slide the artichokes into the hot oil—being careful not to crowd the pan or let the oil temperature drop too much—and fry until the artichokes are golden and crisp. Remove the artichokes from the oil and place on paper towels. Season immediately with salt and a squeeze of lemon. Serve immediately, with black garlic aioli and garnished with black garlic.

creamy artichoke & ramp toast

serves 4

2 lemons, 1 finely zested, both halved
4 large artichokes
⅓ cup (80 ml) Crème Fraîche (page 278)
1 tablespoon extra-virgin olive oil, plus
    extra as needed
2 teaspoons chopped flat-leaf parsley
kosher salt
4 thick slices (1 inch/2.5 cm) Deanie's
    Brioche (page 283)
½ cup (50 g) Pickled Ramps (page 303)
freshly ground black pepper
arugula (rocket) leaves, to garnish

I know that I have a lot of things on toast in this book, but I happened upon this iteration in the kitchen one day and I loved the taste, so I'm adding it.

NOTE If you want to use your artichoke scraps, you can steam or blanch the leaves and then scrape the little bits of meat off of each leaf and add it to things like pasta, soup, or anywhere else you'd like to use artichoke.

directions

Set up a large bowl of cold water and squeeze the juice of 1 lemon into it—this will keep the artichokes from browning.

Trim the artichokes down to just the hearts and a bit of stem. Halve them lengthwise after they've been trimmed and scoop out the fuzzy choke with a spoon. Keep the trimmed artichokes in the acidulated water while you work on the remaining ones.

On a mandoline, slice the artichokes into thin, but not paper-thin, slices—you want them to have a little bit of bite. Immediately squeeze the remaining lemon over the artichoke and dress with the crème fraîche, olive oil, and parsley, and season to taste with salt.

Toast the brioche slices, either in a toaster (mini) oven or with some oil in a preheated cast-iron pan over medium heat, until the bread is golden brown on both sides. Top the brioche slices with the artichoke mixture, followed by the pickled ramps. Finish with lemon zest, pepper to taste, and a few leaves of arugula.

grilled artichoke, celery, meyer lemon & olive

serves 4 to 8

4 large (10 oz/285 g each) artichokes
½ cup (40 g) celery leaves, roughly chopped, plus more for garnish
¼ cup (60 ml) brine from Pickled Green Garlic (page 303) or 2 tablespoons white wine vinegar
¼ cup (60 ml) extra-virgin olive oil, plus more for brushing
2 garlic cloves, germ removed, grated
3 meyer lemons
kosher salt
¼ cup (60 ml) Black Olive Caramel (page 266)

Eating a whole artichoke and peeling off the leaves reminds me of my fourth grade teacher, who, one day, brought in steamed artichokes with melted butter. I felt cool and sophisticated eating vegetables. I still have no idea why she brought steamed artichokes to a bunch of fourth graders, but I'm really glad she did.

directions

I don't trim artichokes too much—I just take off whatever leaves are on the stem. Then, steam the artichokes whole. You can use a steamer basket or bamboo steamer with water underneath. Cook the artichokes until the heart of the stem is tender and the leaves can easily be pulled off, 20 to 30 minutes.

Meanwhile, in a bowl, toss together the celery leaves, pickled garlic brine, olive oil, and garlic. Finely grate the zest of 2 Meyer lemons and add to the salsa. Squeeze the lemon juice in, mix thoroughly, and season to taste with salt.

Remove the artichokes from the steamer and halve lengthwise. Using a small spoon, scoop out the inedible choke, being careful not to nick up any of the actual meat.

Prepare your outdoor gas or charcoal grill (barbecue) and bring to a high heat. Brush the cut sides of the artichokes with oil. Season with salt and grill, cut-side down, until the artichokes get a nice, even char, 3 to 4 minutes. Halve the last lemon and squeeze it over the artichokes while still hot.

Season the artichokes again with salt and transfer to a plate. Spoon the salsa over the artichokes and dot with the olive caramel. Finish with additional celery leaves.

asparagus vichyssoise, black garlic mustard & potato

Traditionally, vichyssoise is a soup with potatoes functioning mostly as a thickener, but here, I'm using them for flavor, and incorporating them after the soup has been cooked. I prefer the flavor of slow-cooked asparagus, even if it's not vibrant green, but if you're worried about the color, you can blanch the asparagus and add it toward the end with the peas. If you have asparagus scraps and peels, you can use them in the purée as well. When pureeing the soup, do not fill the blender more than half way.

NOTE The vichyssoise can be made up to a day in advance—after that it will start to lose its color—and should be made early enough to chill completely before serving. The potatoes, however, should be made within a couple hours of serving—you ideally don't want to have to refrigerate them. They should be served at room temperature.

serves 4

spring vichyssoise
4 ounces (115 g) ramps, greens separated from bulbs, or 1 leek, white and light green parts only
4 ounces (115 g) unsalted butter
kosher salt
2 pounds (910 g) asparagus, preferably pencil-thin, cut into ½-inch (1.25 cm) pieces
2 garlic cloves, germ removed, finely grated
5 cups (1.2 liters) Pea Shell Stock (page 311)
4 ounces (115 g) shelled English peas, from about 9 ounces (255 g) pea pods
¼ cup (60 ml) heavy (double) cream
4 tablespoons chopped cilantro (coriander) leaves and stems
4 tablespoons chopped parsley leaves and stems
25 mint leaves

crushed potato
8 ounces (225 g) yukon gold potatoes
2 tablespoons extra-virgin olive oil
2 tablespoons thinly sliced ramp bulbs
2 tablespoons thinly sliced chives
kosher salt

to serve
¼ cup (60 ml) Black Garlic Mustard (page 296)
2 green jumbo asparagus, shaved
tips of 24 white matchstick asparagus

make the spring vichyssoise

Thinly slice the ramp bulbs. Give the ramp greens a rough chop and set aside.

In a large pot, melt the butter over medium heat. Add the ramp bulbs and season with salt. Cook the bulbs, stirring, until they are translucent—don't let the bulbs take on any color—about 10 minutes.

Add the asparagus and garlic, season with salt, and cook for another 5 minutes, stirring occasionally. Add the pea shell stock and bring everything to a boil. Reduce the heat to low, cover, and simmer, until the asparagus is soft enough to be puréed, 25 to 30 minutes.

Meanwhile, prepare an ice bath in a large bowl and bring a pot of salted water to a boil over high heat. Blanch the peas in the boiling water for around 3 minutes, or until just tender. Shock in the ice bath until completely cool, drain, and transfer to towels to dry.

Add the heavy cream to the soup and bring to a simmer. Remove the soup from the heat and add the reserved ramp greens, peas, cilantro, parsley, and mint leaves. Working in batches, purée the soup in a blender until smooth. Strain the soup through a fine-mesh strainer into a bowl and cool down quickly by placing the bowl of soup into a larger bowl filled with ice, whisking until it's room temperature. Cover and refrigerate until completely cold before serving, and for up to a day in advance.

make the crushed potato

Follow the cooking method for poaching potatoes on page 46. When the potatoes are cool enough to handle, peel them and transfer them to a bowl. Add the olive oil and lightly crush the potatoes with a fork. Add the ramp bulbs and chives, and season to taste with salt. Allow the potatoes to cool to room temperature before serving.

to serve

In 4 individual bowls, pile crushed potatoes and a dollop of the black garlic mustard on one side of each bowl. Garnish with some shaved green asparagus and white asparagus tips, then ladle the soup on the other side of the bowl.

chilled asparagus, saffron, olive & fennel pollen

serves 4

1 pound (455 g) asparagus
kosher salt
juice of 2 lemons
1 teaspoon saffron threads
½ cup (120 ml) Yogurt (page 281)
2 tablespoons extra-virgin olive oil
3 tablespoons Black Olive Caramel
    (page 266)
2 tablespoons chopped toasted almonds
1 teaspoon fennel pollen

I like pencil-thin asparagus spears for this recipe because of the texture. Even though they could be eaten raw, I find that the seasonings don't adhere as well and the asparagus winds up requiring a lot more salt and lemon to make an impact. So for this recipe, I just do a very quick blanch.

Also, unlike with bigger asparagus, you really just need to snap off the bottoms—no need to peel or trim.

directions

Snap off the base of the asparagus—it will have a natural place where it wants to break off.

Bring a 6- to 8-quart (6- to 8-liter) stockpot of salted water to a boil over high heat. Meanwhile, prepare an ice bath in a large bowl.

Cut the asparagus into 1-inch (2.5 cm) pieces and add them to the boiling water for 45 seconds. Drain the asparagus and immediately plunge into the prepared ice bath until completely chilled. Drain the asparagus on towels and set aside.

Place half of lemon juice into a bowl and add the saffron to let it bloom—the acid will help the colors leach out. Add the yogurt and season to taste with salt—the yogurt should have taken on color from the saffron.

Dress the asparagus with the olive oil and season to taste with salt and remaining lemon juice. Arrange the asparagus on the plate. Fill in the gaps with dots of black olive caramel and dollops of the saffron yogurt. Top with the toasted almonds and fennel pollen.

poached asparagus
à la flamande

serves 4

2 tablespoons distilled white vinegar
4 large eggs, cold
kosher salt
½ cup (120 ml) Brown Butter (page 278)
2 teaspoons freshly ground black pepper
10 grates nutmeg
1 tablespoon (15 g) unsalted butter,
  at room temperature
20 stalks jumbo asparagus
1 lemon, quartered and seeded
4 tablespoons Breadcrumbs (page 290)
1 Cured Egg Yolk (page 291)
1 tablespoon chiffonade of flat-leaf
  parsley
flaky sea salt

I have a not-so-secret ambition to open a Belgian restaurant one day. One of my first chefs, Shaun Doty, set me up with a *stage* (an unpaid internship) in Bruges many years ago. I fell in love with the people, the culture, and of course, the food.

I saw a version of poached asparagus on seemingly every menu. We did a similar dish at a restaurant I came up at in Atlanta, Georgia, called Mumbo Jumbo, and that was the first time I had eaten fresh asparagus. I grew up eating the mushy stuff in a can, and this was far superior.

NOTE   Since the asparagus is served hot, you'll want to have all the other parts of the dish ready when you add the asparagus to the boiling water to blanch it.

directions

In a pot, bring 2 quarts (about 2 liters) of water with the vinegar to a boil. In a large bowl, prepare an ice bath. Gently slide the cold eggs into the boiling water and cook at a light simmer for 9 minutes. Transfer the eggs to the ice bath and leave for around 5 minutes. Remove the eggs from the ice bath, then peel, roughly chop, and set aside.

Follow the directions for trimming, peeling, and tying the asparagus in bundles on page 38. Bring a pot of heavily salted water to a boil. (It should have enough water so that you won't lose your boil once you add the asparagus.)

While the water comes to a boil, melt the brown butter in a pan over low heat, being careful not to burn or overcook it. Remove the brown butter from the heat and add the chopped eggs, black pepper, nutmeg, and kosher salt to taste. Quickly add the butter to the brown butter sauce, and fold it in to combine.

Blanch the asparagus in the boiling water. Drain and dry the asparagus briefly on towels, then squeeze over it the juice of your quartered lemon.

To serve, lay the warm asparagus on plates. Spoon the warm egg sauce over the top and then finish with the breadcrumbs, cured egg yolk, parsley, and flaky sea salt.

avocado toast

serves 4

1 tablespoon flaxseeds
1 tablespoon sunflower seeds
4 slices Pain de Mie (page 285),
   1 inch (2.5 cm) thick
kosher salt
2 avocados, halved and pitted
1 tablespoon extra-virgin olive oil,
   plus more as needed
freshly ground black pepper
36 cherry tomatoes, halved
½ cup (120 ml) Sea Moss Tapenade
   (page 272), at room temperature
2 calendula flowers (optional)
flaky sea salt

Avocado toast is ubiquitous on Southern California menus, and as a result, people like to make fun of it. But it's ubiquitous for a reason—California grows a lot of avocados, and also avocado toast can taste really good. This version is sort of an homage to 1990s health food.

directions

Preheat the oven to 350°F (180°C/Gas 4).

Place the flaxseeds and sunflower seeds in separate small baking pans (in case they cook at different speeds) and toast in the oven until fragrant, 4 to 5 minutes. Remove from the oven and transfer to a plate.

Meanwhile, toast the bread in a toaster or toaster (mini) oven, or brushed with olive oil in a preheated cast-iron skillet over medium heat. (Both methods work quite well here.) Once toasted, season the bread lightly with kosher salt.

While the bread is toasting, scoop the avocados into a bowl. Add the olive oil and season with kosher salt and black pepper. Mash it with a fork until chunky but spreadable.

Spread the avocado mixture over the toast and arrange the tomatoes on top cut-side up. Top with dollops of the tapenade, toasted seeds, calendula petals (if using), and flaky sea salt.

bananas, crème fraîche, honey & curry cashews

serves 8

1 cup (240 ml) Crème Fraîche (page 278)
4 bananas, sliced
¼ cup (60 ml) honey
½ cup (115 g) Curry Cashews (page 299), chopped
flaky sea salt

Not every dessert needs to be a fancy, labor-intensive thing. This one is actually based on a dessert I made when I was five years old. So if a five-year-old can do it, so can you. Back then, I just mixed bananas, sour cream, and sugar in a bowl until it was all grainy and crunchy. I hope this version is better—you be the judge.

directions

Spoon a base coat of crème fraîche in each bowl. Arrange the banana slices on top, drizzle with honey, then finish with cashews and flaky sea salt.

lima bean
& sorrel cacio e pepe

Lima beans, also known as butter beans, are probably my favorite shell bean. Fun fact: When I put this dish on the menu at Rustic Canyon with the name "lima bean," nobody buys it, but when I list it as "butter bean," it sells out and everybody loves it.

To me, one of the best things about eating beans is the broth, and when you can add butter, garlic, and pecorino to it, it becomes something really great. The only acidity in this dish comes from the sorrel, which brings a really nice tang.

serves 4

1 pound (455 g) shelled fresh lima (butter) beans

2 garlic cloves, germ removed, peeled and smashed

2 teaspoons fresh rosemary leaves

½ cup (2 oz/60 g) tightly packed torn sorrel leaves, plus 2 tablespoons fine chiffonade of sorrel leaves

1 tablespoon freshly ground black pepper kosher salt

2 tablespoons (30 g) unsalted butter, at room temperature

4 teaspoons Garlic Confit Purée (page 313), at room temperature

½ cup (30 g) finely grated pecorino romano cheese

2 tablespoons oil from Garlic Confit (page 312), at room temperature

1 tablespoon grated Cured Egg Yolk (page 291)

directions

Place the lima beans in a pot filled with 4 cups (1 liter) cold water. Place the garlic and rosemary in a single-layer square of cheesecloth, tie it into a sachet, and add it to the pot with the beans. Bring to a simmer over medium heat, then reduce the heat to low and cook, uncovered, at just below a simmer, until the beans are tender, 30 to 40 minutes.

Remove the pot from the heat, discard the sachet, and add the torn sorrel, black pepper, and salt to taste. (You will notice that the sorrel turns drab quickly, but that's okay. It's about the flavor more than the appearance, with tart sorrel standing in place of lemon to balance out the other ingredients.)

Right before serving, fold the butter into the beans.

To serve, warm the bowls and add 1 teaspoon of the garlic confit purée to the bottom of each bowl. Spoon the beans and their broth into the bowls (since black pepper tends to settle to the bottom of the pot, make sure to re-stir the soup before each ladle).

Finish with the chiffonade of sorrel, grated pecorino, garlic confit oil, and cured egg yolk.

rustic yellow eye
bean stew, torn bread

During the tougher times at Manresa, before the restaurant gained critical esteem, we tried our version of a bar menu, called the "Patio Menu," which focused on straightforward dishes, and this stew came out of that effort. I kept refining the stew over time, and I eventually found a specific bean that I really loved: Rancho Gordo Yellow Eye Bean. The bean held its shape, but stayed creamy and didn't burst or overcook. The stew became really popular at Ubuntu and eventually people would come in just to order it. Brothy and garlicky—one of the heartier things on the menu—it's one of only a handful of dishes that I never get tired of making and eating.

NOTE   Give yourself a one-day lead time for this recipe, as you'll need to soak the beans overnight. You can also start cooking the stew while the beans are cooking. If the beans aren't ready in time, just turn the heat off on the stew and wait for the beans to catch up. After picking the rosemary leaves, keep the stems to use in conjunction with the mirepoix when cooking the beans.

Should you be unable to find yellow eye beans (Rancho Gordo being my favorite source), any dried bean you like will work just fine.

serves 6 to 8

yellow eye beans
stripped rosemary stems
2 celery stalks
1 carrot, halved lengthwise
1 leek, halved lengthwise, tough green parts trimmed off
stems from 1 bunch flat-leaf parsley
1 head garlic, halved horizontally
1 pound (455 g) dried yellow eye beans, soaked overnight
kosher salt

yellow eye bean stew
1 cup (240 ml) extra-virgin olive oil, plus more as needed
8 ounces (225 g) diced carrots
kosher salt
8 ounces (225 g) diced celery
8 ounces (225 g) diced leeks (white and light green parts only; save the tougher green tops for another use, such as vegetable stock)
1 bunch hearty greens like kale or collard greens, ribs removed and roughly chopped
½ cup (200 g) chopped garlic (germ removed)
¾ cup (60 g) chopped fresh rosemary leaves
1 teaspoon chili flakes
1 cup (255 g) tomato paste (purée)

to serve
about 1 pound (455 g) crusty bread, torn into bite-size pieces
extra-virgin olive oil
kosher salt

make the yellow eye beans

Pick the leaves off the rosemary sprigs and set the leaves aside for the stew. Take the rosemary stems and, using kitchen twine, tie them into a bundle with the celery, carrot, and leek. In a double layer of cheesecloth, combine the parsley stems and garlic halves and tie up to make a sachet. Place the beans, aromatics bundle, and sachet in a large pot and cover with 12 cups (2.8 liters) of water. Bring to a simmer over medium heat, reduce the heat to low, and cook the beans just below a simmer, uncovered and skimming off any foam that rises to the top, until they have a creamy texture but are not falling apart. Depending on the freshness of the beans, this could take anywhere from 45 minutes to 2½ hours.

Remove and discard the bundle and sachet and season the beans with salt until the broth tastes good by itself. Remove the pot from the heat and set the beans and cooking liquid aside until you're ready to make the stew. You could let the beans cool to room temperature and then refrigerate until you're ready to make the stew. →

make the yellow eye bean stew

In a large pot, warm the olive oil over medium heat. Add the carrots first (they will take the longest), season with salt, and cook, stirring occasionally, for 5 minutes. Add the celery, leeks, and greens and season with salt. Allow them to cook down, stirring, for about 5 minutes.

Add the chopped garlic, rosemary, and chili flakes—you want the garlic to become fragrant but not browned. Add the tomato paste and stir thoroughly to combine. Cook for about 2 minutes, allowing the tomato paste to toast. At this point, all of the vegetables should be cooked through but still have a bite. Taste them to make sure, and if they have too much bite, let them go a little longer.

Add the cooked beans, along with their liquid, and bring the pot to a simmer. Taste and adjust the seasoning. Remove from the heat.

to serve

Toss the bread with a touch of olive oil and season with salt. Toast over medium heat in a large sauté pan until crispy on the edges, 3 to 5 minutes. Ladle the stew into bowls, and then follow with the toasted bread. Finish with a drizzle of olive oil.

gold beets, nectarine, hazelnut & oregano

serves 4

16 baby golden beets (beetroots), greens
   removed and reserved for another use
3 nectarines
¼ cup (60 ml) fresh orange juice
1 tablespoon champagne vinegar
1 tablespoon extra-virgin olive oil
¼ Preserved Lemon (page 307)
16 blanched hazelnuts, halved
32 fresh oregano leaves

This makes good use of any nectarines that might be too soft or blemished to eat on their own since here they're used to highlight the beets. Blemishes stand out in a raw nectarine, but no one will ever notice it in a cooked purée.

directions

Preheat the oven to 350°F (180°C/Gas 4).

Thoroughly wash and dry the beets and place them in a 12 x 6-inch (30 x 15 cm) baking dish with the whole nectarines and orange juice.

Cover the dish with foil and bake until the beets are tender when a cake tester easily slides in an out of the beets, 30 to 45 minutes. Remove the foil. Let the beets cool down just enough to handle, then, using either gloves or a tea towel, peel off and discard the outer skin. Halve the beets and toss with the champagne vinegar, olive oil, and salt to taste.

Halve and pit the nectarines—which should be as easy as pulling braised meat from the bone—and place in a blender, along with the preserved lemon. Blend together until a fine purée forms. It should be the consistency of baby food, slightly looser than a mousse or pudding. Taste and adjust seasoning if necessary.

To serve, place the nectarine puree around each plate in 8 dollops. Lay a halved beet on each dollop, cut-side up. Place another small dollop of puree on top, then use it to anchor each hazelnut half atop, as well as a leaf of oregano.

beet gazpacho, mustard, cherries & almond

While gazpacho is typically associated with tomatoes and cucumbers, I like using beets (beetroots) in this version, as an homage to cold summer borscht.

serves 4

1 pound 6 ounces (625 g) beets (beetroots), peeled and thinly sliced
1 pound (455 g) white onions, julienned
8 ounces (225 g) red bell pepper, chopped into small pieces
½ cup (120 ml) red wine vinegar
1 generous tablespoon chopped garlic (germ removed) plus 1 tablespoon thinly sliced garlic (germ intact)
kosher salt
4 tablespoons Horsey Goat (page 279)
2 tablespoons Whole-Grain Mustard (page 272)
1 tablespoon extra-virgin olive oil
14 Bing cherries, pitted and halved
1 tablespoon chopped toasted almonds
small florets of flowering brassica; can substitute arugula (rocket), watercress, or other mildly spicy greens, to garnish

directions

In a large pot, combine the beets, onions, bell pepper, vinegar, chopped garlic, and 1 quart (about 1 liter) water. Bring to a simmer over medium heat and cook, uncovered, until the vegetables are very soft, 45 minutes to 1 hour.

Working in batches, blend thoroughly until smooth, then strain through a fine-mesh sieve or chinois. Transfer to a container, cover, and refrigerate until cold, about 4 hours. Season to taste with salt—you will probably find that a cold soup requires more salt than a hot one. The gazpacho will keep for 3 to 5 days under refrigeration.

Meanwhile, in a small bowl, fold the horseradish goat cheese and mustard together until incorporated. Refrigerate until needed. Let stand at room temperature for 30 minutes before serving.

In a small sauté pan, combine the sliced garlic and olive oil and set the pan over medium heat. Set a sieve over a small bowl. Slowly cook the garlic, shaking the pan occasionally as it cooks, until evenly golden throughout, 3 to 5 minutes. Drain the garlic oil through the sieve into the bowl and set the oil aside. Transfer the sliced garlic to a paper towel and sprinkle with salt.

Ladle the cold gazpacho into 4 bowls. Place a quenelle or dollop of mustard-horseradish cheese on top and garnish with cherries, almonds, garlic chips, and garlic oil. Finish with the small florets of flowering brassica.

beets & berries

This dish was on my menu for a long time, and while I was going through a rustic simplicity phase, I thought that perhaps the beet soil was too showy, so I took it off the plate. Two months later, my wife came in and had the salad, then told me that she was really missing the soil. So I told the kitchen staff what she said, and they all said, "We all thought that the whole time." So, it might be showy, but I have to listen to the people, so now it's back on the plate.

serves 4

roasted beets
10 small beets (beetroots), greens removed and reserved for another use
2 tablespoons extra-virgin olive oil
1 tablespoon red wine vinegar
kosher salt

red quinoa
⅔ cup (115 g) red quinoa
3 tablespoons plus 2 teaspoons extra-virgin olive oil
2 teaspoons chopped fresh spearmint leaves
finely grated zest and juice of 1 lemon, plus more as needed
kosher salt
1 cup (150 g) mixed berries

to serve
1 medium avocado
2 tablespoons extra-virgin olive oil
kosher salt
freshly cracked black pepper
4 tablespoons Beet Soil (page 293)
a handful of each: whole mulberries, halved raspberries, and halved blackberries, to garnish

make the roasted beets

Follow the instructions for roasting and peeling beets on page 40. Cut the peeled beets into whatever size and shape you like and toss them with the olive oil, red wine vinegar, and salt to taste. Set the beets aside to cool until plating.

make the red quinoa

Rinse the quinoa under cold running water. In a pot, combine the quinoa and 1⅓ cups (315 ml) cool water. Bring to a boil over medium heat. Cover, reduce the heat to a simmer, and cook until all the water is absorbed, 15 to 20 minutes. Remove from the heat, fluff the quinoa with a fork, and toss it with the 2 teaspoons of the olive oil, the mint, lemon zest and juice, and salt to taste. Cool the quinoa to room temperature or cooler before serving.

In a bowl, toss the berries in a bowl with the remaining 3 tablespoons olive oil, season lightly with salt, and mash them up with a fork until the oil and the juices combine. Right before serving, halve and pit the avocado, then scoop the avocado flesh into a bowl. Add the olive oil, salt to taste, and a healthy dose of black pepper. Mash it with a fork until well combined.

to serve

To serve, either portion onto 4 individual plates or bowls or onto 1 large platter and serve family-style. Lay a dollop of the avocado first, and follow with some quinoa. Arrange the beets over the avocado and quinoa, then spoon the berry mixture on top. Garnish with beet soil and finish with the fresh berries.

beets, greens, figs, blue cheese & walnuts

A beet salad with blue cheese and walnuts is fairly common, so I'm not reinventing the wheel with this flavor combination. But I do love that this is a great way to use every part of the beet (stems, greens and all) in one single dish.

NOTE Malabar spinach (pictured) may be uncommon (and actually, isn't even in the spinach family), but if you happen to find it, definitely use it. You can, however, definitely substitute baby mustard greens, baby spinach, beet greens, or other such greens.

serves 4

beet salad
6 small beets (beetroots), greens and stems set aside for Beet Green Marmalade (recipe follows)
kosher salt
2 teaspoons red wine vinegar
1 tablespoon extra-virgin olive oil

beet green marmalade
stems and greens from 1 bunch beets/beetroots (yielding about 1 quart/1 liter of leaves, and the accompanying stems)
2 tablespoons extra-virgin olive oil
kosher salt
1 cup (240 ml) red wine vinegar
¼ cup (50 g) granulated sugar

to serve
6 fresh figs, sliced ⅛ inch (3 mm) thick
½ cup (120 ml) Beet Green Marmalade
2 ounces (60 g) blue cheese
1 tablespoon chopped toasted walnuts
24 petite clusters malabar spinach (see Note)

make the beets	Follow the cooking instructions for roasting and peeling beets on page 40. While the beets are still warm, cut them into coins, ⅛ inch (3 mm) thick. Season to taste with salt, and dress with the vinegar and oil.
	Meanwhile, thoroughly wash and dry the reserved beet stems—they tend to collect a lot of sand. Tear the leaves into rustic 1-inch (2.5 cm) pieces. Cut the stems into small dice.
make the beet green marmalade	In a large sauté pan, heat the oil over medium heat. Add the stems, season with salt, and cook them gently, stirring, until just tender, about 8 minutes. Add the torn leaves, vinegar, sugar, and a touch more salt.
	Reduce the heat to low and cook gently until the stems and leaves are tender and about 90 percent of the liquid is cooked off, 20 to 30 minutes. Transfer the greens to a plate and let cool to room temperature.
	Chop finely until you have a unified mixture. Taste and adjust the seasonings.
to serve	Arrange the sliced beets in 4 bowls or on plates. Follow with the figs. Form a quenelle (or dollop) with the beet marmalade and set it on the side of the plate.
	Thinly slice the blue cheese with a hot, wet knife and lay it over the top of the bowl (if it crumbles, that's fine too). Sprinkle with the walnuts and garnish with the spinach.

spaetzle, blueberry sauce & corn pudding

serves 4

blueberry sauce
2 cups (100 g) blueberries, rinsed and
    dried
¼ cup (50 g) granulated sugar
1 teaspoon fresh lemon juice

spaetzle
4 large eggs, at room temperature
2 cups (250 g) all-purpose (plain) flour
¾ cup (180 ml) whole (full-fat) milk
2 tablespoons granulated sugar
2 teaspoons kosher salt
2 teaspoons grapeseed oil

to serve
1 tablespoon (15 g) unsalted butter
kosher salt
1 cup (240 ml) Yellow Corn Pudding
    (page 274), chilled
mint leaves, to garnish

The idea for this dish came about when I made spaetzle once, ate it unseasoned, and thought it tasted kind of like pancakes. To me, spaetzle is basically just crispy, misshapen droplets of pancake batter. You can try them with just maple syrup and bananas if you want, or you can eat them like this.

NOTE Spaetzle is best the same day, but it can be boiled in advance and then crisped up in the brown butter just before serving.

make the blueberry sauce	In a small pot, combine the berries, sugar, and ¼ cup (60 ml) water and bring to a boil over medium heat. Reduce the heat to a simmer and cook until the blueberries soften and the liquid begins to thicken, 5 to 10 minutes. Remove the pot from the heat and stir in the lemon juice. Let cool slightly before using, or cool completely, cover, and refrigerate for up to 3 days. Serve the sauce at room temperature.
make the spaetzle	In a bowl, lightly beat the eggs. Add the flour, milk, sugar, and salt and mix until thoroughly combined—the batter should look pretty similar to pancake batter.
	Bring a large pot of water to a simmer. Prepare an ice bath in a bowl.
	Push the batter through a perforated hotel pan, colander, or spaetzle maker into the simmering water and cook until the spaetzle float to the top, about 1 minute.
	Drain and transfer the spaetzle to the ice bath until cool. Drain again, then toss with the grapeseed oil. Transfer to baking sheets, using your fingers to break up the individual dumplings, and let them dry. If you are holding them for longer than a couple of hours, cover and refrigerate for up to 1 day.
to serve	Heat a large sauté pan over medium-high heat. Melt the butter in the pan and cook until it begins to brown. Add the spaetzle and cook until golden brown and slightly crispy. Season lightly with salt and then drain on paper towels.
	When ready to serve, place a dollop of corn pudding on each of 4 plates. Lay 3 mounds of spaetzle around the pudding. Top with blueberry sauce and garnish with mint leaves.

borage & ricotta dumplings in mushroom broth

This recipe is inspired by my good friend Eric Korsh—the executive chef at the North End Grill in New York City. His version had chopped spinach in the dumplings, which he served with mushrooms in a Parmesan broth. He gave me his recipe and I tweaked it minimally (just to standardize the recipe a bit), so I usually list it on my menu as "Malfatti—literally, 'badly made'—alla Korsh." I like to be upfront about where my dishes come from; I'd rather pay homage than rip somebody off. That being said, I came up with this dish all by myself. (Insert wink emoji here.)

NOTES   You'll need to prepare the borage leaves and drain the ricotta the day before you make the dumplings. If you can't find borage, any bright green—kale, nettles, spinach—will do.

If you're making the fresh ricotta (page 279) for this recipe, you will need to make three times the batch size, but you will have a good amount of ricotta left over. If you're using store-bought ricotta, you will still need to drain it overnight.

serves 4 to 6

borage and ricotta dumplings
½ cup (120 ml) minced shallots
¼ cup (60 ml) extra-virgin olive oil, plus more as needed
kosher salt
2 pounds (910 g) borage leaves, washed, dried, and coarsely chopped
3½ pounds (1.6 kg) fresh ricotta cheese, homemade (page 279) or store-bought (see Note)
1½ cups (95 g) finely grated parmigiano-reggiano cheese
1 cup (125 g) "00" flour
15 twists freshly ground black pepper
10 grates nutmeg
1 large whole egg
1 large egg yolk
semolina flour, for dusting

mushroom broth
1½ cups (360 ml) Mushroom Stock (page 311)
kosher salt
2 tablespoons (30 g) unsalted butter

to serve
kosher salt
extra-virgin olive oil
borage flowers, to garnish

make the borage and ricotta dumplings

In a large pot, combine the shallots, olive oil, and a pinch of salt and cook over medium heat, stirring, until the shallots are translucent, 3 to 5 minutes.

Add the borage, season with salt, and cook until all of the natural liquid cooks out, about 30 minutes. Transfer the borage to a baking sheet to cool. Once cooled, squeeze out as much of the liquid as possible (discard the liquid). Transfer the borage to a cutting (chopping) board and chop it very finely. Taste the borage, season with more salt if needed, then wrap in cheesecloth. Squeeze out any remaining juice and leave the borage in a sieve set over a bowl to drain overnight in the refrigerator.

Meanwhile, also make the ricotta as directed and drain overnight.

Set the drained ricotta in a large bowl. Add the Parmigiano, "00" flour, a scant 2 tablespoons kosher salt, the black pepper, and nutmeg. Mix well to combine, then add the borage leaves. Gently whisk the whole egg and egg yolk with a fork and add to the ricotta and borage. Use your hands to thoroughly mix the dough. The result should be like a pasta dough—the dough should not be sticking to your hands. If it is too dry, add a small amount of water; if too wet, add more flour. →

Shape the dough into a ball and place in a lightly oiled bowl with a piece of plastic wrap (clingfilm) gently pressed over the top of the dough—you don't want the dough to dry out. Refrigerate and let the dough rest for at least 2 hours.

Remove the dough from the refrigerator and place on a work surface. Divide the dough into 6 pieces. Work with one piece at a time, keeping the other pieces covered with plastic wrap (clingfilm) while you work. Lightly dust the work surface with semolina flour, then using your hands, roll the dough into a long log, just under 1 inch (2.5 cm) in diameter. If you have the space, repeat until all of the dough pieces have been formed into long logs.

Cut the logs crosswise into 1½-inch (4 cm) dumplings and set them onto semolina-dusted baking sheets (trays). Refrigerate, uncovered, for at least 1 hour and up to 24 hours.

make the mushroom broth

In a saucepot, warm the stock over medium heat until hot. Season to taste with salt and set aside until serving. Just before serving, rewarm the stock and whisk in the butter until incorporated.

to serve

Bring a large pot of water to a lively simmer and season it with enough salt for it to taste seasoned.

Cook the dumplings in the simmering water until they float to the surface, 2 to 3 minutes. Using a sieve, fish the dumplings out of the broth, making sure to drain all the water before you plate them. Divide the dumplings across bowls and then ladle the mushroom broth over them. Finish with a few drops of olive oil and some borage flowers.

brassicas a la catalan

serves 4

1 pound (455 g) florets from assorted
    brassicas, specifically broccoli and
    cauliflower, such as Romanesco, or any
    other cool types you can find
2 tablespoons extra-virgin olive oil
kosher salt
¼ cup (60 ml) Pine Nut Pudding
    (page 301)
2 tablespoons golden raisins (sultanas)
1 tablespoon toasted pine nuts
20 small peppermint leaves
½ cup (120 ml) Pepper Tears (page 309),
    at room temperature

I've always loved raw broccoli and cauliflower. One of my earliest food memories is eating it for lunch every day at the preschool from which I was eventually expelled. But if they're so good raw and dipped in ranch dressing, this version should be even better.

This recipe is all about finding all of the cool, crazy, unique brassicas (a rather large family in the vegetable kingdom, which, in addition to cauliflower and broccoli, includes items such as cabbage and kohlrabi) available in the winter. Don't be afraid to be creative.

directions

Follow the trimming instructions on pages 40-41 for the brassicas. Everything should be in bite-size pieces.

In a bowl, toss the brassicas with the olive oil. Season pretty aggressively with salt, as this is the only salt added to the dish.

To serve, spoon the pine nut pudding on one side of each of 4 bowls and lay down the dressed brassicas on top. Sprinkle with the raisins and pine nuts on top, followed by the mint leaves. Finally, gently pour the pepper tears on the opposite side of the bowl from the pine nut pudding.

bread au chocolat

Brioche, chocolate, and salt is one of my favorite flavor combinations—and subsequently, one of my favorite things to eat as dessert. I started griddling brioche with butter at Rustic Canyon when Zoe Nathan Loeb (acclaimed pastry chef and co-owner of the Rustic Canyon Family of restaurants in Los Angeles) came in and ordered it. Then she showed us a crazy method I'd never seen before. She griddled brioche with butter, spread more butter on it, dipped it in sugar, and then griddled it again. When it came off the heat, she added more butter. Until that day, I feel like I didn't know how to properly cook a dessert brioche. Luckily, my damaged pride was quickly healed by how damn good that brioche tasted.

NOTE Make the ganache well in advance, as it needs to chill for at least 4 hours before serving. The whipped cream can be made a few hours early, but the griddled brioche should be made just prior to serving.

serves 4

chocolate ganache
4 ounces (115 g) 73% chocolate, pistoles, or chips (chop it if it's in block form)
2 tablespoons honey
1 cup (240 ml) heavy (double) cream

whipped cream
½ cup (120 ml) heavy cream
4 teaspoons granulated sugar

griddled brioche
¼ cup (55 g) dark brown sugar
¼ cup (50 g) granulated sugar
5¼ ounces (150 g) unsalted butter, at room temperature
4 slices Deanie's Brioche (page 283), 1 to 1½ inches (2.5 to 3.8 cm) thick
Homemade Salt (page 263) or flaky sea salt

make the chocolate ganache

In a heatproof bowl, combine the chocolate and honey. Heat the cream over medium-low heat to just below a simmer. Pour the cream over the chocolate and honey and let it sit for 2 minutes. Whisk to combine, then refrigerate for at least 4 hours before serving.

make the whipped cream

In a bowl, combine the cream and sugar and whip to soft peaks using a whisk or a hand mixer.

make the griddled brioche

Heat a cast-iron skillet over medium heat.

Meanwhile, in a bowl, mix the two sugars until combined and spread the mixture on a plate.

Spread a healthy (or unhealthy, depending on how you look at it) amount of butter on one side of each slice of brioche. Add the brioche, butter-side down, to the pan. Spread butter on the other side of the bread. Once the bottom of the brioche has browned evenly, flip it over and repeat with the second side.

Remove the brioche from the pan and lightly brush with butter on both sides. Dip the bread into the sugar mixture, coating both sides, and return it to the skillet. You want a crème brûlée, caramelized sort of a situation—just watch the sugar carefully, as it burns easily. It should be dark amber but not blackened.

Remove the brioche from the skillet and sprinkle a pinch of salt on top.

To serve, place the griddled brioche on a plate and spoon a dollop of ganache on top, sprinkle with a touch of salt, and finish with the whipped cream.

simple broccoli di cicco, garlic, lemon & burrata

serves 4 to 6

kosher salt
1 pound (455 g) broccoli di cicco, washed and trimmed
3 tablespoons extra-virgin olive oil, plus more for drizzling
4 garlic cloves, germ removed, finely grated
juice of 1 to 2 lemons, to taste
1 pound (455 g) burrata cheese
flaky sea salt
freshly ground black pepper

This is a really quick, simple dish that's great when you have people coming over. Frankly, if you put old shoes out with buratta, people will love it. So if you replace those old shoes with broccoli, lemon, and garlic, you have a winner. Then you can also donate those old shoes instead of eating them.

directions

Bring a large pot of water to a boil over medium-high heat. Salt it so that it tastes like the sea. Meanwhile, prepare an ice bath in a large bowl. Blanch the broccoli in the boiling water for 1 minute—just long enough to turn the color a more vibrant green—and transfer to the ice bath until cool. Drain and dry the broccoli.

Place a large frying pan over medium-high heat and preheat for 3 minutes. Add the oil, then the broccoli. Cook until hot, giving it a little color if you'd like, 2 to 3 minutes. Remove the pan from the heat and add the garlic, lemon juice, and salt to taste (the lemon will also help to cool down the pan).

Divide the broccoli across plates and place a mound of burrata in the center of each plate. Drizzle the burrata with some olive oil and garnish with flaky sea salt and black pepper.

charred whole broccoli with miso bagna cauda

serves 4 to 8

8 heads (each 2 oz/60 g) young broccoli,
  sliced lengthwise through the stalk
kosher salt
¼ cup (60 ml) extra-virgin olive oil
⅓ cup (80 ml) Miso Bagna Cauda
  (page 269), at room temperature
4 tablespoons Breadcrumbs (page 290)
flaky sea salt
parmigiano-reggiano cheese (optional)

This was my biggest "aha" moment at Ubuntu. We harvested this beautiful broccoli from the garden, which I usually love eating with bagna cauda. But bagna cauda has anchovy in it, so I couldn't serve it at a vegetarian restaurant. To recreate the umami component that the anchovies bring, I started messing around with miso, and the vegetarian bagna cauda really started to come together.

directions

Preheat the oven to 450°F (230°C/Gas 8).

Bring a large pot of water to a boil over medium-high heat. Salt it so that it tastes like the sea. Meanwhile, prepare an ice bath in a large bowl. Blanch the broccoli in the boiling water, until bright green and just tender, about 2 minutes. Drain and immediately transfer the broccoli to the prepared ice bath until completely cool. Drain and dry thoroughly on paper towels.

In a large bowl, toss the broccoli with the olive oil and a light sprinkle of kosher salt. Arrange the broccoli in a single layer on a 12 x 6-inch (30 x 15 cm) baking sheet and roast in the oven until the pieces are tender and nicely charred, 10 to 15 minutes.

Remove the broccoli from the oven, transfer to a platter, and spoon the miso bagna cauda over it. Sprinkle with breadcrumbs and flaky sea salt. Finish with shaved Parmigiano, if desired.

purple haze carrots, yogurt & sumac

serves 4 to 6

1 pound (455 g) young purple haze
    carrots, with tops attached
1½ cups (360 ml) Labneh (page 281)
2 tablespoons extra-virgin olive oil
1 tablespoon ground sumac
1 teaspoon flaky sea salt

The inspiration of having teenage carrots with the greens attached was actually from a dish I was responsible for when I *staged* at St. John in London—one of the least vegetarian restaurants in the world. That dish was just carrots with their greens, served with a dollop of mayonnaise and an uncracked hard-boiled egg. There was something so beautiful and meaningful about that dish: great carrots, amazing mayonnaise, and a perfectly cooked egg. No pretense. It is also the soul of this dish.

NOTE You don't have to use Purple Haze carrots, but they look especially great if you can get them. It's far more important that your carrots be young and still have their tops attached (more mature carrots have tougher tops).

directions

Wash the carrots. (Good carrots don't need to be peeled, but use a bird's beak knife to remove any hairs or fibers.) Dry thoroughly.

Arrange the carrots on a platter and spoon the labneh into a small bowl. Drizzle the olive oil over the labneh and sprinkle it with the sumac and flaky sea salt. Dip your carrots and enjoy.

tandoori carrots, labneh & vadouvan

serves 4

1 pound (455 g) young round carrots, baby to medium, washed but not peeled
3 tablespoons Yogurt (page 281)
2 tablespoons extra-virgin olive oil
kosher salt
¼ cup (60 ml) Vadouvan Butter (page 280)
½ cup (120 ml) Carrot Purée (page 267)
½ cup (120 ml) Labneh (page 281)
flowering cilantro (coriander), or cilantro or mint leaves, to garnish

Tandoori dishes, like chicken tandoori, are named as such because they are typically cooked in a tandoor (a cylindrical oven most famously used in India, usually made of clay). While I don't have a tandoor, I call these tandoori carrots because they're seasoned first with yogurt, which gives them a beautiful blister and char that reminds me of other tandoori dishes.

NOTE   All of the "Larder" ingredients can be made in advance, but the carrots should be roasted just before serving.

directions

Preheat the oven to 500°F (260°C/Gas 10).

In a bowl, toss the carrots with the yogurt, oil, and salt to taste.

Line an 18 x 13-inch (45 x 33 cm) roasting pan with parchment paper and add the carrots in a single layer. Roast the carrots until they are lightly charred and wrinkled on the outside, but soft on the interior, 25 to 40 minutes. Shake the carrots in the pan halfway through cooking.

Meanwhile, in a small pan, warm the vadouvan butter gently over low heat—you want to be careful not to burn or overcook the spices and garlic. In another pan, gently warm the carrot purée over low heat.

To serve, divide the carrot purée, in dollops, across 4 plates. Place the roasted carrots on top. Spoon the vadouvan butter on top and garnish with a quenelle or dollop of labneh and flowering cilantro.

carrot juice cavatelli, tops salsa & spiced pulp crumble

serves 4

carrot juice cavatelli
4¼ cups (530 g) "00" flour, plus more for dusting
1 teaspoon kosher salt, plus more for the cooking water
1 cup (240 ml) fresh carrot juice (from orange carrots), pulp reserved
to serve
¾ cup (180 ml) Carrot Purée (page 267)
4 tablespoons Salsa Verde (page 269), using the leaves of young carrot tops
4 tablespoons Carrot Crumble (page 290)
aged gouda cheese

This dish accomplishes two things: First, it's the purest example of using every single part of a vegetable in one single dish. And second—and what I was really trying to accomplish—the cavatelli look like that bright orange Kraft macaroni and cheese from a box.

If you are making this dish from the ground up, it is pretty exciting, as you can use the tops of your carrots to make the salsa, the juice to make the cavatelli, and the pulp (from juicing) to make the crumble.

NOTE Start cooking the day before you intend to serve this. The carrot pulp and cavatelli dough will need overnight to dehydrate and rest, respectively.

make the carrot juice cavatelli

In a food processor, blend together the flour and salt. With the machine running, slowly add the carrot juice (you may not need all of it), until the dough comes together. Be careful not to overwork the dough in the food processor: The dough may well look crumbly, but if you press it together with your fingers it should very easily combine into dough. You are looking for a texture similar to Play-Doh: elastic, pliable, and not sticking to your fingers when you touch it. If the dough is too dry, add more juice; too wet, add more flour.

Transfer the dough to a lightly floured surface and knead it with the heels of your hands for about 1 minute, until you have a smooth dough.

Wrap the dough tightly with plastic wrap (clingfilm) and let it rest overnight in the refrigerator.

Place the carrot pulp on a dehydrator tray and dehydrate at 135°F (57°C) overnight.

About 1 hour before you plan to make the cavatelli, let the dough come to room temperature—this will make it much easier to work with. Divide the dough into 6 pieces. Lightly flour a work surface. Working with one piece at a time—and keeping the rest of the dough covered—roll the dough into a long, thin rope, about 1/8 inch (3 mm) in diameter. Cut the rope crosswise into ¼-inch (6 mm) pieces. →

Using a cavatelli board, or the tines of a fork, gently but confidently roll the dough pieces against it. The cavatelli may not come out perfect right away, but soon the motion will find its way into your muscle memory.

Once the cavatelli are shaped, lay them in a single layer (not touching) on a baking sheet lined with a tea towel. Repeat this process until all of the dough has been turned into cavatelli. These are best cooked when fresh, so if you are going to be cooking them the same day, you can just leave them out. Otherwise, cover and refrigerate for up to 2 days.

Bring a large pot of water to a boil. Season your water with salt so it tastes like the sea. I think it's important to taste the pasta water to make sure it is seasoned properly. Once seasoned and boiling, add the cavatelli and cook until they float to the surface, about 3 minutes. If you're not sure whether they are done, the best test is just to eat one.

to serve

While the pasta water heats up, gently warm the carrot purée in a small pan over low heat and keep covered (and warm) until serving.

Using a sieve, scoop the cavatelli out of the pasta water and into a wide bowl. Immediately dress them with the carrot top salsa verde and toss to combine. Ladle in some of the starchy, seasoned pasta water, a little at a time, to open up the flavors and create a very light sauce that will coat the cavatelli. Don't add too much water or it will make for a thin, diluted sauce.

Place dollops of the carrot purée on 4 warmed plates. Spoon the cavatelli on top and sprinkle the carrot crumble over the pasta and the plate. I like being able to drag the cavatelli through more of the crumble as I'm eating it. Shave ribbons of Gouda over the top and serve immediately.

cauliflower in a cast-iron pot

serves 4

½ cup (120 ml) melted Vadouvan Butter (page 280), plus more for basting
3 pounds (1.4 kg) cauliflower florets, 2 inches (5 cm) thick (2 to 3 heads, trimmed as directed on page 41)
1 teaspoon kosher salt, plus more as needed
ciabatta or baguette, for toasting
2 lemons
¼ cup (60 ml) whole (full-fat) milk
¼ cup (60 ml) heavy (double) cream
1 orange, segmented, and each segment cut into 3 pieces
flowering cilantro (coriander), to garnish

It seems that when any new restaurant opens, people like to focus on one dish in particular. When Ubuntu opened, this was that dish. For one, the star was a very humble, underappreciated vegetable that is pretty much found in any banquet kitchen's steamed-vegetable medley. For another thing, the dish was very rich and decadent—a surprise for a vegetarian restaurant. It was also cute because it was served in a little black cast-iron pot. I suppose it also tasted good.

directions

Preheat the oven to 400°F (200°C/Gas 6).

Stir the vadouvan butter as you would vinaigrette (so that when you scoop it up, you are getting both the liquid and any spices that might have settled to the bottom), then toss 2 pounds (900 g) of the cauliflower florets with 3 tablespoons of the vadouvan butter and the 1 teaspoon salt.

Place the tossed cauliflower in a single layer on a baking sheet and roast in the oven until the florets are slightly charred and tender, 12 to 15 minutes. Remove from the oven and reduce the oven temperature to 300°F (150°C/Gas 2).

Thinly slice the bread. Stir the melted vadouvan butter and brush the bread with some of it. Sprinkle with some salt and arrange the slices on a baking sheet. Bake until crisp, 8 to 10 minutes. Set aside until serving time. Return the oven temperature to 400°F (200°C/Gas 6).

Chop the cooled cauliflower into bite-size pieces and transfer to a bowl. Finely grate the lemon zest and set it aside for later. Squeeze the juice of the lemons and season the roasted cauliflower with the lemon juice and salt to taste.

Coarsely chop the remaining raw cauliflower and place it in a pot. Add the reserved lemon zest, milk, cream, and a pinch of salt. Bring to a bare simmer over medium-low heat, cover, and reduce the heat to low. Cook until the cauliflower is soft when pierced with a knife, about 30 minutes. Transfer to a blender with the cooking liquid and purée until smooth.

Spread a thin layer of the cauliflower purée in the bottom of each of four 1-cup (240 ml) cast-iron pots. Divide the roasted cauliflower pieces evenly among them and cover with the remaining cauliflower purée. Bake until just bubbling, 5 to 8 minutes.

Remove from the oven and spoon a tablespoon of hot, stirred vadouvan butter over the surface of each pot.

Garnish with orange segments and flowering cilantro and serve with toasted bread.

chickpeas in broth, lots of olive oil & black pepper, pan con tomate

Simple chickpeas, served in their own broth with lots of olive oil and some crusty bread, is one of the great simple pleasures in life. I like to base a dish on the broth, because it gives you incentive to really baby it and pay close attention to the process. You can't fake the great flavor that comes from following all of the proper steps in a great broth.

NOTE The chickpeas and their broth will keep in the fridge for a few days, so you can cook that in advance if you'd like. I like to soak dried beans overnight before cooking them.

serves 4

2 cups (400 g) dried chickpeas, soaked overnight in 6 cups (1.4 liters) water
2 celery stalks
1 carrot
1 leek
stems from 8 fresh thyme sprigs
kosher salt and freshly cracked black pepper
½ cup (120 ml) extra-virgin olive oil, plus more for brushing the bread
48 cherry tomatoes
4 slices crusty, rustic bread
1 or 2 medium tomatoes (I like momotaro or early girl), grated (if they're not in season, you can substitute the juice of good canned tomatoes)
1 to 2 whole garlic cloves
flaky sea salt

directions

Drain the chickpeas, place in a large pot, and cover with 6 cups (1.4 liters) cold water.

Cut the celery, carrot, and leek into smaller chunks. Wrap them up, along with the thyme stems, in a sachet made of cheesecloth and add to the pot. Bring to a simmer over medium heat. Reduce the heat to just below a simmer and cook until the chickpeas are creamy and soft, 1 hour 15 minutes to 2 hours. Remove the chickpeas from the heat (discard the sachet). Generously season with kosher salt (the broth should taste great by itself) and a lot of black pepper. Add the olive oil—I like to use the full ½ cup (120 ml), but you can pull back a bit if you like.

Right before serving, turn the broiler (grill) on high and place the cherry tomatoes in a roasting pan. Pour the grated tomatoes (or canned tomato juices) into a wide, shallow bowl.

Preheat an outdoor grill or skillet to grill the bread. Brush the bread with olive oil and grill it or toast in a hot skillet. While the bread is grilling, toss the cherry tomatoes into the broiler and broil (grill) until the skins crack and soften up, about 3 minutes. Remove from the broiler and lightly season salt with kosher salt.

Once the bread is finished toasting, season it with kosher salt. Rub the cut garlic halves over the toast. Dip one side of the toast into the grated tomatoes so that it soaks up a good amount of juice, then sprinkle it with flaky sea salt.

To serve, ladle the hot chickpeas and broth into four bowls. Place the broiled cherry tomatoes on the top of the chickpeas and serve with grilled tomato-garlic toast.

chickpea panisse, celery, olive & manchego

I think celery is underrated as a vegetable, because it's usually used as an accompaniment or a flavoring agent (like in a mirepoix), and not allowed to shine on its own. There's this old Trader Joe's commercial that I really love—it sounds like Jerry Bruckheimer produced a radio ad for celery with crazy voices and explosion sounds, acting like celery was the must-have ingredient of the summer. Here is a riff on the now-classic San Francisco Zuni Café dish of celery, anchovies, Parmesan, and olives.

NOTE Make the panisse the day before serving, but fry just before serving.

serves 8

2 quarts (2 liters) canola (rapeseed), peanut (groundnut), or grapeseed oil, for deep-frying
1½ cups (355 ml) chopped celery (the inner, pale, thin stalks and leaves from 2 bunches)
1 tablespoon extra-virgin olive oil
juice of 1 lemon
kosher salt
Panisse (page 286), cut into 8 (4 x 2-inch/10 x 5 cm) planks
4 tablespoons Black Olive Caramel (page 266)
4 ounces (115 g) manchego cheese, grated

directions

In a large pot, heat the canola oil until it registers 350°F (180°C) on a deep-frying thermometer.

While the oil is heating, dress the celery with the olive oil and lemon juice and season with salt to taste.

Gently lower the panisse planks into the hot oil and fry until they are browned and crispy, 3 to 4 minutes. Use a sieve or spider/skimmer to pull the panisse out and set them on wire racks or a plate lined with paper towel. Season immediately with salt and divide across individual plates or place on a single large platter.

Using a squeeze bottle or a butter knife, add the black olive caramel. Place the dressed celery salad on top, and finish with freshly grated Manchego.

corn polenta,
curds, whey
& strawberry sofrito

serves 4

4 cups (about 1 liter) Whey (page 279)
2 cups (290 g) coarse polenta
1 cup (240 ml) heavy (double) cream
½ cup (30 g) finely grated parmigiano-
   reggiano cheese
3 tablespoons (45 g) unsalted butter
kosher salt
½ cup (120 ml) Strawberry Sofrito
   (page 314)
1 cup (240 ml) Fresh Ricotta (page 279),
   at room temperature
flaky sea salt
basil leaves, to garnish

This dish is, in a way, a nod to chef David Kinch of Manresa restaurant.
He taught me about using whey to cook polenta, and he was also the guy
who used to substitute strawberries for tomatoes in his gazpacho.

directions

In a medium pot, bring the whey to a boil over high heat. Whisk in the polenta and
cook over medium-low heat, stirring, until the polenta has softened up and is no longer
crunchy or grainy (it will continue cooking in the next step), about 20 minutes.

Add the cream and cook until the polenta is soft and velvety, about 15 minutes.
Remove the pot from the heat and slowly fold in the Parmigiano and butter until fully
incorporated. Season to taste with salt.

Meanwhile, in a saucepot, bring the sofrito up to a bare simmer over low heat and drain
off any excess oil.

To serve, spoon the hot polenta into bowls and add quenelles or dollops of sofrito and
ricotta. Finish with flaky sea salt and garnish with fresh basil leaves.

creamed corn, fig jam & dried vanilla pod

serves 4

creamed corn
4 cups (1.4 kg) corn kernels
2 cups (480 ml) Corn Cob Stock
   (page 310)
kosher salt
to serve
1 scraped vanilla pod
4 tablespoons Fig, Pepper Skin & Riesling
   Jam (page 268)

This is a creamless creamed corn, using the natural starch and thickness of the corn to replace any actual cream. I like this recipe because it shows off, once again, how versatile a single vegetable like corn can be. It's also a great way to use leftover vanilla pods, after the beans have been scraped out.

make the creamed corn

In a medium saucepot, combine the corn kernels and stock with a pinch of salt. Bring to a simmer over medium heat, then reduce to medium-low and cook at a simmer, uncovered, until the kernels are completely tender, 20 to 25 minutes. Remove from the heat. Transfer half of the corn to a blender and purée until smooth. Return the blended corn to the pot and stir to combine. Taste and adjust seasoning, if needed.

to serve

Dry the vanilla pod in a dehydrator for 6 to 8 hours at 135°F (57°C), or until completely dry. Break the pod up with your hands and grind in a coffee grinder to a fine powder. Store, indefinitely, at room temperature in an airtight container.

Divide the corn across 4 bowls and top with a quenelle or dollop of jam. Finish with ground vanilla pod.

vegan 4x corn polenta

5 cups (1.2 liters) Corn Cob Stock
  (page 310)
2 cups (290 g) polenta
2 cups (480 ml) Creamed Corn (page 114)
1½ cups (360 ml) Yellow Corn Pudding
  (page 274)
kosher salt

This is how to make the best bowl of corn polenta that I can possibly come up with, using multiple layers and concentrations of corn—and then infusing it back within itself.

directions

In a medium saucepot, bring the stock to a boil over high heat. Whisk in the polenta, add a pinch of salt, then reduce the heat to medium-low and cook, uncovered, stirring occasionally, until the polenta is just tender and no longer grainy, about 20 minutes.

Fold in the creamed corn, stir to combine, and cook until just hot, about 5 minutes. Add the corn pudding, then cook for an additional 2 to 3 minutes, stirring occasionally, until hot. Season to taste with salt.

To serve, divide the polenta across 4 bowls.

grilled corn on the cob, calabrian chili butter & ash salt

serves 4

4 ears yellow corn
1 cup (240 ml) Corn Cob Stock (page 310)
8 ounces (225 g) Calabrian Chili Butter
(page 277)
2 tablespoons flaky sea salt
½ teaspoon Onion Top Ash (page 289)

This is another example of the value of building up your larder in your spare time, and then using it to elevate a simple dish. Grilled corn with delicious things from your larder: What could go wrong?

Well, come to think of it a lot could go wrong. I mean, it's a hot grill. Be safe out there. But in any case—this recipe is delicious.

directions

Preheat the oven to 375°F (190°C/Gas 5).

Trim any dark outer husks from the corn—just make sure to keep it wrapped. Place the corn in an 18 x 13-inch (46 x 33 cm) rimmed baking sheet or baking dish with the corn cob stock. Cover with foil and bake until the kernels start to soften up, 25 to 30 minutes. Remove the corn from the oven and allow it to cool, then remove the husks and silk.

Heat a grill (barbecue) to medium-low.

Place the corn on the grill and cook on all sides—you're looking for a bit of color (some of you may prefer more color than others).

In a sauté pan, melt the chili butter over medium-high heat and cook the butter for about 3 minutes—it will bubble and clarify a bit, so let it do its thing—just don't let it burn. Meanwhile, in a small bowl, stir together the flaky sea salt and onion top ash to make ash salt.

Serve the corn on a platter and top with chili butter and ash salt.

crosnes, brown butter & sage

serves 4 to 6

4 tablespoons (60 g) unsalted butter
20 to 30 fresh sage leaves
kosher salt
1 pound (455 g) crosnes, washed, dried,
    and trimmed of strings
juice of 1 lemon, plus more as needed

Usually when you get crosnes (page 42), they're pretty clean. If you grow them yourself you will realize why they're expensive and not readily available—basically, they're a huge pain to harvest and clean. They grow underground, attached to vines, and snap in half really easily.

Since they're such a unique and rare item, if you find them, it's a shame to do anything that hides or covers them up too much.

directions

In a wide sauté pan, melt the butter over medium-high heat. Add the sage leaves and toast them in the butter until crisp and their color changes to a pine green.

Using tweezers or a fork, pull out the sage leaves and place them on paper towels to dry. Lightly sprinkle with salt and set aside.

Meanwhile, keep cooking the butter until it starts to foam and the solids turn brown, 2 to 3 minutes. Add the crosnes, season with salt, and cook, stirring and tossing occasionally, until just tender but still with some crunch, 3 to 5 minutes. Be careful and don't burn the butter (you don't want it to turn bitter).

Season the crosnes in the pan to taste with lemon juice and additional salt, if needed. Plate, topped with the crispy sage leaves.

cucumber, potato, olive, pine nut & parmesan

Cucumbers are quite mild, so they do really well when contrasted with briny olives, crispy potatoes, sharp parmesan, and toasty pine nuts.

serves 4

kosher salt
6 ounces (170 g) fingerling potatoes
1 pound (455 g) mixed cucumbers
   (persian, lemon—whatever you like, but
   some variety is nice)
2 quarts (about 2 liters) canola
   (rapeseed), rice bran, or peanut
   (groundnut) oil, for deep-frying or
   extra-virgin olive oil, for baking
juice of 1 lemon
24 mint leaves, cut into chiffonade
½ cup (120 ml) Pine Nut Pudding
   (page 301)
¼ cup (60 ml) Black Olive Caramel
   (page 266)
parmigiano-reggiano cheese, to serve

directions

Bring a medium pot of aggressively salted water to a boil. Add the potatoes, reduce to a simmer, and cook until the potatoes are soft when pierced with a cake tester, about 30 minutes. Drain and set aside to cool.

Meanwhile, cut up the cucumbers. This is where you want to get a bit creative and artful. Keep the pieces bite-size—it is a salad, after all—but explore your options: Shave the cucumbers into thin ribbons and roll them; slice them into rings; cut them into oddly shaped chunks; or even just cut up pieces of the tender, seeded interior. Regardless, it's the variety—both in the cuts and the types of cucumbers—that makes for a really nice salad.

The potatoes now get cooked again. The ideal method will be to fry them, but you can also bake them. Using the flat side of a cleaver (if you have one) or a chef's knife, firmly press the potatoes flat, breaking them up into smaller pieces (those small pieces get nice and crispy, almost like croutons).

If frying, in a Dutch oven, heat the canola oil until it registers 350°F (180°C) on a deep-frying thermometer. Carefully place the potatoes in the hot oil and fry until crunchy, 3 to 5 minutes. Transfer the cooked potatoes to a wire rack or plate lined with paper towels. Season immediately with salt.

If baking, preheat the oven to 350°F (180°C/Gas 4). Lightly coat the potatoes with olive oil and arrange on a baking sheet (tray). Bake until crispy, 5 to 10 minutes. Transfer to a plate lined with paper towels and season with salt.

In a bowl, dress the cucumbers with some olive oil, the lemon juice, mint, and salt to taste.

Arrange the cucumbers on a plate. Using squeeze bottles, randomly, but equally, distribute dots of the pine nut pudding and black olive caramel.

Scatter the crispy potatoes on top and, using a vegetable peeler, grate ribbons of Parmigiano over the potatoes.

cucumbers with green goddess

Green Goddess dressing dates back to 1920s San Francisco, but is probably best known as the go-to salad dressing of kitschy 1970s dinner parties. My version is enlivened with homemade aioli and crème fraîche and serves as a refreshing base for lemon-marinated cucumbers and pickled gherkins.

NOTE If you can't find Persian or lemon cucumbers, substitute other cucumbers in their place—though the more variety the better. Bronze fennel is a type of fennel that is mainly used just for the fronds. It's a little more intense than regular fennel, but if you can't find bronze fennel, just substitute the regular varietal.

serves 4

1 cup (240 ml) Mayonnaise (page 268)
½ cup (120 ml) Crème Fraîche (page 278)
½ cup (15 g) chopped flat-leaf parsley leaves
½ cup (15 g) chopped fresh tarragon leaves
½ cup (15 g) thinly sliced scallions (spring onions)
¼ cup (8 g) finely chopped flat-leaf parsley stems
kosher salt
4 persian cucumbers
4 small lemon cucumbers (the size of ping pong balls)
1 tablespoon extra-virgin olive oil
finely grated zest and juice of 1 lemon
24 Dill Pickles (page 304), made with gherkins, halved
bronze fennel fronds (can substitute dill or regular fennel fronds), to garnish
new zealand spinach (tetragonia) leaves, to garnish

directions

In a bowl, whisk together the mayonnaise, crème fraîche, parsley leaves, tarragon, scallions, and parsley stems until incorporated. Season to taste with salt. Set the dressing aside.

Thinly slice the cucumbers on a mandoline. I love it when the shapes of the cucumbers vary. As long as the thickness of the slices stays relatively the same, you can slice some of the cucumbers on an angle, while others can be cut into ribbons, rounds, or slants. Season the cucumbers with the olive oil, lemon zest and juice, and salt to taste.

To serve, spoon dollops of the dressing on a plate and top it with cucumbers and gherkins. Garnish with fennel fronds and spinach.

daikon piccata, lemon butter & nasturtium capers

serves 4

1 cup (50 g) panko breadcrumbs
1 teaspoon kosher salt, plus more
    as needed
½ cup (10 g) loosely packed flat-leaf
    parsley leaves plus 2 tablespoons
    chopped parsley leaves
1 large (1 pound/455 g) daikon radish
3 large eggs, lightly beaten
1 cup (125 g) all-purpose (plain) flour
1 cup (240 ml) grapeseed oil
1 tablespoon brine from Nasturtium
    Capers (page 306)
3 Meyer or regular lemons
4 ounces (115 g) unsalted butter, at room
    temperature
2 tablespoons Nasturtium Capers
    (page 306), drained
assorted leaves and herbs, such as pea
    tendrils, fennel fronds, and chervil,
    to garnish

I was surprised to discover that daikon radish worked really well as a meat substitute. It gets tender, but also holds its shape, even after you cut it. Between the crispy, fried daikon and the sharp buttery sauce, this is one satisfying dish.

NOTE   The daikon is breaded and then refrigerated for 1 to 2 hours (for the coating to set) before being pan-fried, so you'll want to start the daikon at least 2 hours before you plan on frying.

directions

In a food processor, combine the panko, salt, and ½ cup (10 g) parsley leaves. Process until the mixture is a vibrant green. Set the herbed breadcrumbs aside.

Slice the daikon into ½-inch (1.25 cm) thick rounds. If you wish, using a round cutter, punch the largest perfect rounds out of the slices.

Set up three shallow bowls on your work counter: one with the eggs, one with the herbed breadcrumbs, and the last with the flour. Keeping one hand for wet coating and the other for dry, coat the daikon first in the flour, then the egg, and finally the bread-crumbs—making sure that each ingredient gets a full coating. Set the breaded daikon on a baking sheet in a single layer and refrigerate for at least 1 and up to 2 hours to allow the coating to set.

In a wide pan, warm the grapeseed oil over medium heat until hot but not smoking.

Carefully place the first daikon round in the oil—it should sizzle as it hits the pan. Arrange more daikon in the pan without overcrowding. Working in batches, cook the daikon for 6 to 7 minutes on the first side, and then carefully flip so that you don't splash any oil on yourself and fry on the other side until cooked through and each side is gol-den brown with hints of green, 4 to 5 minutes longer. Transfer to a baking sheet lined with paper towels and sprinkle with salt. Repeat with the remaining daikon.

In a small saucepot, combine the caper brine and 1 tablespoon water. Finely grate the zest of 1 lemon into the pan. Squeeze the juice of the lemon and add it to the mixture. Set the saucepot over medium heat to warm up, but do not let it get hot or the sauce will break. Add the butter, and as it slowly melts, whisk it to emulsify. Add the capers and 2 tablespoons of chopped parsley. Taste and adjust the seasonings, if needed. Remove from the heat and set aside.

Heat a grill, grill pan (griddle pan), or cast-iron skillet over high heat.for the lemons. Halve the remaining 2 lemons through the equator, and trim the pointed ends as well so they can stand up straight, cut-side up. Using tweezers or a fork, seed the lemons. Place the lemons on the grill, cut-side down, and cook until they are charred, but not burnt.

To serve, drizzle the butter sauce on the bottom of 4 plates and place the fried daikon over it. Garnish with a charred lemon half and with the assorted herbs and leaves.

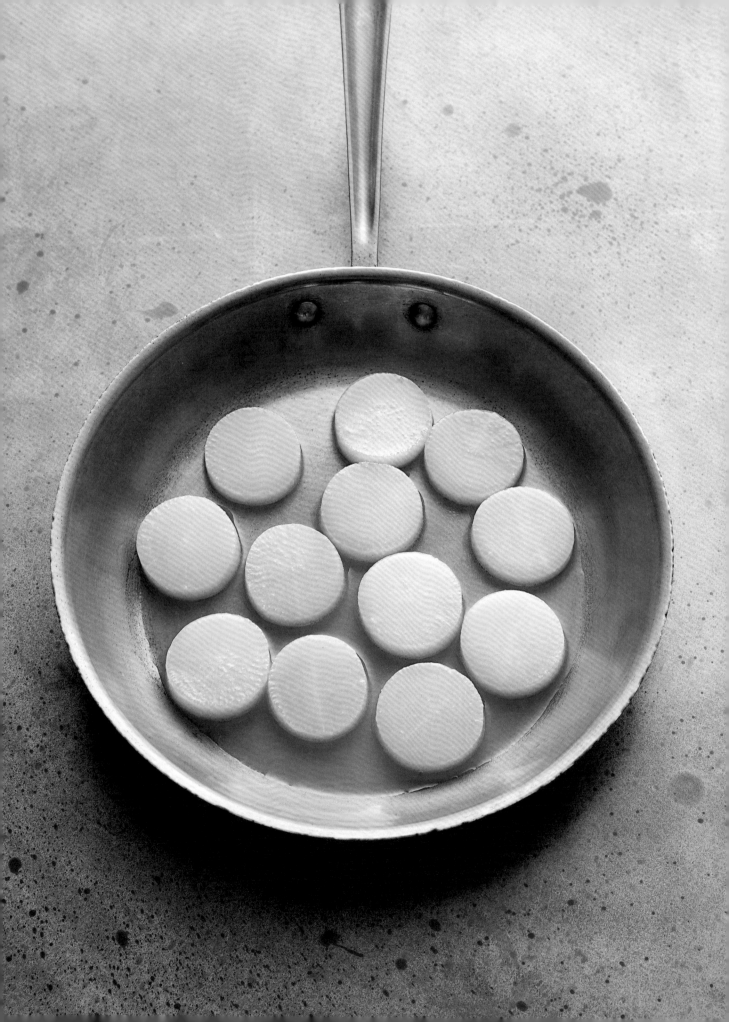

daikon braised in orange juice

serves 6

1 very large (2 pounds/910 g) daikon radish, cut into slices ½ to ¾ inch (12 to 20 mm) thick
2½ cups (600 ml) strained fresh orange juice (6 to 7 oranges)
2 teaspoons kosher salt

This has become one of my favorite ways to cook a vegetable. It's great right after it's made, and is also terrific the next day straight out of the fridge. I know this to be true, because I'm eating it cold as I write this. If you want perfect rounds from your daikon slices, use a round cutter to punch the circles out.

directions

In a pan at least 12 inches (30 cm) wide, combine the daikon, orange juice, and salt in a single layer. Set the pan over medium heat and cook the daikon until the orange juice evaporates below the surface of the daikon. Carefully flip the slices—they should be fairly soft at this point, and easily damaged if you're not careful.

As the daikon continues to cook, gradually baste it with the reducing orange juice until the daikon is quite tender but still holding together well. It will be around 35 to 40 minutes of total cooking time.

Eat immediately—or later. But I probably like this best when it's fresh.

eggplant, tahini, honey & caper

serves 4

2 pounds (900 g) Japanese eggplants
 (aubergines), about 8
kosher salt
¼ cup (60 ml) olive oil
2 lemons
½ cup (120 ml) tahini
2 tablespoons honey
4 teaspoons drained capers
2 teaspoons white sesame seeds
20 large fresh spearmint leaves, cut into
 a chiffonade
20 small fresh spearmint leaves

The beauty of this dish is its freeform style: Just roast eggplant (aubergines), drizzle delicious things over it, and make as much of a mess as you want. It's beautiful in its chaos—like confetti being thrown at a party.

directions

Preheat the oven to 350°F (180°C/Gas 4). Line a baking sheet with foil.

Using a fork, poke the eggplants a few times in places and place them on the lined baking sheet. Bake until the eggplants are completely soft, 35 to 45 minutes. Remove from the oven and set aside to cool.

Once they are cool enough to handle, use a bird's beak knife to peel off the skin, being careful not to puncture the flesh. The goal is wind up with 8 whole, tender, skinless eggplants—don't beat yourself up if you puncture some flesh though. We all make mistakes.

Now cut the eggplants into irregular chunks, roughly 1 to 1½ inches (2.5 to 4 cm) in length. Season to taste with salt and let come to room temperature.

Pour the olive oil into a bowl and finely grate lemon zest directly into the oil (this will help keep the zest fresh while you finish). Halve the lemons.

To serve, divide the eggplants across 4 plates. Holding your lemon halves over a small mesh sieve, squeeze the juice over all of the eggplants, then drizzle with the zested olive oil. Thoroughly stir the tahini, then drizzle it on top, followed by the honey.

Top with the capers, sesame seeds, chiffonade of mint, and whole small mint leaves.

whole roasted young favas with their pesto & pistachio

A treat for being the early bird at the farmers market is that you get to fish through the pile of fava beans—especially early in the season—and pick out all the small, young tender ones that you can just roast really quickly and are completely edible, pods and all.

NOTE   The pesto is best when made the same day.

serves 4 to 6

roasted favas
40 tender, young fava pods, trimmed
    and cleaned
about ¼ cup (60 ml) extra-virgin olive oil
    (just enough to coat the fava pods)
kosher salt
flaky sea salt
6 lemon quarters, plus more for garnish
1¾ cups (415 ml) Fava Bean Pesto
    (recipe follows)
1 tablespoon chopped pistachios,
    to garnish
fava bean pesto
kosher salt
1½ cups (340 g) double-shucked fava
    beans
1¼ cups (300 ml) extra-virgin olive oil
4 tablespoons finely grated parmigiano-
    reggiano cheese
2 tablespoons chopped pistachios
20 fresh mint leaves, finely chopped
1 teaspoon grated garlic (germ removed)
juice of 1 lemon

make the roasted favas

Preheat the oven to 500°F (260°C/Gas 10). Warm an 18 x 13-inch (46 x 33 cm) baking sheet or large cast-iron skillet in the preheated oven for about 20 minutes, so it's hot when you add the fava pods to it.

Toss the fava pods in the olive oil and season with a pinch of kosher salt. Add the favas, in a single layer, to the pan and roast, stirring occasionally, until the pods are tender and caramelized, 5 to 10 minutes. Remove the favas from the oven, season with flaky sea salt, and squeeze the lemon wedges on top.

To serve, divide the roasted fava pods across plates, spoon the pesto over them, sprinkle with chopped pistachios and flaky salt, and garnish with lemon.

make the fava bean pesto

It's a bit more advanced, but I also like using an alternative method for the pesto, utilizing every last bit of scraps from the favas. For this method, after you shell the favas, scrape the white pith off the interior of the fava pods and roast them in the oven until crispy but tender. Meanwhile, blanch the fava bean skins. They can then both get rough chopped and then pulsed in a food processor. After that, you can use them to replace some of the fava beans in the recipe.

Bring a pot of aggressively salted water to a boil over high heat. Prepare an ice bath in a large bowl and set aside. Blanch the fava beans in the boiling water until tender, 2 to 4 minutes. Transfer immediately to the ice bath until they completely cool. Drain the favas and dry on towels.

Place the fava beans in a food processor and pulse until you have a coarse texture. Transfer the pulsed favas to a bowl and, with a silicone spatula (which works better to mix a pesto), combine with the olive oil, Parmigiano, pistachios, mint, and garlic. Season to taste with salt and set aside.

Right before serving, season to taste with the lemon juice and stir to combine.

pane frattau: fennel, strawberry sofrito, carta da musica & egg

We were making *carta da musica* (page 147) at Ubuntu, but not all of them were coming out perfectly enough to serve to patrons. Some of them would also break. As a result, we had a surplus of *carta* shards, which we started to fry into these delicious little things that came out like wonton crisps. So those inspired me to create my freeform version of a traditional Sardinian dish called *pane frattau*.

Make layers in whatever order you like. It will be delicious. I believe in you.

serves 4 to 6

stewed fennel
2 fennel bulbs or roughly 4 cups (950 ml) scraps from preparing Fennel Confit (page 134)
½ cup (120 ml) extra-virgin olive oil
kosher salt
4 tablespoons chopped fennel fronds
2 tablespoons minced shallots

broken carta da musica
1 or 2 handfuls broken Carta da Musica (page 147)
olive oil
fennel pollen
kosher salt

scrambled eggs
12 large eggs
1 teaspoon kosher salt, plus more as needed
3 tablespoons (45 g) unsalted butter

to serve
1 cup (240 ml) Strawberry Sofrito (page 314)

make the stewed fennel	Preheat the oven to 275°F (135°C/Gas 1).
	If you're using whole fennel bulbs, halve them through the core, remove the cores, and roughly chop. If you're using scraps, roughly chop the pieces.
	Place the fennel in a saucepot or baking dish and add the oil. Season with salt. Cover the dish with foil and bake until the fennel is completely soft and broken down, 1 to 1½ hours. Toss in the fennel fronds and shallots and set aside. Gently reheat before serving.
make the broken carta da musica	Preheat the oven to 450°F (232°C/Gas 8).
	I don't want to get too prescriptive here: Use your judgment and take whatever leftover scraps you have from making carta da musica. You'll want some big chunks, and not just crumbs. Brush the pieces with olive oil and sprinkle them with some fennel pollen and salt.
	Place the pieces on a baking sheet and bake until golden and crisp but not burnt, 2 to 4 minutes. Set aside while you make the scrambled eggs.
make the scrambled eggs	Lightly beat the eggs and season with the salt. In a large nonstick pan, melt the butter over medium-low heat. Pour in the eggs and using a silicone spatula, move the eggs in a pattern—sides, then bottom, then center—so that each area only has a few seconds to cook before it gets moved. Take your time. Cook slowly. Don't rush.
	Once the eggs begin to tighten, you can taste them for salt and adjust seasoning. Cook the eggs, stirring, until rich and custardy. Remove from the pan to a plate.
to serve	In a small covered pan, gently heat the sofrito until hot.
	Make layers with stewed fennel, strawberry sofrito, scrambled eggs, and carta da musica. Think lasagna or napoleons: Any combination of these ingredients, in whatever order you prefer, will be delicious.

fennel confit, kumquat, feta, chili & oregano

serves 4 to 8

4 large fennel bulbs
kosher salt
3 cups (710 ml) olive oil
4 ounces (115 g) Calabrian Chili Butter
   (page 277)
2 tablespoons Black Olive Caramel
   (page 266)
3 tablespoons Salsa Verde (page 269),
   using the fronds from the fennel
4 ounces (115 g) feta cheese, crumbled
4 ounces (115 g) seedless kumquats
   (15 to 20), thinly sliced
1 tablespoon fresh oregano leaves

I was thinking about a Greek salad when putting this dish together. Somewhere between my brain and my hands, this dish happened. The fennel is cooked slowly so that it's soft and sweet, but still holds up against the strong flavors of feta, the Black Olive Caramel, and the Calabrian Chili Butter.

directions

Preheat the oven to 275°F (135°C/Gas 1).

Trim the fennel at very end of the root and remove any particularly unsavory or discolored bits. Cut the bulbs vertically through the core into slices, 1 inch (2.5 cm) thick. You should wind up with 2 to 3 slices per bulb. Reserve the fennel fronds for the salsa verde, and any scraps for another use (like the pane frattau on page 134).

Lightly salt the sliced fennel and let sit for about 15 minutes—this is a quick cure for the fennel.

Place the fennel in a single layer in a 20 x 12-inch (50 x 30 cm) baking dish, cover them with the olive oil, and cover the pan with foil. Bake until the fennel is completely tender and spreadable but still holds its shape, 1 to 1½ hours. Set aside.

In a sauté pan, melt the chili butter over medium-high heat and cook the butter about 3 minutes—it will bubble and clarify a bit, so let it do its thing—just don't let it burn.

To serve, pour the melted chili butter onto the bottom of a platter. Carefully place the cooked fennel over it (try your best to let it hold shape). Dot the fennel with the black olive caramel, drizzle with the salsa verde, and top with the feta, kumquats, and oregano.

figs, celery, almonds & pickled grapes

It may seem arduous, but peeling grapes for pickling is actually a really key step, otherwise they won't take on the flavor of the pickling liquid.

serves 4

pickled grapes
24 red flame seedless grapes
½ cup (120 ml) muscat vinegar
¼ cup (50 g) granulated sugar
1 teaspoon kosher salt
celery ribbons
8 celery stalks, peeled of their fibrous
    layer and cut into 4-inch (10 cm) lengths
¼ cup (60 ml) extra-virgin olive oil
finely grated zest and juice of 2 lemons
kosher salt
to serve
4 tablespoons almond butter
8 fresh figs, cut into wedges
20 almonds, toasted and carefully sliced
¼ teaspoon fennel seeds, crushed in
    a mortar and pestle
40 small leaves new zealand spinach
    (tetragonia) or baby spinach
fennel fronds, to garnish
flaky sea salt

make the pickled grapes

Using a bird's beak knife, very gently peel the grapes. Place them in a nonreactive heatproof bowl.

In a small saucepot, combine ¼ cup (60 ml) water, the vinegar, sugar, and kosher salt and bring to a boil over high heat. Remove from the heat and pour the brine immediately over the grapes. Let sit at room temperature for 1 hour. Transfer to a glass jar, seal, and refrigerate indefinitely.

make the celery ribbons

With a knife, halve the celery pieces lengthwise.. Using a vegetable peeler or a mandoline, shave the celery sticks lengthwise into thin ribbons. In a bowl, combine the shaved celery with the olive oil, and lemon zest and juice. Season to taste with kosher salt.

to serve

Place a dollop of almond butter in the center of each of 4 plates. Place the celery ribbons on top. Arrange the figs and pickled grapes over the celery and sprinkle with the almonds, fennel seeds, and flaky sea salt. Finish with the spinach leaves and fennel fronds. (You may be inclined at this point to season your garnish with salt, but I'm of the opinion that a garnish should taste like what it tastes like. I find that leaving your garnish unseasoned actually grounds your taste buds.)

baby kiwi & burrata

serves 4

30 baby (hardy) kiwi, halved lengthwise
¾ pound (340 g) burrata cheese
¼ cup (60 ml) extra-virgin olive oil
24 small basil leaves
flaky sea salt
freshly cracked black pepper

The skins of baby kiwi are really tender and don't have any fuzz. I had never seen them before, but the day we were shooting the photos for the book, I happened to find them, so I used them. If you can't find baby kiwi, regular ones will work fine too—just make sure you peel the skins and cut them into smaller pieces.

directions

Arrange the kiwi halves, cut-side up, and divide among 4 plates. Lay dollops of burrata next to the kiwi and then drizzle with the olive oil. Garnish with the basil leaves and then sprinkle with flaky sea salt and black pepper to taste.

kohlrabi kraut, dill spaetzle, poached egg & pickle powder

This is my version of traditional German spaetzle with sauerkraut, but using the flavors of classic Jewish deli. The spaetzle are best the same day, but can be boiled in advance and then crisped up in butter before the final plating.

NOTE Make sure you use clean hands, gloves, or a utensil when pulling the kraut from its container. Any contaminant that makes it into your kraut could wind up spoiling the rest of the batch.

serves 4

spaetzle
4 large eggs
2 cups (250 g) all-purpose (plain) flour
¾ cup (180 ml) whole (full-fat) milk
a handful of chopped fresh dill
2 tablespoons granulated sugar
1 tablespoon kosher salt, plus more as needed
3 tablespoons (45 g) unsalted butter
2 teaspoons grapeseed oil (optional)
braised kohlrabi kraut
1 small white onion, julienned
2 teaspoons grapeseed or olive oil
2 teaspoons kosher salt, plus more as needed
2 cups (140 g) drained Kohlrabi Kraut (page 297)
½ cup (120 ml) light beer (not IPA)
1 tablespoon chopped fresh dill, plus more as needed
freshly ground black pepper
poached eggs
4 large eggs
2 tablespoons white wine vinegar
flaky sea salt
freshly ground black pepper
to serve
2 to 3 tablespoons Whole-Grain Mustard (page 272)
1 tablespoon powdered Dried Pickle Powder (page 291)

make the spaetzle

In a bowl, lightly beat the eggs. Add the flour, milk, dill, sugar, and kosher salt and mix until thoroughly combined—the batter should have a texture similar to pancake batter.

Bring a pot of water to a simmer over medium-high heat. If serving the spaetzle right away, have a large sauté pan set over medium-high heat and melt the butter in it. If you plan to serve the spaetzle later, prepare an ice bath in a large bowl.

Once the water is simmering, push the batter through a perforated pan, colander, or spaetzle maker directly into the pot. The dumplings will rise to the surface when ready—which will be very quickly—in 1 to 2 minutes.

If serving spaetzle right away, scoop them out with a sieve or spider/skimmer and transfer to the pan with the melted butter. Cook the spaetzle, stirring occasionally, until they have turned a bit brown and crispy, 2 to 3 minutes. Season to taste with kosher salt.

If serving spaetzle later, drain the dumplings and then shock in the ice bath. Drain the spaetzle thoroughly, then toss in the grapeseed oil. Transfer to a baking sheet, using your fingers to separate the dumplings. If you are holding them for longer than a couple of hours, cover and refrigerate. Right before serving, cook the spaetzle in butter, as explained above. Season to taste with kosher salt. →

**make the braised
kohlrabi kraut**

In a bowl, toss the onion with the oil and kosher salt and set aside for 10 minutes.

Place the onion with their oil in a large sauté pan over medium heat and cook, stirring occasionally, until the onion is soft and translucent, 7 to 8 minutes. Add the kraut and beer and cook, uncovered, stirring occasionally, until the beer has completely evaporated, 5 to 7 minutes. Stir in the dill and season to taste with kosher salt and black pepper. Serve warm.

**make the
poached eggs**

Crack the eggs into individual small dishes, pouring out any of the excess water that lingers around the outer edges of the egg (these turn into those messy white strands on a poached egg).

In a pot, combine the vinegar and 2 quarts (about 2 liters) water and bring to just below a simmer. Swirl the water with a spoon to create a whirlpool in the center, then carefully add the eggs one at a time. Keep the eggs in the water until the whites are just set, about 3 minutes, then remove them with a slotted spoon. Season to taste with flaky sea salt and black pepper.

to serve

Divide the spaetzle across 4 plates and spread it over the base of the plate in an even layer. Lay the kraut on top, making a nest to hold a poached egg. Gently place the egg in the "nest," add a small quenelle or dollop of mustard next to the egg, then sprinkle with the pickle powder.

carta da musica, leaves, things & truffled pecorino

makes 8

carta da musica
½ teaspoon active dry (fast-action) yeast
1¾ cups (220 g) durum wheat flour
1 teaspoon kosher salt
extra-virgin olive oil for greasing the bowl
all-purpose (plain) flour, for dusting
to serve
assorted leaves, herbs, and shaved
   vegetables (see Note)
1 pound (455 g) boschetto al tartufo
   cheese (or aged pecorino or
   parmigiano-reggiano)
extra-virgin olive oil, for brushing
1 tablespoon chopped rosemary
1½ teaspoons chili flakes
kosher salt
lemon wedges
flaky sea salt

When I worked at Mumbo Jumbo in Atlanta, Georgia, we used to purchase ready-made Sardinian flatbread (also called *carta da musica*). On its own it's not that tasty, but brushed with olive oil and toasted, it turns into something great. Whenever we had a VIP in the restaurant we would send it out topped with herbs and truffles—and the like—and I always dreamed that one day, if I had a pizza oven, I would start making these myself. When I opened Ubuntu I got to do just that, and as a result, this was probably my favorite dish on the menu. It is basically a vehicle for everything great that we happened to have on hand. Just for fun, and despite Ubuntu being a vegetarian restaurant, we always served it on a pig-shaped wooden board.

NOTE For the "leaves and things," I like to use pea tendrils, nasturtiums, calendula, young beet (beetroot) greens, fava (broad bean) leaves, parsley, shaved carrots, and shaved radishes. But really whatever is seasonal, fresh, and sounds good to you will work great.

Once the *carta da musica* is dried out in the oven, it will keep for a very long time—so that step can be done very far in advance.

make the carta da musica

Fill a 1-cup (240 ml) measuring cup (measuring jug) with ⅔ cup (160 ml) warm (105° to 115°F/40° to 46°C) water, sprinkle in the yeast, and stir it to blend. Let stand for about 10 minutes to activate the yeast.

In a stand mixer fitted with the paddle attachment, combine the flour and kosher salt and mix on low speed to blend.

With the mixer running, pour in the yeast/water mixture, increase the speed to medium, and beat the dough until it is smooth and elastic, about 4 minutes. The dough will be slightly sticky to the touch.

Lightly coat a medium bowl with the olive oil. With your hands lightly oiled as well, shape the dough into a ball and place in the bowl. Turn the dough ball over so that it is coated all over with the olive oil. Cover the bowl with plastic wrap (clingfilm) and let the dough proof in a warm area for around 2 hours—the dough will rise very slightly, but will not double in volume.

Once the dough is proofed, place a pizza stone on a rack positioned in the center of the oven and begin preheating the oven and stone to 500°F (260°C/Gas 10). Give the stone at least 1 hour to preheat so that the *carta* will cook evenly and consistently. (Although a pizza stone has much better heat retention and will create a superior product, you can also use an 18 x 13-inch/46 x 33 cm baking sheet. Stick it in the oven upside down; this gives you a flat surface with no lip, making it easier to lay down and remove the dough.) →

While the oven and pizza stone are preheating, roll out the dough. Sprinkle some flour over a work surface. Divide the dough into quarters. Working with one piece at a time while keeping the others covered, use a rolling pin to roll out the dough to an 8-inch (20 cm) round, about 1/16 inch (1.5 mm) thick. The round doesn't need to be perfect, but it does need to be of consistent thickness and of an appropriate size to fit on your stone. But most important, it needs to be totally flat. If the rolled-out dough has any tears or crimps, it will not inflate, and thus won't cook properly.

Rest the rolled-out dough on a floured baking sheet or work surface for 30 to 45 minutes.

Dust flour over a pizza peel or an upside-down 8-inch (20 cm) tart pan—you're going to use this to slide your dough rounds onto the stone, so the flour helps keep the dough from sticking to the peel. Transfer the dough round to the pizza peel or tart pan and give the peel a light shake to ensure that the dough can move around.

Open the oven door and bring the peel in flat, over to the far edge of the pizza stone. Tilt it up slightly—but don't let it bunch up—and jostle the peel gently until the edge of the dough round hits the far end of the stone. The dough will immediately catch on the stone, so you should be able to pull the peel back at a flat angle, leaving the dough on the pizza stone with no wrinkles or crimps (that last part is, again, important to it cooking properly). Immediately close the oven door to maintain temperature.

The dough should puff up and fill with air in 2 to 3 minutes. The carta da musica is done when it is puffy, hollow, and dry to the touch. Remove it from the oven and let it cool for 5 minutes. Repeat the process with the remaining dough rounds.

After an initial 5-minute rest, use scissors to cut around the outer seam of the carta (like a pita), carefully peeling back the top layer from the bottom to remove the two layers into separate round sheets. The layers toward the center may want to stick a bit, so use extra care when peeling it apart. You should wind up with two disks of even thickness.

As the breads are baked and separated, stack the sheets cut-side down. Once the last piece of dough is baked, reduce the oven to its lowest setting, ideally below 200°F (95°C). Remove the pizza stone.

Once your oven has cooled down, place the cut rounds, cut-side down, directly on the oven racks in single layers (you can use multiple oven racks) and let the bread dry out until completely crispy, at least 2 hours.

Once dry, the breads can be stored indefinitely in an airtight container. Just continue to store them cut-side down, as the cut-side is not as pretty or even, and will be kept face down when you assemble the finished dish.

to serve

Preheat the oven to 500°F (260°C/Gas 10).

Prepare the leaves, herbs, and vegetables. These can be as rustic or precise as you like, but the real goal is to have things that will be delicious to eat raw, on top of crispy bread.

Place the carta da musica cut-side-down on an 18 x 13-inch (46 x 33 cm) rimmed baking sheet (tray)—it is rimmed to keep the olive oil from leaking onto the oven floor and burning.

Meanwhile, using a vegetable peeler, peel around the perimeter of the wheel of Boschetto al Tartufo—the goal is to have as long of a peel as possible.

Brush the bread disks evenly and generously with olive oil. Sprinkle with the rosemary, chili flakes, and kosher salt to taste. Bake the carta until they are golden brown and crisp, about 2 minutes.

As the disks come out of the oven, pour off any excess oil that has not been absorbed and immediately drape the cheese over the surface so it starts to melt from the residual heat. Place the carta da musica on a plate and dress it with the prepared herbs, greens, flowers, and vegetables. Finish it with a squeeze of fresh lemon juice and flaky sea salt.

Eat this immediately—and with your hands. Basically, just have fun.

lentils, garlic & parmesan

serves 4 to 6

1 pound (455 g) green or black lentils, rinsed and picked over
4 ounces (115 g) finely diced carrots
4 ounces (115 g) finely diced celery
4 ounces (115 g) finely diced leeks, white and light green parts only
4 ounces (115 g) finely diced celery root (celeriac)
4 ounces (115 g) finely diced rutabaga (swede)
kosher salt
2 tablespoons (30 g) unsalted butter
2 tablespoons chopped flat-leaf parsley
1 cup (60 g) grated parmigiano-reggiano cheese
1 to 2 tablespoons Garlic Powder (page 293), to taste
extra-virgin olive oil, for serving

My mom didn't cook a lot, but one thing she did "cook" was canned Progresso lentil soup with a ton of garlic powder and canned Kraft Parmesan cheese. Those things thickened it into a gloppy, grainy sort of mass, but I loved it anyway. I feel that a lot of what drives a chef is nostalgia, and a desire to re-create poignant food memories from their lives. As unsophisticated as this is, it's a deeply ingrained food memory for me. Here is my grown-up version of the canned lentil soup of my childhood.

NOTE The homemade garlic powder must be made in advance, as it takes about 2 days to dehydrate.

directions

In a large pot, combine the lentils and 6 cups (1.5 liters) water. Bring to a light simmer over medium-high heat and cook the lentils for 20 minutes, skimming off any foam that floats to the surface. Add the carrots, celery, leeks, celery root, and rutabaga. Season with a little salt—just not too much, as it will continue to cook down. Cook the soup, uncovered, until the lentils and vegetables are tender, 15 to 20 minutes. Taste and adjust seasoning as needed. Stir in the butter and parsley until incorporated.

To serve, ladle the soup into bowls. Sprinkle with freshly grated Parmigiano, garlic powder, and a few drops of olive oil.

cool melon &
coconut milk curry

This is a dish I look forward to making any summer, especially since I really love the flavor and texture of the melons that grow at Weiser Family Farms (page 24). This dish really works because melon plays well with salt—think melon and prosciutto—and it seems to be a natural fit for the Thai curry flavors, with the herbs, kaffir lime, and coconut milk.

NOTE   You'll want to get at least a day ahead on this recipe. The coconut milk should be held in the refrigerator overnight so that you can more easily separate out the cream (for garnish) from the liquid (for the soup). Meanwhile, the soup can be made up to three days in advance. Keep in mind that it must be completely chilled before being served.

serves 4

melon curry
2 cups (475 ml) plus 1 tablespoon
   grapeseed oil
3 shallots, sliced as thinly as possible
¼ cup (30 g) all-purpose (plain) flour
kosher salt
1 (3 pound/1.3 kg) cantaloupe or another
   orange-fleshed melon
4 ounces (115 g) lemongrass (about
   3 stalks), trimmed of tough base and
   outer leaves and very thinly sliced
1 fresh jalapeño pepper, seeded and
   minced
1 tablespoon minced peeled fresh ginger
1 small white onion, julienned
6 fresh kaffir lime leaves
stems from 1 bunch of cilantro (coriander)
stems from 1 bunch of basil
stems from 1 bunch of mint
3 cups (710 ml) coconut milk with cream
   (full-fat), refrigerated overnight
fresh lime juice

to serve
purple basil leaves (or any herb leaves
   you like)
sliced, seeded jalapeño pepper
extra-virgin olive oil

make the melon curry

In a medium saucepot, heat the 2 cups (475 ml) grapeseed oil over medium-high heat until it registers 300°F (150°C) on a deep-frying thermometer.

Meanwhile, using a fork or your fingers, pull the shallots into rings. In a bowl, combine the flour and 1 teaspoon salt. Toss the shallots in the mixture, until each shallot is fully coated. Transfer the shallots to a sieve or basket to shake off excess flour.

Fry the shallots until golden brown, 2 to 3 minutes. (Be careful of overfrying, as the heat tends to carry over and they will continue cooking out of the oil.) Season with additional salt. Transfer the fried shallots to a plate lined with paper towels and set aside until you're ready to serve.

Halve the melon and scoop out the seeds into a fine-mesh sieve set over a bowl. Using a spoon, press on the seeds until you've extracted as much juice as possible. Discard the seeds and set the juice aside.

Roughly chop the melon until you have about 8 cups (800 g), reserving any remaining melon for garnish.

In a pot or large saucepan, warm the remaining 1 tablespoon grapeseed oil over medium-low heat. Add the lemongrass, jalapeño, ginger, onion, and a pinch of salt. Cook, stirring, until the onion is translucent. Don't let the vegetables take on color.

Using a single layer of cheesecloth, make a sachet with the lime leaves and herb stems and add it to the bottom of the pot. Add the melon and season with a pinch of salt. Reduce the heat to low, cover, and cook, stirring occasionally, until the melon has nearly melted in the pot, about 30 minutes. →

Remove the coconut milk from the refrigerator and separate out the coconut cream. Measure out ½ cup (120 ml) of the cream and refrigerate until serving. Add the coconut milk and the remaining cream to the pot with the melon. Increase the heat to medium-high and bring the mixture to a boil. Remove the pan from the heat and add the reserved melon juice. Discard the sachet. Working in batches, transfer the contents of the pot to a blender and blend thoroughly. Strain through a fine-mesh sieve pressing on the solids.

Let the soup come to room temperature, then transfer to the refrigerator until completely chilled. Once cold, season to taste with lime juice and salt.

to serve

Ladle the soup into bowls. Garnish with the fried shallot rings, dollops of the reserved coconut cream, the melon chunks, jalapeño, and herbs. Finish with a drizzle or dots of olive oil.

king trumpet mushrooms, potato purée, puntarelle & bordelaise

This is my vegetarian version of steak and mashed potatoes. You can prepare this recipe in stages. The Bordelaise can be made up to a few days in advance. It is delicious used in many other dishes too, so feel free to make a double batch and freeze some for later. (If you do make a double batch, just set aside some extra time for everything to reduce.) The sauce is great emulsified with butter and tossed with pasta; for glazing a steak; or to use in *oeufs en meurette* (eggs in a red wine sauce—a classic French bistro dish).

NOTE   You can get a bit ahead on the potato purée if you like, and keep it warm in the oven while you are cooking the mushrooms.

The puntarelle (a bitter green plant in the chicory family) and Spigarello (heirloom broccoli) should be dressed just before serving, but you can prepare the puntarelle a couple of hours in advance and hold it in the ice water.

The king trumpets should be cooked right before serving.

serves 4

mushroom bordelaise
2 cups (480 ml) red wine
4 ounces (115 g) shallots, sliced into thin rings
2 bay leaves
1 cup (240 ml) unfiltered apple juice
1 quart (about 1 liter) Mushroom Stock (page 311)
kosher salt

potato purée
3½ pounds (1.6 kg) yukon gold potatoes (or other yellow-fleshed potato)
2 cups (480 ml) heavy (double) cream
14 ounces (400 g) unsalted butter, at room temperature, cut into chunks
kosher salt

puntarelle and spigarello
1 small puntarelle
a handful of young spigarello, washed and dried
2 tablespoons Miso Bagna Cauda (page 269)
kosher salt

roasted king trumpet mushrooms
1½ pounds (680 g) king trumpet mushrooms
1 teaspoon kosher salt, plus more as needed
3 tablespoons (45 g) unsalted butter
1 tablespoon chopped flat-leaf parsley

make the mushroom bordelaise

In a heavy large pot, combine the red wine, shallots, and bay leaves and bring the liquid to a simmer over medium heat. Let it simmer, uncovered, until the wine has been reduced by three-quarters of the original volume, 20 to 30 minutes.

Add the apple juice and return the liquid to a simmer. Reduce the liquid by half, 10 to 15 minutes. Add the mushroom stock and return the liquid to a simmer. Cook, uncovered, until the liquid reduces to about 1 cup (240 ml), about 30 minutes.

Remove the pot from the heat and strain the reduction through a fine-mesh sieve into a bowl. Salt to taste. If not using right away for the trumpet mushrooms (below), let cool to room temperature and store, covered, in the refrigerator for up to 3 days.

make the potato purée

Preheat the oven to 200°F (95°C).

Peel the potatoes and cut into 1-inch (2.5 cm) chunks. Place the potatoes in a sieve and rinse under cold, running water to remove some of the starch. Place the potatoes in a steamer basket.

Fill a large pot with 2 inches (5 cm) water (just enough to not evaporate out while cooking, but not so much that it touches the steamer basket). Bring to a simmer over medium-high heat, reduce to medium, and place the steamer basket in the pot. Cover and steam until the potatoes are soft, about 45 minutes. →

Meanwhile, in a saucepan, warm the heavy cream (cold cream will cool down the potatoes and make them gummy).

While still warm, pass the potatoes through a ricer into a bowl. Add the warm cream and butter to the riced potatoes and whisk, working quickly, until fully combined. Season to taste with salt and then pass the potatoes through a tamis (highly recommended if you don't have one)—the goal is to wind up with potatoes that have the texture of good pastry cream. Transfer the potatoes to a serving dish, cover with foil, and keep warm in the oven at 200°F (95°C) until ready to serve.

make the puntarelle and spigarello

Separate the puntarelle and reserve any small, tender leaves for garnish. Now take the tubes and cut them in half lengthwise. Cut them into matchsticks and then soak them in ice water—they will start curling up, which is what you want, for 30 minutes.

Right before serving, drain and dry the puntarelle and toss in a bowl with the spigarello, reserved puntarelle leaves, miso bagna cauda, and salt to taste.

make the roasted king trumpet mushrooms

King trumpets don't need to be washed, so you can jump right into cutting them. Slice the mushrooms into 2 to 3 equal pieces (some pieces will just be stems). Season the mushrooms with 1 teaspoon of salt and let sit for 15 minutes to let the salt penetrate the mushrooms.

In a large skillet, melt the 2 tablespoons (30 g) of the butter over medium heat. Add the mushrooms, being extra careful not to break the delicate caps. Cook the mushrooms, without moving, for 5 to 7 minutes. As the mushrooms cook and brown, their caps will become sturdier—after this you can move them around a bit. Once the mushrooms turn golden brown, flip them over. You can also roll them in the pan to try to get as much color as possible on every part of the mushroom. They should look great after 10 to 12 minutes.

Add the bordelaise and bring it to a simmer. Using a spoon, glaze the mushrooms with the sauce until they are shiny and look delicious. Add the remaining 1 tablespoon (15 g) butter and the parsley and stir to combine. Season to taste with salt and prepare to serve.

To serve, spoon the potato purée onto 4 plates and scatter the mushrooms on top. Pour the bordelaise sauce over the mushrooms and potatoes and top with the dressed puntarelle and spigarello.

braised matsutake mushrooms, delicata squash, tomatillo & pumpkin seeds

It's seemed to me that matsutake mushrooms were always cooked in a delicate, gentle way and seasoned with subtle Japanese flavors. So I decided to try cooking them in precisely the opposite way to see if they could stand up to more bold, aggressive Tex-Mex flavors.

serves 4

tomatillo sauce
1 pound (455 g) tomatillos (I prefer smaller ones), husked and washed
1 medium white onion, cut into eighths
3 garlic cloves, germ removed, finely grated
1 tablespoon extra-virgin olive oil
1 tablespoon chopped cilantro (coriander)
1 teaspoon chopped flat-leaf parsley leaves
kosher salt

delicata squash
1 small delicata squash
1 tablespoon Brown Butter (page 278), melted
kosher salt

matsutake mushrooms
1 pound (455 g) matsutake mushrooms
2 cups (480 ml) Mushroom Stock (page 311)
kosher salt
3 tablespoons (45 g) unsalted butter, at room temperature

to serve
2 tablespoons hulled pumpkin seeds, lightly toasted

make the tomatillo sauce	Preheat the oven to 500°F (260°C/Gas 10). Line a baking sheet with foil.
	Arrange the tomatillos and onion on the baking sheet in a single layer. We want a dry char, so oil isn't necessary—but foil is (it will save you a lot of time on cleanup). Roast the vegetables until charred all over, 15 to 20 minutes. If the tomatillos are soft but not yet blackened, and the onion is done, you can finish the former under the broiler.
	Transfer the charred vegetables to a food processor and add the garlic, olive oil, cilantro, and parsley. Process until the vegetables turn into a smooth, textured sauce and season to taste with salt. Right before serving, gently warm the sauce in a saucepan over low heat.
make the delicata squash	Preheat the oven to 325°F (160°C/Gas 3). Line a baking sheet with parchment paper.
	Cut the squash (unpeeled) into slices, about 1/8 inch (3 mm) thick. Toss them in a bowl with the brown butter and salt to taste. Spread them on the baking sheet in a single layer. Roast until the squash is tender but not mushy, 10 to 12 minutes. Remove from the oven and set aside. Right before serving, return to the oven to warm up.
make the matsutake mushrooms	This is a gentle, gradual cooking process, so take your time and be patient.
	Using a bird's beak knife, carefully peel the whole exterior of the mushrooms (stalk and cap) and set the peels aside for use in another dish (such as Mushroom Stock, page 360, or the peel fondue on page 166). Halve the mushrooms lengthwise and place them cut-side down in a pan wide enough to fit them in a single layer. Pour the mushroom stock over the mushrooms and sprinkle conservatively with salt. (As the mushrooms cook, the stock will reduce dramatically, so the salt will become quite concentrated.)
	Set the pan on the stove over medium heat and cook the mushrooms, uncovered, until the stock reduces to a demi-glace (a thick glaze) and the mushrooms are cooked through. Remove from the heat and add the butter to the pan, shaking the pan to combine. Taste and adjust seasoning, if needed.
to serve	Divide the tomatillo sauce in dollops across 4 plates. Place the mushrooms on top of the sauce, allowing the tomatillo sauce to anchor the mushrooms to the plate. Follow with squash, and spoon the mushroom sauce on top. Finish with a sprinkling of toasted pumpkin seeds.

stracciatella with morel mushrooms, ramps & saffron

serves 4

12 ounces (340 g) fresh morel mushrooms
6 cups (1.4 liters) Mushroom Stock
  (page 311), chilled
12 saffron threads
30 ramp leaves, roughly chopped
3 large eggs, lightly whisked
kosher salt

I'd never actually had stracciatella soup until my wife made it for me—and it was delicious. My variation on this traditional Italian soup is to use morels and ramps, which impart a lot of extra flavor to the broth. Just be sure to properly clean the morels, as they have lots of little nooks and crannies that love hiding dirt.

directions

To clean morels, fill up 2 medium containers with tepid water. Trim the very tips of the mushroom stems, halve the mushrooms lengthwise, and shake out any grit that falls out. Submerge the mushrooms in the first container of water and agitate the water so that the grit falls to the bottom of the container. Carefully lift the mushrooms out of the water and repeat in the second container. Rinse out the first container, refill with water and wash the mushrooms again. Repeat until no grit falls to the bottom of the container.

In a medium saucepot, combine the stock and saffron threads. Submerge the morels in the stock and set the pot over medium heat. Bring the stock to a simmer, reduce the heat to low, and cook at a low simmer until the mushrooms are not too raw or firm but also not overcooked, about 5 minutes. (Morels are special and expensive and—once mushy—are a waste.) Add the ramp leaves and cook for no more than 1½ minutes—they are delicate and will break down quickly.

Using a wooden spoon, stir the soup quickly to create a vortex (like when poaching an egg) and slowly pour in the eggs in a steady stream. Remove from the heat, let sit for 30 seconds, then stir again.

Taste the soup and season with salt. Serve immediately.

country-fried morel mushrooms with green garlic gravy

Morels are a meaty mushroom, and it's a fairly classic move to stuff them with chicken mousse. In keeping with those flavors, I went back to my Southern roots and country-fried the morels, serving them with white country gravy. The morels kind of look like fried chicken hearts, and it's a really rich, decadent dish, which gets brightened by the addition of green garlic.

serves 4

green garlic gravy
2 tablespoons (30 g) unsalted butter
¼ teaspoon kosher salt
4 tablespoons thinly sliced green garlic
2 tablespoons all-purpose (plain) flour
½ cup (120 ml) whole (full-fat) milk
½ cup (120 ml) Mushroom Stock
  (page 311)

country-fried morels
3 to 4 cups (700 to 950 ml) canola
  (rapeseed), peanut (groundnut),
  or grapeseed oil, for deep-frying
¼ cup (60 ml) buttermilk
3 large eggs
2 cups (250 g) all-purpose (plain) flour
2 teaspoons kosher salt, plus more as
  needed
1 teaspoon smoked paprika (pimentón)
1 teaspoon freshly ground black pepper
1 pound (454 g) fresh morel mushrooms,
  washed and dried (for washing
  instructions, see Stracciatella with
  Morel Mushrooms, Ramps & Saffron,
  page 156)
miner's lettuce leaves or flat-leaf parsley
  leaves, to garnish

make the green garlic gravy

This is essentially a play on classic Southern country gravy. In a pan, melt the butter over medium heat. Add the salt and green garlic and sauté, stirring, until just fragrant, about 1 minute. Add the flour, whisking to incorporate, but don't let it brown.

Combine the milk and mushroom stock, then gradually add it to the pan, whisking constantly, until all of the liquid is incorporated and does not have any lumps.

Bring the sauce to a simmer. Adjust the heat to maintain a low simmer, stirring to make sure the sauce does not stick or burn, and cook until it thickens to the consistency of hearty gravy. Remove the pan from the heat and set aside, continuing to stir occasionally as the gravy cools. When ready to serve, gently reheat over low heat until warm.

make the country-fried morels

In a deep pot, heat the oil until it registers 350°F (180°C) on a deep-frying thermometer.

Meanwhile, in a bowl, whisk together the buttermilk and eggs. In a separate bowl, combine the flour, 2 teaspoons of salt, paprika, and pepper and mix thoroughly.

Once the oil reaches the desired temperature, begin to dredge the morels. Working with one mushroom at a time, coat the morels first in the egg mixture, then lift them up and allow the egg to drain from the cavity. Next, put them in the flour mixture, working the mix into all of the little crevices—it will create all of those nice little crispies.

Working in batches, fry the mushrooms until golden brown and cooked through, 6 to 8 minutes. Remove with a spider (skimmer), drain on paper towels, and season immediately to taste with salt.

To serve, spoon the warm gravy on the bottom of 4 plates, place the mushrooms on top, and garnish with lettuce leaves.

mushroom conserva, ricotta & gochugaru

serves 4 to 6

1½ pounds (680 g) Whipped Ricotta
(page 281)
kosher salt
1 cup (240 ml) Mushroom Conserva
(page 305)
½ cup (120 ml) Garlic Confit (page 312)
1 tablespoon chopped fresh rosemary
2 teaspoons *gochugaru* (korean chili
powder)
sliced bread, for serving

This is a simple recipe that highlights what you can do with a well-stocked larder. Once you have things like homemade ricotta, mushroom conserva, and garlic confit, you can make lots of great dishes relatively quickly.

directions

Preheat the oven to 350°F (180°C/Gas 4).

Taste the ricotta and season with additional salt, if needed. Divide the ricotta across 1-cup (240 ml) cast-iron pots and spoon the mushroom conserva over it. Top with the garlic confit and place the pots in the oven. Bake until warmed through, 8 to 10 minutes.

Sprinkle with *gochugaru* and serve either warm or at room temperature, with bread.

porcini mushrooms en papillote, fondue of the peels & egg

serves 4

peel fondue
12 ounces (340 g) porcini peels, scraps, and pieces of broken cap (reserved from the porcini for the papillote, see below)
4 ounces (115 g) shallots, thinly sliced
1 cup (240 ml) Mushroom Stock (page 311)
4 tablespoons (60 g) unsalted butter
4 garlic cloves, halved lengthwise, germ removed
1 sprig fresh rosemary
¼ cup (60 ml) heavy (double) cream
papillote
2 pounds (910 g) porcini mushrooms, trimmed (see Note)
3 ounces (85 g) unsalted butter, cut into 4 pieces
16 sprigs fresh thyme
4 garlic cloves, germ removed
8 fresh bay leaves
4 tablespoons (60 ml) madeira
eggs
4 tablespoons (60 g) unsalted butter
4 large eggs
kosher salt
freshly ground black pepper

Fun fact #1: I didn't invent porcini en papillote. Fun fact #2: I made this dish as an audition for a job, and when I did it, I spilled butter all over someone's rug. Fun fact #3: I still got the job. When purchasing porcini, look for ones that are dense and not spongy. If they're wet and mushy, that often means that there are worms inside.

NOTE   To clean porcini, brush the grit from them with a soft, clean toothbrush and trim the stems. Using a bird's beak knife, start from the bottom of the stem and peel—as thinly as possible—toward the cap, curving around the base so that you get (ideally) one clean peel.

make the peel fondue

In a large pot, combine the porcini peels, scraps, and pieces with the shallots, stock, butter, garlic, and rosemary. Bring to a simmer over medium heat. Reduce the heat to low and cook, stirring occasionally, until everything is tender, about 40 minutes. Remove the pot from the heat and stir in the cream. Purée the mixture in a blender until smooth. Strain through a fine-mesh sieve and set aside. Right before serving, warm the fondue over gentle heat.

make the papillote

Preheat the oven to 400°F (200°C/Gas 6).

Slice the porcini lengthwise into slices about the thickness of a coin.

Set out 4 large pieces of parchment paper, fold them in half to form a center crease, and then open them back up. Dividing evenly, place the porcini next to the center crease of the parchment. Place a piece of butter on top, followed by the thyme, garlic, and bay leaves. Drizzle the Madeira over the mushrooms. Fold the parchment over on itself, then either fold or roll the edges as tightly as possible—you do not want any air to escape. Transfer the parchment packets to an 18 x 13-inch (46 x 33 cm) baking sheet. Bake in the oven for 12 minutes. While baking, you can set about frying your eggs (see below).

make the eggs

While the papillotes are baking, in a pan, melt the butter over medium heat. Crack in the eggs and fry until the whites are set but the yolks are still runny, 3 to 4 minutes. Season to taste with salt and black pepper.

When ready to serve, remove the papillottes from the oven and present one of the parcels to the diners. Cut it open in front of them on a plate (there will be juices), so that they can take in the smell when it escapes the package.

Once you've presented the papillote, bring it back into the kitchen. Open the remaining papillotes and then discard the bay leaf, thyme, and garlic. Transfer the contents of the papillotes to a large sauté pan or braiser. Gently warm the ingredients, shaking the pan to unify the sauce if needed.

Divide the fondue evenly across 4 plates. Place a fried egg in the center. To finish, spoon the mushrooms and their juices around the egg.

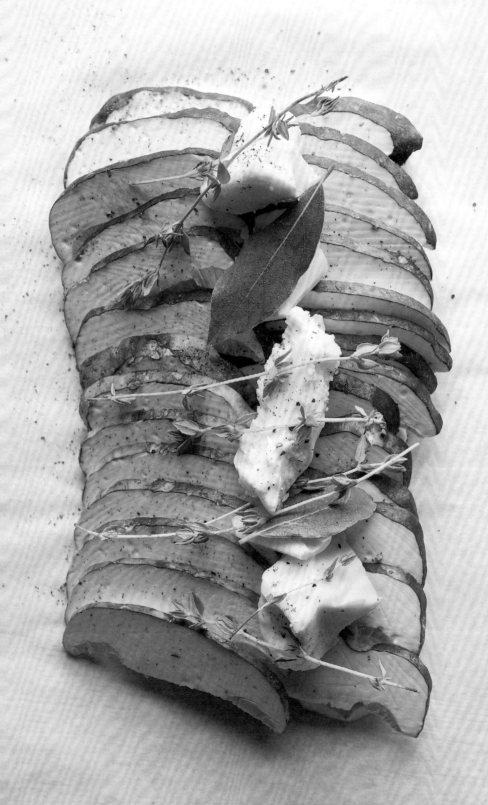

nasturtium dolmas, black rice & sesame

Usually, people just use the small leaves of nasturtiums as a garnish, but here I use the larger leaves—which in this instance mimic grape leaves, and are stuffed as dolmas.

serves 4 to 6

nasturtium panade
2 ounces (60 g) nasturtium flowers
3 ounces (85 g) Pain de Mie (page 285),
   crusts removed and cut into small dice
4 tablespoons (60 g) unsalted butter
juice of ½ lemon
kosher salt
dolmas
1 cup (200 g) black rice
30 large nasturtium leaves
¼ cup (60 ml) Brittany's Pepper Jam
   (page 267)
1 tablespoon white sesame seeds
1 tablespoon extra-virgin olive oil
kosher salt
to serve
small nasturtium leaves

make the nasturtium panade

In a small pot, combine the flowers and 1 cup (240 ml) water. Bring to a boil over medium-high heat, then remove immediately from the heat and add the bread and butter, and let sit for 15 minutes, allowing the bread to soak up the liquid. Add the lemon juice and then purée the mixture in a blender until smooth. Season to taste with salt and refrigerate for at least 2 hours.

make the dolmas

Thoroughly rinse the rice under cold, running water and drain. Place the rice in a pot, add 1¾ cups (415 ml) cold water, and bring it to a boil over medium-high heat. Reduce the heat to low, cover, and cook until all of the water is absorbed, 30 to 40 minutes.

While the rice is cooking, roughly chop 10 of the nasturtium leaves.

Once the rice is cooked, flake it with a fork and add the pepper jam, the chopped nasturtium leaves, sesame seeds, and olive oil. Stir to combine, season to taste with salt, and set the rice aside until ready to stuff the dolmas.

Bring a pot of generously salted water to a boil over high heat. Prepare an ice bath in a bowl. Working with one leaf at a time, blanch the remaining nasturtium leaves for 5 seconds, lift out of the water using a spider/skimmer, and transfer to the ice bath until cool. Carefully lay them on paper towels. (The leaves are delicate and if you try to blanch them all at the same time, there is a good chance that they will be much more difficult to lay out and keep whole.)

Take a small mound of the rice mixture and place it on a blanched nasturtium leaf about a quarter of the way from the edge closest to you. Roll up the bottom, fold in the sides, then roll the rest of the way. Repeat until all of the dolmas are rolled.

to serve

When ready to serve, divide the dolmas across multiple plates or place all on one plate, if you prefer. Adorn each plate with a few dollops of the panade—I like to form it into a cascade, almost like a breaking wave. Finally, garnish with tiny nasturtium leaves if you have them.

vanilla ice cream with nasturtium flower

People like to imply that vanilla is boring or plain, but it's probably one of the most complex flavors in existence—and one of my favorite flavors of ice cream. This ice cream is closer to the texture of a semifreddo than a traditional ice cream. No eggs, no churning—it's just cream, condensed milk, and a little vodka to keep it from overfreezing. The texture is almost like pure, frozen cream, which I love. I think churned ice creams get icier over time, while this kind just stays smooth.

NOTE   The ice cream is best if made the day before. Meanwhile, the panade will hold under refrigeration for a day or two. The candied nasturtium flowers take 4 to 6 hours to dehydrate.

serves 6 to 8

no-churn vanilla bean ice cream
2½ cups (600 ml) heavy (double) cream
1 vanilla bean, split lengthwise
1 can (14 oz/400 g) sweetened
   condensed milk
2 tablespoons vodka
candied nasturtium flowers
1 cup (200 g) granulated sugar
20 nasturtium flowers
sweet nasturtium panade
1½ ounces (45 g) nasturtium flowers
¼ cup (50 g) granulated sugar
½ teaspoon kosher salt
3 ounces (85 g) Pain de Mie (page 285),
   crusts removed and cut into small dice
4 tablespoons (60 g) unsalted butter,
   at room temperature
juice of ½ lemon

make the no-churn vanilla bean ice cream

Pour the cream into a chilled mixer bowl, then scrape the vanilla seeds into the cream (reserve the vanilla pod for another use, like the Creamed Corn on page 114). Whip the cream to soft peaks. Add the condensed milk and continue to whip until you have a texture similar to Cool Whip (the texture is somewhat like Greek yogurt, but lighter and fluffier). Fold in the vodka until incorporated, cover, and freeze for at least 6 hours and preferably overnight.

make the candied nasturtium flowers

In a saucepot, combine the sugar and ½ cup (120 ml) water and bring to a boil over high heat. Immediately remove from the heat and let the syrup cool to room temperature. Gently dip each flower leaf into the syrup to coat, and arrange on trays in a food dehydrator.

Dehydrate at 135°F (57°C) for 4 to 6 hours, flipping after the first 45 minutes to prevent sticking, until the leaves are just crisp on the outside and candy-like on the inside. Set aside until ready to serve.

make the sweet nasturtium panade

In a pot, combine the flowers, sugar, salt, and 1 cup (240 ml) water and bring to a boil over high heat. Remove from the heat and add the bread, butter, and lemon juice and set aside for 15 minutes, allowing the bread to soak up the liquid. In a blender, purée the mixture until smooth and let cool to room temperature. Cover and refrigerate until ready to serve. After the panade is completely chilled, rewhip it with a whisk to achieve a creamy sauce before serving.

To serve, scoop the ice cream into bowls and spoon the panade on top. Garnish with candied nasturtium flowers.

oca crudo, persimmon, citrus & avocado

Oca (sometimes called a New Zealand yam) is a South American tuber common in Peru. I used to grow them in Napa—they grow underground like potatoes, attached to the vine—and I love how the leaves look like clover and they have beautiful, lemony, edible yellow flowers. Oca is actually a difficult ingredient to find, but if you happen upon it, wherever you are, grab it.

Oca is visually striking to me: I love all its wrinkles and colors. Good to eat raw when they're small, oca have a texture similar to water chestnut. When cooked, they tend to lose their striking color.

NOTE   Variety is key with the citrus, so if you can't find these exact fruits, you can substitute others. Just don't substitute regular lemons for the pink, as they will be too tart. Instead of pink lemons you could use pink grapefruit or even another type of orange.

serves 4

avocado crema
1 medium avocado (4 to 5 oz/110 to 140 g), halved and pitted
1 cup (240 ml) Crème Fraîche (page 278)
finely grated zest and juice of 1 lime
1 garlic clove, germ removed, roughly chopped
1 jalapeño pepper, seeded and roughly chopped
kosher salt

fuyu persimmon purée
2 ripe fuyu persimmons, peeled, seeded (if any), and chopped
½ Preserved Lemon (page 307)
1 tablespoon extra-virgin olive oil
kosher salt

oca & citrus
½ pound (225 g) oca, washed and dried
1 tablespoon extra-virgin olive oil
kosher salt
2 pink lemons
2 blood oranges
1 navel orange
1 cara cara orange

to serve
oca leaves and flowers

make the avocado crema

Scoop the avocado flesh into a blender. Add the crème fraîche, the lime zest, 2 tablespoons lime juice, the garlic, jalapeño (you can use more or less of jalapeño, depending on taste), and salt to taste. Begin blending, then taste for salt and heat. Adjust as needed and then continue to blend until the crema is fully whipped. (I don't recommend blending more jalapeño in after it is fully blended, as it will wind up in chunks and not fully incorporated into the crema.)

Cover and refrigerate the crema until ready to serve, but try to use it as soon as possible, as the color will begin to brown over time, and the flavor will turn with it.

make the fuyu persimmon purée

In a blender, purée the persimmons with the preserved lemon and olive oil until you have a velvety, custardy mixture. Season to taste with salt. Set aside. →

**make the oca
& citrus**

If the oca are of a nice small size (the size of your thumb, or a little smaller), you can leave them whole. If they're larger, halve them in either direction.

In a bowl, toss the oca with the olive oil and some salt and set aside for about 15 minutes. The salt will essentially give the oca a quick cure, allowing the seasoning to penetrate the vegetable—this will keep oca from having a seasoned exterior and a bland interior. Just don't let it sit for so long that it starts to break the oca down —15 minutes is perfect.

Cut the tops and bottoms off the citrus so that you get clean, flat surfaces and also expose the fruit. Slide your knife into the side of the citrus until it is just through the pith. Moving your knife around the whole fruit, remove all of the peel and pith. The result should be beautiful fruit with no white pith or peel. Repeat this process with the remaining citrus. Slice the citrus crosswise into thin wheels, ⅛ inch (3 mm) thick. Using tweezers or the tip of a knife, remove the seeds.

to serve

Evenly divide the citrus slices across 4 plates; feel free to let them stack and overlap a bit, leaving room on the plate for the rest of the ingredients. Using a squeeze bottle, dot the plate with the persimmon purée. Place the dressed oca over the persimmon dots, using it as glue to help anchor the oca. Fill in the gaps with dots of avocado crema and garnish with the leaves and flowers.

olives marinated with garlic, fennel & orange

serves 4

1 pound (455 g) various olives, drained
½ cup (120 ml) extra-virgin olive oil
1 tablespoon grated garlic (from 4 to 5 cloves, germ removed)
1 tablespoon ground fennel seed
zest and juice of 2 oranges

This is a very common flavor combination for a reason: It's a great thing to snack on, really at any time. I like Castelvetrano olives because they're really meaty and briny.

directions

Bring a medium pot of water to a simmer over medium-high heat.

Meanwhile, in a metal bowl, combine the olive oil, garlic, and fennel seed.

Cover the bowl tightly with plastic wrap (clingfilm) and set it over the pot of water so it fits snugly, but the bottom of the bowl doesn't touch the water. Cook until the garlic is fragrant and no longer raw, about 30 minutes.

Remove from the heat and toss with the olives, and orange zest and juice. Serve immediately, while warm, or refrigerate for up to 2 days and serve chilled.

french onion soup

French onion soup is universally beloved. If it's on a menu, I'm almost guaranteed to order it. Even bad versions are pretty good, as long as there's plenty of melty cheese. This version is all about celebrating onions. It is basically nothing more than onions, cheese, and bread.

serves 4

4 cups (about 1 liter) plus 2 teaspoons grapeseed oil

4 spring onion (salad onion) bulbs, peeled and halved lengthwise (reserve the tops for Onion Top Ash, page 289)

kosher salt

1 bunch whole wild onions, preferably with blossoms

freshly ground black pepper

1 leek, white part only, julienned, rinsed, and dried completely

¼ cup (60 ml) dry sherry

4 cups (1 liter) Caramelized Onion Stock (page 310)

4 slices Pain de Mie (page 285), 1 inch (2.5 cm) thick

½ pound (225 g) raclette cheese, thinly sliced

directions

Preheat the oven to 350°F (180°C/Gas 4).

Heat a cast-iron pan over high heat until hot. Add 1 teaspoon of the grapeseed oil followed by the spring onions, cut-side down. Place a plate that fits inside the pan over the onions to weight them down—it will help to get an even sear. Cook until the onions have a nice char, 7 to 10 minutes, then remove from the pan. (If the onions are not cooked all the way through, place them on a baking sheet and finish in the oven.) Separate the cooked onions into petals, season with salt, and set aside until ready to serve.

If the wild onions have blossoms, remove them and set aside for garnish. Then, in a bowl, toss the wild onions with 1 teaspoon of the grapeseed oil and season with salt and pepper. Transfer to a baking sheet and bake until the onions loose their rawness, 8 to 10 minutes. Set aside. (Leave the oven on.)

In a deep pot, heat the remaining 4 cups (1 liter) oil until it registers 275°F (135°C) on a deep-frying thermometer. Gently lower the leek whites into the oil and fry until just golden and crisp, 2 to 4 minutes—don't let them turn too dark or bitter. Fish the leeks out with a spider/skimmer and drain on paper towels. Season immediately with salt.

In a medium pot, bring the sherry to a lively simmer over medium-high heat and cook until it is reduced by half, about 2 minutes. Add the onion stock, bring up to a boil and then reduce heat to keep warm. Season to taste with salt.

In a cast-iron pan, in a toaster, or in the oven, toast the bread until lightly browned and slightly crisp. Arrange the toast on a baking sheet and top with the raclette, making sure to completely cover the bread (otherwise it will burn). Place it in the oven until the cheese is melted and just beginning to brown, 3 to 5 minutes. You can reheat your charred onion in the oven at this point too.

To serve, place a piece of toast on the bottom of each of 4 bowls. Top with the charred spring onions, wild onions, blossoms, and fried leeks. Ladle the hot, seasoned onion stock over the top and serve.

spring onions, roasted in their skins with ash honey

serves 4

12 medium spring onions (salad onions),
  bulbs untrimmed, greens separated
1 tablespoon extra-virgin olive oil
½ teaspoon kosher salt
3 tablespoons honey
flaky sea salt

I like this dish because you can just start cooking—no prep work required. You don't even have to peel the onions ahead of time, but rather, you do it after, and have a deep roasted flavor but with better texture than if they were exposed to direct heat.

Delicious on their own, these are particularly good with crispy skinned duck breast and turnips. When shopping for spring onions (salad onions), make sure that they have a decent bulb and aren't too scrawny.

NOTE If you have a convection (fan-assisted) oven, don't use that feature here, as the fan will blow the onions all over the place.

directions

Preheat the oven to 450°F (230°C/Gas 8).

Place the onion greens on a baking sheet and bake until the greens are completely brittle, blackened, and crumbly, about 30 minutes, rotating the pan halfway through. Remove from the oven and set aside to cool. Reduce the oven temperature to 350°F (180°C/Gas 4).

Roughly chop the blackened greens and grind in a spice grinder until mostly finely ground but with a little texture. Set the ash aside.

Toss the onion bulbs with the olive oil and kosher salt. Arrange on a baking sheet and bake until the skins are crisp and the onions are soft, 20 to 25 minutes. When the onions can be handled, use a bird's beak knife to carefully peel the skins off, leaving the root end intact.

In a small pot, gently warm the honey and stir in 2 teaspoons of the ash (save the rest for another use; it will last pretty much forever in an airtight container).

To serve, divide the onions evenly across 4 plates. Drizzle with ash honey and finish with flaky sea salt.

plöppenschmëar:
parsnip cream,
meringue & citrus

Plöppenschmëar is a made-up word that sounds vaguely German, and is my version of the British dessert called Eton Mess. I, personally, find it way more fun to say, "plöppenschmëar." It's also a great use for any ugly, malformed meringues when you make Pavlova (page 233).

NOTE All of these components actually last pretty well and could be made the day before and then assembled when you're ready for dessert, making it perfect for a dinner party. For the whipped cream: Some people like to add sugar once the cream is already whipped, but I prefer to add it at the beginning.

serves 6

meringue
1¼ cups (280 g) superfine (caster) sugar
1½ teaspoons cornstarch (cornflour)
½ cup (120 ml) egg whites, from about 4 or 5 large eggs
⅛ teaspoon cream of tartar
⅛ teaspoon kosher salt
1 teaspoon vanilla extract
1 tablespoon apple cider vinegar

parsnip cream
2 pounds (900 g) parsnips, peeled and roughly chopped
¼ cup (60 ml) plus 2 tablespoons grapeseed oil
½ teaspoon kosher salt, plus more as needed
1 cup (240 ml) heavy (double) cream
1 cup (240 ml) whole (full-fat) milk
½ cup (100 g) granulated sugar
½ vanilla bean, split lengthwise
2 large egg yolks
¼ cup (28 g) cornstarch
2 tablespoons (30 g) unsalted butter, cut into cubes, at room temperature

whipped cream
1½ cups (360 ml) heavy cream
3 tablespoons granulated sugar

to serve
a variety of citrus—such as pomelo, oroblanco, tangelo, blood orange—ideally seedless, peel and pith removed and cut into segments

make the meringue

Preheat the oven to 225°F (110°C/Gas ¼).

In a bowl, combine the sugar and cornstarch and mix well. Set aside.

In a stand mixer fitted with a whisk attachment, whip the egg whites, cream of tartar, and salt on low speed. Increase the speed to medium and whisk until the mixture becomes frothy, 2 to 3 minutes.

Add the sugar and cornstarch mixture in three equal parts—it's okay if the sugar doesn't quite dissolve all the way right now—and continue to whisk until the egg whites start to form peaks, 2 to 3 minutes. Add the vanilla and vinegar and continue whisking until stiff peaks form, 3 to 5 minutes.

Turn the mixer off. Line an 18 x 13-inch (46 x 33 cm) baking sheet with parchment paper or a silicone baking mat. Using a 3-ounce (45 ml) ice cream scoop, form 6 individual meringues on the lined pan. Bake for 1 hour, rotating the pan every 15 minutes. Then reduce the temperature to 200°F (95°C) and bake for 1 more hour (you don't need to rotate anymore)—the meringues should not take on color. When the meringues are done, they should peel off easily from the parchment and have a hard exterior with a soft interior. Let the meringues cool to room temperature. →

**make the
parsnip cream**

In a bowl, toss the parsnips with 2 tablespoons of the grapeseed oil, ½ teaspoon salt, and ¼ cup (60 ml) water. Set aside for 15 minutes to let the salt draw out some of the moisture.

Transfer the parsnips and their juices to a pot. Cover and cook over low heat, stirring occasionally, until the parsnips are soft enough to mash with a spoon against the side of the pot, about 45 minutes. Add a few drops of water, if needed, to prevent any caramelization. Transfer the parsnips to a blender and purée until smooth. With the machine running, slowly drizzle in the remaining ¼ cup (60 ml) grapeseed oil. Transfer to a container, cover with plastic wrap (clingfilm) pressed directly over the surface to prevent a skin from forming, and refrigerate until chilled.

While the parsnips are cooking, in a medium saucepan, combine the cream, milk, ¼ cup (50 g) of the sugar, the vanilla bean, and a pinch of salt. Cook, stirring, until the mixture comes to a simmer, then remove from the heat and set aside.

In a medium bowl, whisk together the egg yolks, cornstarch, and remaining ¼ cup (50 g) sugar. Whisking constantly, slowly drizzle in about ½ cup (120 ml) of the hot cream mixture and continue adding, ½ cup (120 ml) at a time, until fully incorporated. Return the custard to the saucepan and cook over medium-high heat, whisking constantly, until it thickens and registers 160°F (70°C) on an instant-read thermometer, about 2 minutes. Remove from the heat and discard the vanilla pod.

Transfer the custard to a stand mixer fitted with a paddle attachment (you can also use a hand mixer if you like). Add the butter and beat on medium speed until the butter melts and the mixture cools, about 5 minutes.

Cover the pastry cream with plastic wrap pressed directly over the surface to prevent a skin from forming, and refrigerate until chilled, at least 2 hours and up to 2 days.

Once both the parsnip purée and pastry cream are chilled, fold them together and refrigerate, covered, until ready to serve.

**make the
whipped cream**

In a chilled bowl (or a chilled bowl of a stand mixer fitted with a whisk), combine the cream and sugar and whip until stiff peaks form, 2 to 3 minutes.

to serve

Using either 6 individual glasses or a large trifle bowl, build the dessert. Start with some parsnip cream on the bottom, follow with a layer of merengue, then citrus, then whipped cream. Make as many layers as you desire, or that the vessel will allow, and don't worry too much about getting sloppy with it. It is called plöppenschmëar, after all.

peas & pecorino

serves 4 to 6

1½ pounds (680 g) peas in their pods
kosher salt
a handful of pea tendrils, to garnish
3 tablespoons extra-virgin olive oil
1½ tablespoons red wine vinegar
1 tablespoon minced shallot
1 tablespoon chiffonade of mint
freshly ground black pepper
4 ounces (115 g) pecorino romano cheese

The first restaurant I worked at after culinary school was Mumbo Jumbo in Atlanta, Georgia, and that's where I ate really good blanched peas for the first time. They made a dish of peas with pecorino that made me realize I actually liked peas. So obviously, the Mumbo Jumbo concoction was a huge inspiration for this version.

directions

Shuck the peas (see the method on page 46); you should get about 2 cups (460 g) of shucked peas. (Reserve the pods for Pea Shell Stock, page 311, or Smoked Split Pea Shell & Carrot Soup, page 200.)

Bring a pot of water to a boil over medium heat. Season it with enough salt that it tastes like the sea. Prepare an ice bath in a large bowl. Add the peas to the boiling water and cook, at a simmer, until they are tender but not mushy (this can vary based on the size of the peas), 2 to 4 minutes. Drain the peas and immediately transfer to the ice bath until completely cool. Drain and spread the peas on paper towels and allow to dry completely.

In a bowl, combine the peas with the pea tendrils, olive oil, vinegar, shallot, and mint. Season to taste with salt and pepper.

To serve, divide the dressed peas across plates. Shave pecorino on top and finish with more pepper.

peas & pecorino, version 2.0

serves 6 to 8

pea purée
kosher salt
½ cup (115 g) shucked peas (from about ½ pound/225 g peas in the pods)
a few drops of Pea Shell Stock (page 311) or water, if needed

pecorino custard
1 cup (240 ml) whole (full-fat) milk
1 cup (240 ml) heavy (double) cream
1 cup (60 g) grated pecorino romano cheese
3 ounces (85 g) diced, crustless Pain de Mie (page 285) or any good white bread
4 large egg yolks
½ teaspoon kosher salt
½ teaspoon freshly ground black pepper

to serve
a handful of pea tendrils
pecorino romano cheese
flaky sea salt
cracked black pepper

The original version (page 189) is a faithful homage to the dish that made me like fresh peas in the first place. This one is a creamier, more decadent version. But to be honest, after trying them both, I kind of want to eat them together.

NOTE   The pea purée can be made slightly in advance, and the pecorino custard should be chilled for at least 2 hours before serving. If you want to make use of the leftover pea solids from sieving the purée, dehydrate them in a food dehydrator and then grind into pea powder. It is quite delicious.

make the pea purée	Bring a pot of water to a boil over medium-high heat. Add enough kosher salt so it tastes like the sea. Prepare an ice bath in a large bowl. Add the peas to the boiling water and blanch until tender, about 3 minutes. Drain and transfer immediately to the ice bath until cool. Drain and dry the peas on paper towels, then purée in a blender until smooth. If you can't quite get it to blend all the way, add a few drops of stock or water to help it along.
	Push the pea purée through a fine-mesh sieve into a bowl, pressing on the solids (see Note). Season to taste with kosher salt and transfer to a squeeze bottle until ready to serve.
make the pecorino custard	Preheat the oven to 350°F (180°C/Gas 4).
	In a pot, combine the milk and cream and bring to a simmer over medium heat. Whisk in the pecorino, then submerge the diced bread. Let sit at room temperature for 20 minutes.
	Working in batches if necessary, in a blender, combine the soaked bread mixture with the egg yolks, kosher salt, and ground black pepper and blend until smooth.
	Wrap the outside of a 9½-inch (24 cm) round tart pan with a removable bottom tightly with foil (this will prevent the mixture from leaking before it sets). Pour the custard into the tart pan and set on a baking sheet. Bake until set and lightly caramelized, 15 to 20 minutes, or until a cake tester inserted in the center comes out clean.
	Transfer the pan to a cooling rack and let cool to room temperature. Refrigerate for at least 2 hours or until completely cold.
to serve	When ready to serve, let the custard sit at room temperature for about 20 minutes. Unwrap the tart pan, remove the outer ring (but keep the custard on the removable bottom; it's really not worth trying to remove it), and transfer the custard to a plate. Dot the top of the custard with the pea purée. Garnish with pea tendrils, ribbons of pecorino, flaky sea salt, and cracked black pepper.

peas, white chocolate & macadamia

There are certain circles in the culinary world that say that this is one of the greatest dishes of all time. People went crazy for it at Ubuntu.

Marco Canora at Hearth in New York City loved the dish when he had it there, so he asked me to cook it with him in New York once. He seemed genuinely surprised by how simple the preparation was—he was expecting a lot more modern, complicated cooking techniques.

serves 6

kosher salt

2 pounds (about 900 g) shucked peas (from about 4½ pounds/2 kg peas in the pods)

2 tablespoons extra-virgin olive oil, plus more as needed

2 teaspoons fresh lemon juice

¾ cup (180 ml) Pea Shell Stock (page 311), chilled

1 tablespoon champagne vinegar

3 tablespoons chopped white chocolate

3 tablespoons chopped and toasted macadamia nuts

chocolate mint or spearmint leaves, to garnish

pea tendrils and blossoms, to garnish

directions

Bring a pot of water to a boil over medium-high heat. Add enough salt so it tastes like the sea. Prepare an ice bath in a large bowl. Add the peas to the boiling water and blanch until tender but not too soft, about 2 minutes. Drain and immediately transfer to the ice bath until completely cool. Drain the peas and allow to dry on a tea towel.

Gently squeeze each pea to remove the two halves inside the skin and transfer to a nonreactive bowl. (Save the outer skins, if you like, to use in Risi e Bisi, page 199.) Season the pea halves with the olive oil, lemon juice, and salt to taste.

Combine the pea shell stock and champagne vinegar and season to taste with salt.

To serve, divide the peas across 6 bowls. Top with the white chocolate and macadamia nuts. Garnish with the mint leaves, pea tendrils, and blossoms. Bring the bowls to the table, then pour the seasoned pea shell stock into the bowls tableside, and garnish with dots of olive oil using a squeeze bottle.

peas, white chocolate & macadamia . . . sweet version

serves 8

pea anglaise
kosher salt
1 cup (230 g) shucked peas (from about
 1 pound/500 g peas in the pod)
1 to 2 tablespoons Pea Shell Stock
 (page 311) or water
5 large egg yolks
a generous ¼ cup (60 g) granulated sugar
1 cup (240 ml) whole (full-fat) milk
1 cup (240 ml) heavy (double) cream
seeds from ½ vanilla bean or 1 teaspoon
 vanilla extract

white chocolate-macadamia blondies
4 ounces (115 g) unsalted butter, at room
 temperature, plus more for greasing
 the pan
2 cups (250 g) all-purpose (plain) flour
1 teaspoon baking soda (bicarbonate
 of soda)
1 teaspoon kosher salt
½ cup lightly packed (110 g) light
 brown sugar
½ cup (100 g) granulated sugar
½ cup (120 ml) Labneh (page 281)
2 teaspoons vanilla extract or seeds
 scraped from 1 vanilla bean
1 large egg
2 cups (240 g) roughly chopped
 white chocolate
1½ cups (6 ounces/170 g) macadamia
 nuts, toasted and roughly chopped
mint leaves, to garnish

If I'm able to use white chocolate in a savory way (page 193), why can't I use peas in a sweet way?

NOTE   You can make the base of the anglaise the day before, but everything else is best made the same day you plan to serve this dessert.

make the pea anglaise

Bring a pot of salted water to a boil over high heat. Prepare an ice bath in a bowl. Add the peas to the boiling water and blanch until soft, about 3 minutes. Drain the peas and transfer to the ice bath until cool. Drain and spread the peas out on towels until dry. Transfer the peas to a blender and purée with as little of the pea stock as possible—just enough to create a smooth purée. Set aside.

In a bowl, prepare another ice bath. In a stand mixer fitted with a whisk attachment, beat the egg yolks, granulated sugar, and a pinch of salt on high speed until the mixture turns pale yellow and thick, about 5 minutes. Turn off the mixer motor and set the mixture aside.

In a large saucepan, combine the milk, cream, and vanilla and bring to a boil over medium heat, stirring occasionally to prevent scorching. Immediately remove from the heat.

Turn the mixer back on with the speed set to low. Gradually mix half of the hot milk mixture into the yolk mixture until just combined. Return the saucepan to the stove and pour the warmed yolk mixture into the saucepan. Cook over low heat, stirring constantly with a wooden spoon, until the custard is thick enough to coat the back of a spoon and hold a line drawn by your finger, 5 to 7 minutes.

Strain the custard through a fine-mesh sieve into a bowl, then set the bowl on top of the ice bath. Let the crème anglaise sit, stirring occasionally, until the mixture has completely cooled. Fold in the pea purée, cover, and refrigerate until ready to serve. →

POOR MAN

CAPERS

LABNEH

CECI MISO

Preheat the oven to 350°F (180°C/Gas 4). Lightly grease a 12 x 8 x 2-inch (30 x 20 x 5 cm) baking pan with butter and line it with parchment paper. Grease the top of the parchment with butter as well.

In a bowl, combine the flour, baking soda, and salt and mix the ingredients together.

In a stand mixer fitted with a paddle attachment, beat the butter and both of the sugars on medium speed, scraping the bowl as needed, until the mixture is light and fluffy, about 4 minutes. Add the labneh and vanilla and beat for 1 more minute until just combined. Add the egg and continue beating. Slowly add the flour mixture and mix until thoroughly combined. Turn the mixer off and fold in the white chocolate and nuts until combined. Transfer the batter to the greased pan and spread evenly.

Bake until a cake tester comes out clean, about 30 minutes, rotating the pan front to back halfway through baking. Be rather careful not to overbake and dry out the blondies. Cool completely in the pan before cutting and serving.

To serve, cut the blondies into 8 (3-inch/7.5 cm) squares, avoiding any of the rounded edges. Pour a nice pool of the pea anglaise on a plate. Lay a blondie square on top and garnish with mint leaves.

risi e bisi, pea husk purée, wild rice & herbs

serves 4 to 6

½ cup (80 g) plus 2 tablespoons wild rice
6 cups (1.4 liters) Pea Shell Stock (page
   311), plus more if needed
⅛ teaspoon kosher salt, plus more as
   needed
2 cups (480 ml) grapeseed oil
1½ to 2 cups (around 250 g) blanched pea
   skins or blanched peas (from about
   2 pounds/1 kg peas in the pod)
1 tablespoon extra-virgin olive oil
2 tablespoons minced shallots
1 cup (175 g) arborio rice
¼ cup (60 ml) dry white wine
2 tablespoons chopped flat-leaf parsley
2 tablespoons chopped tarragon leaves
2 tablespoons (30 g) unsalted butter
2 tablespoons finely grated parmigiano-
   reggiano cheese
wood sorrel flowers, to garnish (optional)

This is a great way to use the skins (though I actually like to call them "husks") from double-shucking your peas for the Peas, White Chocolate & Macadamia (page 194). It is sort of a brothy version of a bright, spring risotto.

NOTE The wild rice can be cooked the day before and refrigerated, as it will be used as part of a larger component later.

directions

In a small pot, combine the wild rice, 1 cup (240 ml) of pea shell stock, and the salt. Bring to a boil over medium heat. Reduce the heat to low to maintain a gentle simmer, cover, and cook the rice until all of the liquid is absorbed, about 30 minutes. Fluff the rice with a fork and set it aside until later.

In a small saucepan, heat the grapeseed oil over high heat until it is just smoking. Grapeseed oil has a very high smoke point, so you can strain this oil off after frying and use it to cook again. Add the remaining 2 tablespoons uncooked wild rice—it will puff up after just a few seconds while it fries. Fish it out quickly with your spider/skimmer and lay it on a plate lined with paper towels. Season to taste with salt and set aside until time to serve.

Place the blanched pea skins and 2 tablespoons of the pea shell stock in a blender and purée. If you need to add more liquid to the purée to get a nice consistency, add 1 tablespoon at a time until you get the consistency you like.

In a large pot, warm the olive oil over medium heat. Add the shallots and a pinch of salt and cook, stirring, until the shallots turn translucent, 3 to 4 minutes. Add the Arborio rice and toast it, stirring, until the rice is coated in oil and smells nutty—you don't want it to take on color, about 3 minutes.

Meanwhile, in another pot, warm the remaining 5 cups (1.2 liters) pea shell stock over low heat until hot.

Add the wine to the pot with the Arborio rice and deglaze, then let it cook for another 3 minutes. Add the hot pea shell stock all at once. Unlike with a typical risotto, the stock here can be added at once to create more of a porridge. Bring the rice to a light simmer and cook, uncovered, until the rice is tender, about 20 minutes.

Stir in the boiled wild rice and pea skin purée, and season to taste with salt. Add more pea shell stock, if needed—the porridge should be brothy and not too thick. Remove the pot from the heat and fold in the parsley, tarragon, butter, and Parmigiano.

To serve, ladle the hot porridge into bowls, top with the fried wild rice, and garnish with sorrel flowers.

smoked split pea shell & carrot soup

serves 8

2 pounds (910 g) empty pea pods (from around 4 pounds/1.8 kg of whole pea pods; see page 46 for how to shell peas)
2 pounds (910 g) carrots, chopped
1 pound (455 g) yellow or white onions, sliced
½ pound (225 g) celery, chopped
10 cups (2.4 liters) Pea Shell Stock (page 311)
kosher salt
1 pound (455 g) bread, cut into slices 1 inch (2.5 cm) thick
extra-virgin olive oil
Crème Fraîche (page 278), to garnish
chickweed or chives, to garnish

One of my favorite things my grandmother used to make was split pea soup with ham hock. I'm not even sure if it was puréed, or just cooked so much that it totally broke down, but I have this memory of flavorful soup with little bits of ham and croutons—as well as a strong carrot taste. I've since discovered that by smoking the vegetables and thickening the soup with carrots and bread, I could recapture that memory without having to use the smoked pork. I like to smoke my vegetables in an outdoor smoker using a low heat over applewood. The goal is to have them take on the smoke flavor, without worrying about cooking them, as they will be cooked later.

NOTE The smoked ingredients can be prepared the day before and refrigerated. The pea shell stock can be made up to three days in advance.

directions

Smoke the empty pea pods, carrots, onions, and celery at around 180°F (82°C) until they taste smoky but are not fully cooked through, about 40 minutes.

In a large pot, combine the pea pods, onions, and celery with the pea shell stock. Season lightly with salt. Bring the liquid to a simmer over medium heat and cook, uncovered, until the vegetables are soft. Working in batches, purée the soup in a blender, then pass it through a fine-mesh sieve and return the soup to the pot.

While the soup cooks, brush the bread on both sides with olive oil and grill over medium heat or toast in the oven at 350°F (180°C/Gas 4) until golden. Add the smoked carrots to the pot and cook on low heat, at a simmer until they are soft.

Tear the bread into bite-size pieces, then add 10 ounces (285 g) of it to the soup, reserving the rest for garnish. Using a hand or stand blender, purée the soup until it has a coarse, rustic texture. Taste and adjust seasoning if needed.

To serve, ladle the soup into bowls. Garnish each with a dollop of crème fraîche, the torn bread, drizzled olive oil, and chickweed.

peach & almond gratins, noyaux cream

serves 6

noyaux cream
20 peach pits (stones)
1½ cups (355 ml) heavy (double) cream
2 tablespoons granulated sugar
peach & almond gratins
¾ cup (70 g) almond meal (flour)
⅔ cup (85 g) all-purpose (plain) flour
2 tablespoons plus 2 teaspoons
  granulated sugar
½ teaspoon kosher salt
a pinch of ground cinnamon
3 ounces (85 g) unsalted butter,
  at room temperature
6 peaches, halved and pitted (pits
  reserved)

The *noyaux* cream is great example of ingredients usually thrown away. Instead of tossing peach pits (stones), I roast them first to destroy the cyanide in them—though the amount is so small that it shouldn't matter much—and then use them to infuse cream with their delightful flavor, which tastes of bitter almond extract or amaretto.

NOTE   The noyaux cream needs to be refrigerated for 4 to 6 hours before whipping. It can also be made the day ahead, if need be.

**make the
noyaux cream**

Preheat the oven to 350°F (180°C/Gas 4).

Crack open the peach pits—they are tough, so use something heavy like a brick, a cleaver, or a really heavy pot. Spread the pits on a baking sheet and roast for 15 minutes. They will look slightly caramelized, but this is all about destroying the cyanide rather than looking for a particular color or texture.

Transfer the roasted pits to a saucepan and add the cream and sugar. Heat the mixture over medium-low heat to 150°F (65°C) on an instant-read thermometer, regularly checking the temperature and adjusting the flame to maintain an even heat. Cook at 150°F (65°C) for 20 minutes. Remove from the heat and pour into a container. Refrigerate for 4 to 6 hours or overnight.

Strain out any bits of peach pits and, using a whisk, stand mixer, or hand mixer, whip the cream to soft peaks. Refrigerate until ready to serve.

**make the peach
& almond gratins**

Preheat the oven to 350°F (180°C/Gas 4).

In a bowl, mix together the almond meal, all-purpose flour, sugar, salt, cinnamon, and butter until combined and crumbly.

Place the peaches, cut-side up, on a rimmed baking sheet. Divide the crumble mixture evenly across the cavities of the peaches. Bake until the peaches are soft but not falling apart and the crumble is golden, 20 to 25 minutes.

To serve, divide the hot peaches across plates and garnish with the noyaux cream.

poached pears, seeded granola & sunchoke milk

I like a good bowl of cereal. It is crunchy, salty, sweet—
all the things I'm looking for. Sunchoke (Jerusalem artichoke) milk
is the unique flavor in this dish that elevates it from a bowl of cow milk
and cereal into something that might make you think a little differently
about what you're eating for dessert—or breakfast.

NOTE   The poached pears, sunchoke milk, and granola can all be made
in advance and then put together when ready to serve.

serves 8

granola

4 ounces (115 g) unsalted butter, melted,
   plus more for greasing the pan 1½ cups
   (135 g) barley flakes
½ cup (120 ml) maple syrup
½ cup (110 g) light brown sugar
¼ cup (30 g) macadamia nuts, halved
¼ cup (35 g) raw sunflower seeds
¼ cup (30 g) raw shelled pistachios
1 tablespoon vanilla extract
¼ teaspoon kosher salt

sunchoke milk

½ pound (225 g) sunchokes (jerusalem
   artichokes), scrubbed, trimmed, and cut
   into 1-inch (2.5 cm) pieces
1 teaspoon grapeseed oil
2 cups (480 ml) whole milk
2 cups (480 ml) heavy (double) cream
½ cup (100 g) granulated sugar
½ teaspoon kosher salt

poached pears

1 cup (200 g) granulated sugar
1 cup (240 ml) white wine
juice of 1 lemon
1 vanilla bean, split lengthwise
4 anjou pears, halved and cored

make the granola

Preheat the oven to 250°F (120°C/Gas ½). Lightly grease a baking sheet with butter.

In a bowl, mix together the barley flakes, melted butter, maple syrup, brown sugar, macadamia nuts, sunflower seeds, pistachios, vanilla extract, and salt until thoroughly combined. Spread the granola on the greased pan.

Bake, stirring every 15 minutes, until the granola is golden brown, crisp, and dry, about 45 minutes. Transfer the pan to a cooling rack and when cool, break the granola into clusters and store, covered, at room temperature, until needed.

make the sunchoke milk

Preheat the oven to 350°F (180°C/Gas 4).

In a bowl, toss the sunchokes with the grapeseed oil. Transfer to a baking sheet and roast until soft and golden, 30 to 40 minutes.

In a saucepan, combine the milk, cream, granulated sugar, and salt and bring to a simmer over medium heat. Remove from the heat, add the sunchokes, and cover tightly with plastic wrap (clingfilm). Let steep for 1 hour 30 minutes, then strain and refrigerate until cold. →

make the poached pears

In a wide pot (the pears will ideally poach in a single layer), combine the granulated sugar, white wine, 2 cups (480 ml) water, the lemon juice, and vanilla bean and bring to a boil over medium-high heat.

Cut a piece of parchment into a round (a cartouche) that will fit snugly inside the pot. Add the pears, then cover with the cartouche—it will rest directly on top of the pears and their liquid—and cook just below a simmer until the pears are tender, 20 to 30 minutes. Gently remove the pears from the poaching liquid and allow them to cool to room temperature. If you are not planning to serve them soon, cover the pears and refrigerate for up to 1 week.

Remove the vanilla bean from the poaching liquid (you can save the vanilla bean and dehydrate it for the Fig, Pepper Skin & Riesling Jam, page 268. Meanwhile, you can also reserve the poaching liquid for another use; I happen to think that it is very nice reduced down and added to a meat jus, then served with a piece of duck or pork).

To serve, divide the granola across 8 bowls. Slice some of the poached pears, while cutting others into irregular chunks. Place the pears over the granola, add the sunchoke milk, and serve.

salt mine potatoes, coraline chicory & gribiche

This is a fun dish based on potatoes made by salt miners in Syracuse, New York, in the northeast United States. Irish salt miners would bring substandard, small unpeeled potatoes to work, and at lunch would boil them in the salt springs. When the potatoes cooled off, they were encrusted in salt crystals.

NOTE The gribiche is sort of a chips-and-dip counterpoint—something creamy and bright to contrast the salty potatoes. The gribiche will hold in the fridge for around three days.

serves 6 to 8

gribiche
1 teaspoon sherry vinegar
6 large eggs
1 cup (240 ml) Mayonnaise (page 268)
2 tablespoons finely diced cornichons
2 tablespoons chopped capers
1 tablespoon chopped flat-leaf parsley
1 tablespoon chopped fresh tarragon
1 tablespoon dijon mustard
½ teaspoon freshly ground black pepper
kosher salt

salt mine potatoes
1 pound (455 g) fingerling potatoes, washed
1 pound (455 g) kosher salt, plus more as needed

coraline chicory
2 heads coraline chicory (can substitute frisée or escarole), separated into leaves
1 tablespoon extra-virgin olive oil
kosher salt
freshly ground black pepper

make the gribiche

Fill a pot with water and bring it to a boil over high heat. Add the vinegar and gently lower the eggs (being careful not to crack them) into the water. Reduce the heat to maintain a light simmer and cook the eggs for 9 minutes. While the eggs cook, prepare an ice bath in a bowl. Remove the eggs from the water, transfer to the ice bath, and cool for at least 10 minutes.

Peel the eggs, then push them through a mesh sieve (you could also finely chop them) into a bowl. Add the mayonnaise, cornichons, capers, parsley, tarragon, mustard, black pepper, and salt to taste. Refrigerate the gribiche until needed.

make the salt-mine potatoes

Place the potatoes and salt in a pot with 8 cups (about 2 liters) cold water. You want a pot that is deep and not too wide. If the water does not totally submerge the potatoes, add more water, as well as more salt, too (keeping the same ratio of salt to water).

Bring the pot to a boil over high heat. Reduce the heat to maintain a simmer and cook the potatoes until tender, 25 to 30 minutes.

Using a slotted spoon, transfer the potatoes to a rack. As the potatoes dry, a salt crust will begin to form (this usually takes around 5 minutes).

make the coraline endive

Just before serving, dress the endive lightly in olive oil and season to taste with salt and black pepper.

To serve, evenly distribute the gribiche, potatoes, and endive in separate mounds on each plate.

potato tostones, horsey goat & persian cress

serves 4

1 pound (455 g) small fingerling potatoes, rinsed
3 fresh bay leaves
2 tablespoons extra-virgin olive oil
kosher salt
2 quarts (2 liters) grapeseed, canola (rapeseed), or peanut (groundnut) oil, for deep-frying (optional)
1 cup (240 ml) Horsey Goat (page 279)
a handful of persian cress, watercress, arugula (rocket), or any spicy, tender green, washed and dried
horseradish root

I first started making tostones years ago with Ozette potatoes that I found in the farmers markets of Northern California. They looked really cool with all these little wrinkles on them, but turned out to be dry and didn't roast particularly well. Then I discovered that when I cooked them, pounded them, and fried them, the texture was great. Now I like that method with any potato. This recipe calls for fingerling potatoes rather than Ozettes, which does allow for the option to roast, rather than fry, them.

directions	Poach the potatoes with the bay leaves (see the method on page 46). Drain the potatoes and toss in the olive oil. Gently flatten each potato with the side of a chef's knife. You want the potatoes to maintain their structure, so don't let them break up into multiple chunks. Each potato should make one, flattened piece.
if frying the potatoes (my preferred method)	In a heavy pot, heat the grapeseed oil until it registers 350°F (180°C) on a deep-frying thermometer. Fry the flattened potatoes until they are golden brown and crispy, 3 to 5 minutes. Transfer the potatoes a wire rack or a plate lined with paper towels and season immediately with salt.
	To serve, divide the potato tostones across 4 plates (or serve on a platter). Accompany with a nice dollop of the horsey goat. Garnish with the cress and freshly grate the horseradish, like falling snow, over the top.
if roasting the potatoes	While the potatoes are poaching, preheat the oven to 400°F (200°C/Gas 6). Once cooked, drained, and flattened, season them to taste with salt and spread on a baking sheet . Roast until they are golden and crisp, 10 to 15 minutes.

raclette
& potato gratin

serves 4

1½ cups (360 ml) heavy (double) cream
kosher salt
freshly ground black pepper
1 pound (455 g) fingerling potatoes,
    rinsed and sliced paper thin on
    a mandoline
½ pound (225 g) raclette cheese,
    shredded
2 teaspoons chopped rosemary
12 cornichons, sliced lengthwise (you
    should get 4 to 5 slices per cornichon)
a few parsley leaves, to garnish

Who doesn't love gooey, molty cheese and potatoes? I grew up eating scalloped potatoes made from a box and this is my fancy version with sticky, oozing raclette—kind of a reconstruction rather than deconstruction: a classic version of potatoes with raclette and pickles.

directions

Preheat the oven to 350°F (180°C/Gas 4).

In a large bowl, add the cream and generously season with salt and pepper so that the cream tastes a bit overseasoned (you will not be adding any other salt or pepper to the dish). Add the potatoes, half of the raclette, and the rosemary and mix thoroughly to combine. Transfer the mixture to a baking dish large enough to fit it in a shallow layer. Cover the dish with foil and bake until the potatoes are tender when pierced with a knife, about 30 minutes.

Add the remaining shredded raclette on top of the gratin in one even layer, then return to the oven and bake until the cheese is melted and bubbling, about 4 minutes longer. Remove the gratin from the oven, divide across bowls or plates, sprinkle with the cornichons and parsley, and serve.

potato beignets, romesco & charred scallion

This recipe is inspired by Catalan *calçots*, those big charred green onions that are served on newspaper, dipped in romesco sauce and swallowed whole—frequently with rather a lot of wine. These fried beignets are also an excellent use of the whey that results from making ricotta.

NOTE   The scallions (spring onions) can be charred in advance and then refreshed quickly in the oven before serving. The pâte à choux, meanwhile, can be made up to 24 hours in advance and held in the fridge before frying.

serves 4

charred scallions
16 scallions (spring onions), trimmed and cleaned of any discolored outer layers, left whole
grapeseed or canola (rapeseed) oil, for drizzling
kosher salt

potato beignets
1⅔ cups (400 ml) whey (page 279) or whole (full-fat) milk
2 tablespoons oil from Garlic Confit (page 312)
1 teaspoon finely grated garlic (germ removed)
1 cup (125 g) all-purpose (plain) flour
4 large eggs
3 large russet (baking) potatoes, scrubbed
3 fresh bay leaves
kosher salt
freshly ground black pepper
⅓ cup (80 ml) Garlic Confit (page 312)
4 quarts (4 liters) grapeseed or canola (rapeseed) oil, for deep-frying

to serve
about 1 tablespoon Onion Top Ash (page 289), made with leek tops
1 cup (240 ml) Romesco (page 271), at room temperature

make the charred scallions	Preheat the oven to 400°F (200°C/Gas 6).
	Place the scallions on a baking sheet, drizzle with a little grapeseed oil, and sprinkle with salt. Roast until the scallions are charred but tender, 10 to 15 minutes. Remove from the oven and set aside (rewarm the scallions in the oven before serving).
make the potato beignets	Start with the pâte à choux (beignet dough). In a medium saucepan that's not too deep, combine the whey, garlic confit oil, and grated garlic and quickly bring to a boil over high heat, so as not to evaporate too much of the liquid. Add the flour and stir vigorously over high heat with a wooden spoon until the dough is thick enough that you can bat it around the saucepan. →

Transfer the dough to a stand mixer fitted with a paddle attachment. With the mixer on low speed, add the garlic confit and mix the dough until smooth, cohesive, and cooled to room temperature, 7 to 10 minutes. Add the eggs, one at a time. With each egg addition, the pâte à choux will look almost broken, so wait for it to turn smooth again in the mixer before adding the next egg. While mixing, occasionally pause the mixer to scrape the sides and bottom of the bowl. Once all the eggs are incorporated and the dough looks smooth, transfer to a bowl, cover, and refrigerate for at least 2 hours, or until thoroughly chilled.

Now cook the potatoes. Place them whole (cutting the potatoes before boiling will waterlog them) in a pot. Cover with cold water and season with bay leaves and salt (it should taste salty like the ocean). Bring to a boil over high heat. Reduce the heat to maintain a simmer and cook until a cake tester can be inserted into a potato with no resistance. (I prefer a cake tester to a paring knife, which can be a bit invasive. Regardless, make sure it is tender, as an undercooked potato will become grainy.) Drain the potatoes and let sit until cool enough to handle but still warm. Using a bird's beak knife, peel the potatoes and set both—the potatoes and their skins—aside.

Meanwhile, preheat the oven to 300°F (149°C/Gas 2). Place the reserved potatoes and their skins on two separate baking sheets (trays), and bake until the potatoes are dry, about 5 minutes. (Dry potatoes will ensure that you won't have an overly wet pâte à choux.) Remove the potatoes from the oven and set aside, but leave the skins in to dry for another 10 minutes.

Meanwhile, while still warm, push the potatoes through a ricer or food mill.

Add the riced potatoes to the pâte à choux and then crumble in the potato skins, folding until just combined. Season to taste with salt and pepper. Use the dough right away or refrigerate for up to 24 hours.

To make beignets, in a heavy-bottomed pot, heat the oil over medium-high heat until it registers 350°F (180°C) on a deep-frying thermometer. Scoop the dough with a large spoon and use a second spoon to gently slide the dough off the first spoon into the oil, being careful not to splash the oil. Repeat with a few more beignets. Cook beignets until deep golden-brown, 3 to 4 minutes. Fish out of the oil with a spider/skimmer and set aside on a plate lined with paper towels. Season immediately with salt and the leek ash.

to serve

Serve immediately, on newspaper if you have it, garnished with dollops of romesco and a scattering of warm charred scallions.

patatas bravas,
aioli & tomato sauce

serves 4

4 russet (baking) potatoes, peeled and
   cut into 2-inch (5 cm) cubes
6 tablespoons kosher salt, plus more as
   needed
4 cups (about 1 liter) canola (rapeseed)
   or rice bran oil, for frying
freshly ground black pepper
1 cup (240 ml) Tomato Sauce (page 315)
1 cup (240 ml) Aioli (page 265)

I love the texture of triple-cooked potatoes. It reminds me of the little
nubs at the bottom of a box of McDonald's French fries—crispy,
saturated, and bubbly. While these are much more laborious than your
standard fried potatoes, they're totally worth it—especially when served
with homemade Tomato Sauce (page 315) and Aioli (page 265).

NOTE You are going to fry these things twice, so make sure to rinse the
starch from the potatoes carefully.

directions

Place the potatoes in a large bowl with cold water and agitate them, stirring gently.
Gently pour out the water and repeat until the water no longer turns cloudy.

Place the potatoes in a large pot and cover with 8 quarts (7.5 liters) cold water and add
the salt. Bring to a boil over medium-high heat, then immediately shut off the heat and
leave uncovered. Let the potatoes sit until they are just starting to fray at the edges, about
30 minutes. Gently transfer the potatoes to a rack set over a baking sheet and refrigerate
for 2 hours.

In a large pot, warm the oil over medium heat until it registers 250°F (120°C) on a
deep-frying thermometer. Gently lower the potatoes in the oil and fry them for about 10
minutes, making sure that they remain pale blonde. Using a spider/skimmer, return the
potatoes to the cooling rack set over a baking sheet and refrigerate for another 2 hours.

Reheat the oil over medium-high heat until it registers 350°F (180°C) on a deep-frying
thermometer. Gently lower the potatoes into the oil and fry again until they turn golden
brown and crispy, 3 to 4 minutes.

Using a spider/skimmer, transfer the potatoes to paper towels to drain briefly, then
place the potatoes in a bowl and toss with salt and pepper to taste. Serve immediately
with the tomato sauce and aioli.

potatoes, ramp kimchi, radish & soft-boiled egg

serves 4

2 tablespoons distilled white vinegar
2 large eggs, cold
kosher salt
½ pound (225 g) assorted baby potatoes
2 teaspoons extra-virgin olive oil
1 teaspoon seasoned rice vinegar
2 watermelon radishes, the size of ping-
   pong balls
3 tablespoons Ramp Kimchi (page 296)
3 tablespoons Mayonnaise (page 268)
freshly ground black pepper
a handful of ruby streaks mustard greens
   or similar peppery greens
1 teaspoon Chili Salt (page 262)

A little bit after we opened our wine bar, Esters, I was worried that I hadn't been spending enough time at Rustic Canyon. One day, while driving to work, I was thinking about our menu, and this dish just came to me. I like a mustardy potato salad, but I also like the creamy richness imparted by the mayo and egg—and the crispy texture from the potato that rounds everything out. This dish has all the elements I like, mixed together on one plate.

directions

In a saucepot, combine 2 quarts (about 2 liters) water and the vinegar and bring to a boil over medium-high heat. Prepare an ice bath in a bowl. Gently add the cold eggs to the boiling water, adjust the heat to maintain a light simmer, and cook for 6 minutes. Transfer the eggs immediately to the ice bath and let cool completely. Right before serving, peel the eggs and then halve them lengthwise.

In a pot, combine 2 quarts (about 2 liters) cold water with enough kosher salt so the water tastes like the sea. Add the potatoes and bring to a light simmer over medium-high heat. Cook until the potatoes are tender, 20 to 25 minutes. Drain and set aside until cool enough to handle (they should be cool but not cold when served). Using a bird's beak knife, carefully peel off the skin; I like to have a little bowl of water nearby to dip my fingers and the knife to keep my hands from getting too starchy. Dress the potatoes in the oil and rice vinegar, then season to taste with kosher salt.

Slice the radishes to coin thickness, then, using a small, round ring cutter, punch out rounds (thus discarding the tough outer skin). Set aside.

To serve, divide the ramp kimchi across 4 shallow bowls or plates, placing it in the center. Dot with mayonnaise. Arrange the potatoes on top and add half of an egg to each plate. Season with kosher salt and pepper. Finish with the radish rounds, greens, and a sprinkle of chili salt.

radishes, goat cheese, nori & mustard

serves 4 to 6

2 toasted nori sheets
4 ounces (115 g) fresh goat cheese,
    at room temperature
28 french breakfast radishes (1 to 1½
    inches/2.5 to 4 cm long) with nice
    greens still attached
3 tablespoons Red Wine–Mustard
    Vinaigrette (page 274)
flaky sea salt or kosher salt

Radishes with butter and salt is obviously a classic dish. At Ubuntu we were growing beautiful radishes and I wanted to do something with them. David Kinch once taught me the value in doing something recognizable, but changing it so that you can flex your creativity while still keeping the soul of the dish intact. This is a play on classic French radishes with butter and salt and was just one of those things that sounded right in my head. The response from our patrons was great. It also turned out to be my signature recipe for the *Food & Wine* Best New Chef issue in 2008.

directions

Using a pair of kitchen scissors, cut the nori into strips, then cut the strips into smaller pieces. Place the pieces in a spice grinder and process to a smooth powder. Measure out 1 tablespoon of the nori powder and set aside. Reserve the remaining nori powder in an airtight container for another use.

Put the goat cheese in a bowl and use a spatula to fold in 1 tablespoon water until combined. Add the 1 tablespoon nori powder next and continue to fold—it should look sort of like a cookies and cream ice cream. Set aside.

Rinse and trim the radishes, removing any dirt and any discolored leaves. If the little stringy bits that hang off the ends of radishes are especially long, you can trim some of that off too. There is also a little collar where the radish meets the stem (they're like two little flaps) that I like to trim off. But, really, the goal is to highlight these lovely, raw radishes, so just try to take away any bits that make them look less pretty and leave the rest.

To serve, divide the radishes across plates with a dollop of the nori goat cheese, a dollop of the vinaigrette, and a small pile of salt. When eating, dip the radishes into the goat cheese, then the vinaigrette, followed by the salt.

rhubarb, ricotta
& radish toast

I really like working with a color palette, while also not having it be the main purpose of the dish. I want it to taste great, but also play off a certain set of colors. This one works with shades of pink and light red, and is one of my favorite dishes to make at the moment.

NOTE You'll probably end up with a little bit of extra rhubarb purée and pickled rhubarb—congratulations—as both are delicious on almost everything and keep well, too. Alternatively, you could just double the amount of toast you make.

serves 4

rhubarb purée and pickled rhubarb
1 pound (455 g) rhubarb
¾ cup (150 g) granulated sugar
¾ cup (180 ml) plus 2 tablespoons white wine vinegar
1 tablespoon kosher salt
to serve
10 baby red radishes (tops reserved for other uses, such as Salsa Verde, page 269)
4 slices Deanie's Brioche (page 283) or Pain de Mie (page 285), 1 inch (2.5 cm) thick
extra-virgin olive oil
kosher salt
11 ounces (315 g) Whipped Ricotta (page 281)
2 ounces (60 g) pickled rhubarb, or to taste
4 tablespoons rhubarb purée, or to taste
flaky sea salt
freshly ground black pepper

make the rhubarb purée and pickled rhubarb

Trim the discolored ends of the rhubarb, as well as any of the whiter and light pink bits near the root end. Slice the stalks on an angle into ¼-inch (6 mm) pieces. Set half of the rhubarb aside in a heatproof bowl.

In a pot, combine the sugar, 2 tablespoons of the vinegar, ¾ cup (180 ml) water, and the kosher salt. Stir over medium heat until the sugar and salt have dissolved. Toss in the remaining half of the rhubarb and bring the pot to a bare simmer. Cook the rhubarb, uncovered, until the rhubarb is completely soft and broken down, about 30 minutes.

Remove from the heat, drain the cooking liquid through a sieve into a small pot and set it aside for the pickled rhubarb.

Transfer the cooked rhubarb to a blender and purée until smooth. If the purée is too thick, add some of the reserved liquid in small quantities, until the blender can blend. The result should be a velvety, shiny, custard-like purée. Press plastic wrap (clingfilm) directly over the top of the purée so that it does not form a skin. Use immediately or refrigerate for up to 1 week.

Add the remaining ¾ cup (180 ml) vinegar to the pot of cooking liquid and bring to a boil over medium-high heat. Immediately pour it over the reserved rhubarb in the heatproof bowl and cover the bowl with plastic wrap—this will help keep in the heat and fully break down the rhubarb. Cool to room temperature and refrigerate for at least 1 day before using. Store, refrigerated, for up to 1 month.

to serve

Using a mandoline, thinly shave the radishes to a ¹⁄₁₆-inch (1.5 mm) thickness. Brush both sides of the bread with olive oil. Heat a cast-iron skillet over medium heat and toast the bread on each side until golden, about 3 minutes per side. Sprinkle the bread with kosher salt.

Slather the toast with ricotta. Arrange the sliced radishes and pickled rhubarb on top and fill in the gaps with dots of rhubarb purée, using a squeeze bottle.

Finish with flaky sea salt, pepper, and a drizzle of olive oil.

shaved squash, basil & pine nut

serves 4

2 pounds (910 g) assorted long summer
   squash
kosher salt
¼ cup (60 ml) extra-virgin olive oil
3 lemons
24 medium-large basil leaves, cut into
   a chiffonade
¼ cup (60 ml) Pesto (page 270)
2 tablespoons pine nuts, toasted until
   golden brown and roughly chopped
a small wedge of parmigiano-reggiano
   cheese, to garnish
20 whole small basil leaves, to garnish
20 baby (thumb-size) pattypan squash,
   heels and stem ends trimmed

This is a clean, simple preparation that highlights beautiful summer squash, and requires that you seek out and use the best quality produce, as there's nothing to hide behind or manipulate through cooking. I like to use an assortment of various summer squash: green zucchini (courgettes), gold bar zucchini, Costata Romanesco, and/or pattypan. Just avoid especially seedy ones, like yellow crookneck.

directions

Using a mandoline or a vegetable peeler, shave the long squash lengthwise into thin ribbons. Place the ribbons in a bowl, season with salt, and set aside for 5 to 10 minutes. Discard any water that leaches out. Add the olive oil and grate the lemon zest directly into the oil. Juice the lemons and add to the bowl along with the basil chiffonade. Toss to combine.

To serve, spoon pesto onto each of 4 plates. Gently arrange the squash ribbons on top. Sprinkle with the pine nuts and thinly shave Parmigiano into airy strips, using them to lightly dust the whole of the dish. Garnish with small basil leaves and baby squash.

butternut squash & ricotta mousse, spiced bread

My mom basically cooked three things: lentil soup with granulated garlic, stuffed pork tenderloin with garlic cloves, and pumpkin bread. All of which, she says, are world famous.

This is a slight tweak on my mom's "world-famous" pumpkin bread recipe. Instead of canned pumpkin, I use roasted squash, and in place of vegetable oil, I prefer brown butter. Though I'm the only person she's given this recipe to, she gave me permission to share it with you.

NOTE Keep in mind that the ricotta needs to be hung overnight before it is used to make the mousse. If you don't have the space to hang it, wrap it in cheesecloth and set it in a strainer set over a bowl. Just weight the ricotta down to drain out as much liquid as possible.

serves 8

mashed roasted squash
5 pounds (2.25 kg) butternut squash
   (about 2 squash)
4 tablespoons (60 g) unsalted butter
¼ cup (55 g) light brown sugar
2 teaspoons kosher salt

spiced bread
butter, for greasing the pan
3 cups (675 g) mashed roasted squash
   (see above)
4 large eggs, lightly beaten
3 cups (600 g) granulated sugar
½ cup (120 ml) Brown Butter (page 278),
   melted but not too hot
3½ cups (438 g) all-purpose (plain) flour
2 tablespoons Fox Spice (page 263)
2 teaspoons baking soda (bicarbonate
   of soda)
2 teaspoons kosher salt
1 cup (125 g) chopped walnuts
1 cup (150 g) golden raisins (sultanas)

butternut squash & ricotta mousse
1½ cups (360 ml) Fresh Ricotta cheese
   (page 279), wrapped in cheesecloth
   and hung overnight (see Note)
½ cup (120 ml) maple syrup
kosher salt

to serve
a knob of unsalted butter
a handful of broken pieces of Frosted
   Nuts (page 300), made with walnuts

make the mashed roasted squash

Preheat the oven to 325°F (160°C/Gas 3).

Halve each squash lengthwise. Scoop out the seeds and reserve them for use in the Squash Seed Gremolata (page 273).

Arrange the squash, cut-side up, in a pan that is deep enough to hold some liquid (a baking dish or hotel pan would both work well). Fill the cavities with the butter and brown sugar and sprinkle with the salt. Add enough water to the pan to cover the bottom (this will help to steam the squash while it roasts).

Cover the pan with foil and bake until the squash is soft when pierced with a knife, about 45 minutes. Scoop the squash, butter, and brown sugar into a bowl, then coarsely mash it with a fork. Use immediately or cover and refrigerate for up to 3 days. →

make the spiced bread

Preheat the oven to 325°F (160°C/Gas 3). Grease a 16 x 4-inch (40 x 10 cm) Pullman loaf pan with butter.

Place mashed squash in a bowl. Add the eggs, granulated sugar, and brown butter and mix thoroughly. In another bowl, combine the flour, spice mix, baking soda, and salt.

Add the flour mixture to the squash mixture and mix to combine. Fold in the walnuts and raisins and pour the mixture into the greased loaf pan. Bake until the bread reaches an internal temperature of 190°F (88°C) on an instant-read thermometer, 1 hour to 1 hour 15 minutes. Let sit for 5 minutes in the pan, then carefully remove from the pan and cool on a wire rack. Inverted, it should slide out easily on its own, but if not, try using a knife to loosen around the edges. Slice it into ½-inch (1.25 cm) thick pieces. You will have some bread leftover.

make the butternut squash & ricotta mousse

In a food processor, combine 2 cups (450 g) of the mashed squash, the ricotta, maple syrup, and salt to taste and process until smooth. The mousse may look grainy at first, but in a few minutes it will smooth out. Transfer the mousse to a squeeze bottle and, if desired, refrigerate until cold.

to serve

In a cast-iron skillet, melt the butter over medium heat. Add the slices of spiced bread and toast on both sides, until golden. Transfer to plates. Squeeze (or spoon) dots of the mousse on the bread and garnish with pieces of frosted walnuts.

strawberry pavlova, yogurt & black pepper

serves 6

dehydrated strawberry powder
9 ounces (255 g) strawberries, hulled
meringues
1¼ cups (280 g) superfine (caster) sugar
1½ teaspoons cornstarch (cornflour)
½ cup (120 ml) egg whites, from about
    4 or 5 large eggs
⅛ teaspoon cream of tartar
⅛ teaspoon kosher salt
1 teaspoon vanilla extract
1 tablespoon apple cider vinegar
macerated strawberries
1 pound (455 g) strawberries, hulled and
    roughly chopped
1 tablespoon granulated sugar
¼ teaspoon kosher salt
½ teaspoon freshly ground black pepper
¼ teaspoon rosewater
yogurt cream
½ cup (120 ml) heavy (double) cream
1 cup (240 ml) Yogurt (page 281)

Dehydration is a fun way to use any strawberries that you might not be able to get through in time. But what I really like here is the combination of black pepper and strawberries.

Meanwhile, you can set aside your extra egg yolks and use them to make Cured Egg Yolks (page 291).

NOTE   The meringues can be made a day in advance and the dehydrated strawberries will keep for quite some time, but the other components should be made the day you plan to serve the Pavlovas.

make the dehydrated strawberry powder	Arrange the strawberries on dehydrator trays and dehydrate at 135°F (57°C) for 12 to 16 hours, until completely dehydrated. Transfer to a spice grinder or a mortar and pestle and grind to a fine powder.
make the meringues	Preheat the oven to 225°F (110°C/Gas ¼).
	In a bowl, combine the superfine sugar and cornstarch and mix well. Set aside.
	In a stand mixer fitted with a whisk attachment, whip the egg whites, cream of tartar, and salt on low speed. Increase the speed to medium and whisk until the mixture becomes frothy, 2 to 3 minutes.
	Add the sugar and cornstarch mixture in three equal parts—it's okay if the sugar doesn't quite dissolve all the way right now—and continue to whisk until the egg whites start to form peaks, 2 to 3 minutes. Add the vanilla and vinegar and continue whisking until stiff peaks form, another 3 to 5 minutes. Turn the mixer off.
	Line an 18 x 13-inch (46 x 33 cm) baking sheet with parchment or a silicone baking mat. Using a 3-ounce (45 ml) ice cream scoop, form 6 individual meringues on the lined pan. Bake for 1 hour, rotating the pan every 15 minutes. Then reduce the oven temperature to 200°F (95°C) and bake for 1 more hour (you don't need to rotate anymore). When the meringues are done, they should peel off easily from the parchment and have a hard exterior with a soft interior. Let the meringues cool to room temperature.
make the macerated strawberries	In a bowl, combine the strawberries, granulated sugar, salt, pepper, and rosewater and toss to combine. Set aside for at least 30 minutes and refrigerate until ready to serve.
make the yogurt cream	In a bowl, whip the cream to stiff peaks and fold in the yogurt until combined. Refrigerate until ready to serve.
	To serve, slice through the meringues horizontally, like splitting a burger bun. Place a bottom piece on each plate and spoon the yogurt cream onto it. Add macerated strawberries, then drizzle some of the juices over them. Place the top of the meringue over the strawberries. With a fine-mesh sieve, sift the dehydrated strawberry powder over the Pavlova.

crispy sunchokes, burrata, grapefruit & fennel

serves 4

1½ pounds (680 g) sunchokes (jerusalem artichokes), cleaned and trimmed
½ cup (120 ml) grapeseed oil
kosher salt
¾ pound (340 g) burrata cheese
3 to 4 ruby red grapefruit, peel and pith removed and cut into segments
1 fennel bulb, stalks trimmed, and thinly sliced, plus fennel fronds

I love the combination of hot sunchokes (Jerusalem artichokes) with cold burrata, crisp fennel, and juicy grapefruit. Go with ruby red grapefruit if possible, and think of the juice as an added bonus—just to drink and enjoy.

directions

Cut the sunchokes into irregular 1-inch (2.5 cm) pieces and flush in a bowl under cold, running water, agitating with your hands as you go to remove as much starch as possible. Drain on paper towels and blot with more towels until the sunchokes are completely dry, as any residual moisture will cause them to splatter and pop in the hot oil.

In a heavy-bottomed pan (wide enough to cook all of the sunchokes in a single layer), heat the grapeseed oil over high heat until it just starts to smoke. Add the sunchokes in an even layer, letting them sit undisturbed, until caramelized on the bottom, 3 to 4 minutes.

Reduce the heat to medium and then cook the sunchokes, stirring occasionally, until they are crisp on all sides and soft on the inside, 12 to 15 minutes. Transfer to a tray lined with paper towels and season immediately with salt to taste.

To serve, spoon a few dollops of burrata on each of 4 plates. Add the warm sunchokes and top with grapefruit segments, fennel slices, and fennel fronds.

cream of sunchoke soup, persimmon red-eye gravy

Red eye gravy, often known as "poor man's gravy," is a classic Southern accompaniment to ham, biscuits, grits—or really anything. I think it works well as a smoky sauce that complements the flavors of roasted sunchokes (Jerusalem artichokes) and caramelized onions. As this gravy lacks the traditional meat drippings, it is layered with slow-cooked onions, mushrooms, and peppers, and fortified with coffee and cream.

NOTE   The red-eye gravy takes time to make, but your patience will be well rewarded with a wonderfully layered sauce. You'll wind up with more gravy than you need here, but you can refrigerate the extra for a few days. It is a delicious addition to anything that might taste good with gravy on it.

serves 4

red-eye gravy
4 tablespoons (60 g) unsalted butter
kosher salt
2 cups (220 g) julienned white onions
8 ounces (225 g) cremini (chestnut) mushrooms, cleaned and sliced
3 fuyu persimmons, peeled, seeded, and roughly chopped
8 ounces (225 g) Roasted Peppers and Pepper Tears (page 309)
1½ cups (360 ml) brewed coffee
¼ cup (60 ml) heavy (double) cream

sunchoke chips
2 quarts (about 2 liters) grapeseed oil, for deep-frying
6 thumb-size sunchokes (jerusalem artichokes), scrubbed and trimmed
kosher salt

sunchoke soup
4 tablespoons (60 g) unsalted butter
1½ pounds (680 g) sunchokes, scrubbed, trimmed, and roughly chopped
4 cups (440 g) julienned white onions
1 tablespoon finely grated garlic (germ removed)
6 cups (1.4 liters) Caramelized Onion Stock (page 310), plus more as needed
2 cups (240 ml) heavy (double) cream
kosher salt

to serve
extra-virgin olive oil
4 tablespoons Crème Fraîche (page 278)
½ teaspoon finely ground coffee beans

make the red-eye gravy

In a medium pot, melt the butter and a pinch of salt over medium heat. Add the onions and cook slowly, stirring from time to time, until the onions are caramelized, about 45 minutes. If the onions or butter are browning too quickly, add a few drops of water.

Add the mushrooms, season with salt, and cook, stirring from time to time, until caramelized, about 30 minutes. Add the persimmon, the roasted peppers and pepper tears, and a pinch of salt, and cook another 30 minutes.

Add the brewed coffee and cook until the liquid is reduced by about two-thirds, 10 to 12 minutes. Add the cream and continue to cook until the liquid is reduced by two-thirds again, 10 to 12 minutes. Remove the gravy from the heat and strain through a fine-mesh sieve into a bowl, pressing on the solids. Taste and adjust the seasoning, if needed. Cover and refrigerate the gravy until it is dense and custard-like. Once cold, taste and adjust seasonings, if needed—cold food tends to require more salt than hot food. →

make the sunchoke chips

In a deep-fryer or a large, heavy pot, heat the oil until it registers 300°F (150°C) on a deep-frying thermometer.

Using a mandoline, slice the sunchokes lengthwise as thinly as possible and drop into a bowl of cold water. With your hand, rinse and agitate them in the bowl while the water is still running over them. Continue until the water runs clear. Dry the sunchokes thoroughly as any residual moisture will cause the hot oil to sputter.

Gently lower the sunchokes, in batches if necessary, into the oil and fry until golden and no longer bubbling, 3 to 4 minutes. Transfer the chips to a plate lined with paper towels and season immediately with salt. Set aside until ready to serve.

make the sunchoke soup

In a soup pot, melt the butter over medium heat. Add the sunchokes and cook, stirring, until the sunchokes are evenly browned, 12 to 15 minutes. Add the onions and continue to cook, stirring, until the onions are golden, about 10 minutes. Add the garlic and cook until fragrant, about 1 minute. Add the stock, stir, and bring the liquid to a simmer. Reduce the heat to low and cook the soup until the vegetables are completely soft, about 45 minutes.

Add the cream, increase the heat to medium, and bring the soup to a simmer. Once it reaches a simmer, remove from heat and purée directly in the pot with a hand blender or in batches in a stand blender. Strain the soup through a fine-mesh sieve, pressing on solids. If the soup is too thick, add more onion stock. Season to taste with salt. Serve immediately or refrigerate for up to 3 days.

to serve

Ladle the soup into 4 warmed bowls. Spoon several dollops of cold gravy on top and drizzle with olive oil. Top with sunchoke chips, crème fraîche, and a light dusting of ground coffee.

tomato raw bar

serves 4

2 pounds (900 g) tomatoes, many
  varieties, cored
1 pound (455 g) burrata cheese
3 to 4 tablespoons extra-virgin olive oil
flaky sea salt
cracked black pepper
2 tablespoons saba
basil leaves, for garnish

A tomato raw bar—which is a bit loose as far as recipes go and asks for a little creativity on your end—is a fun way to serve tomatoes while highlighting their delicious simplicity. Just as many varieties of oysters pique people's curiosity, tomatoes deserve equal attention. Jeff Dawson, the head farmer at Ubuntu, used to grow over thirty different varietals of tomatoes for me, some of which—such as Copia, Sharon's Surprise, and Foxheart (which he named after me)—he even bred himself.

directions

Cut the tomatoes into various shapes and sizes—have fun with it. You can even take an apple corer and cut out some funky little tube shapes.

Divide the tomatoes across plates and place a generous dollop of burrata alongside. Drizzle with olive oil and season with flaky sea salt and cracked pepper. To finish, garnish with the saba and basil.

poor man's lox: salted tomato, horsey goat, capers, shallots & seeds

serves 6

6 orange or red tomatoes, cored and very
  thinly sliced
kosher salt
1 cup (240 ml) Horsey Goat (page 279)
6 Jun's Focaccia (page 286), made
  without rosemary, halved across (like
  a bagel)
2 or 3 shallots, sliced
2 tablespoons drained capers
1 english cucumber, sliced
fresh dill, to garnish
2 teaspoons white sesame seeds, lightly
  toasted
2 teaspoons poppy seeds
1 teaspoon flaxseeds
1 teaspoon sunflower seeds
flaky sea salt

This spread is inspired by a Sunday morning staple in my house growing up. In my Jewish household—and every other as far as I knew—lox and bagels were just what you ate on Sunday. But quite often we could not afford the steep price tag that real lox carried, so this assortment of toppings was the next best thing. The saltiness of the tomatoes made it pretty easy to close your eyes and imagine it was the real deal.

directions

Sprinkle the tomatoes with kosher salt. They should be nice and salty, but not inedible. Smear the goat cheese on half of each focaccia, and top with the salted tomatoes. Add the shallots, capers, cucumber, and dill. Sprinkle with sesame, poppy, flax, and sunflower seeds and finish with flaky sea salt.

fried green tomatoes, burrata & green tomato preserves

serves 6 to 8

1 pound (455 g) unripe green tomatoes, cored and cut into slices, ¼ inch (6 mm) thick

1 cup (240 ml) buttermilk or Whey (page 279)

4 cups (about 1 liter) grapeseed, peanut (groundnut), or canola (rapeseed) oil, for frying

¾ cup (100 g) cornmeal

¼ cup (30 g) all-purpose (plain) flour

1 teaspoon smoked paprika (pimenton)

1 tablespoon kosher salt, plus more as needed

1 teaspoon freshly ground black pepper

½ pound (225 g) burrata cheese

½ cup (120 ml) Green Tomato Preserves (page 305)

basil leaves, to garnish

Fried green tomatoes make a great starter, offering lots of flavor in just one or two bites. And for a Southern boy such as myself, it's hard not to love these. Give yourself at least a couple of hours for the green tomatoes to soak in buttermilk before they are breaded and fried. The soaking will really help the breading to adhere and add flavor to the final product.

directions

Soak the tomatoes in the buttermilk in the refrigerator for at least 2 hours and up to overnight.

Add the oil to a large pot (not filling it up more than 60 percent) and warm over medium-high heat until it registers 350°F (180°C) on a deep-frying thermometer.

Meanwhile, in a bowl, whisk together the cornmeal, flour, paprika, 1 tablespoon salt, and the pepper until combined.

Keeping one hand for wet coating and the other for dry, lift each tomato slice out of the buttermilk and place it in the cornmeal. Using the other hand, thoroughly coat the tomatoes in the dredge. Carefully lower the tomatoes in the hot oil and fry until golden and crisp, 3 to 5 minutes. Drain on paper towels and sprinkle immediately with salt. Let the tomatoes cool for 5 to 10 minutes—just so they don't melt the burrata.

To serve, top the cooled tomatoes with some burrata, followed by a dollop of the tomato preserves. Garnish with basil.

pappa al pomodoro: tomato-bread stew, ramp kimchi & burrata

I just love this dish. This dish resulted from me wanting to do something with tomatoes and bread, but wanting to focus more on flavor than on a uniform texture. So I started making this broken tomato and bread soup, and then for some reason I wanted to put kimchi in it, too. Then I found that as I started making the dish, it just wanted more and more kimchi, so I kept adding more. You might think it's weird to combine two peasant foods from two totally different cultures, but it really works here. The rich olive oil and the spicy funky flavors of kimchi play really well together.

If you can, try to eat this stew the day after it was made—the flavors taste better and deeper.

serves 6 to 8

pappa al pomodoro
5 pounds (2.25 kg) red tomatoes, cored
¾ cup (180 ml) extra-virgin olive oil
2 white onions, finely diced
2 tablespoons grated garlic (germ removed)
1 bunch basil, leaves picked and roughly chopped, stems reserved
1 bunch oregano, leaves picked, stems reserved
kosher salt and freshly ground black pepper

garlic bread
1 pound (455 g) country bread, cut into 1-inch (2.5 cm) chunks
3 ounces (85 g) unsalted butter, melted
2 tablespoons finely grated parmigiano-reggiano cheese
2 teaspoons finely grated garlic (germ removed)
kosher salt
freshly ground black pepper

to serve
1 pound (455 g) burrata cheese
1 to 2 cups (240 to 480 ml) chilled Ramp Kimchi (page 296), to taste
small basil leaves
extra-virgin olive oil

make the pappa al pomodoro

Preheat the oven to 400°F (200°C/Gas 6). Line a baking sheet with foil.

Place the tomatoes, cored-side down, on the baking sheet. Carve a little "x" into the top-facing side of the tomatoes, then roast them in the oven until you can easily and gently peel off the tomato skins with a pair of tweezers or a bird's beak knife, 12 to 15 minutes.

Once the tomatoes are peeled, heat a large pot over medium heat. Add the olive oil and onions and cook, stirring, until the onions are translucent, 12 to 15 minutes. Add the garlic and cook just until it is fragrant but has no color, about 1 minute.

Tie the basil and oregano stems into a bundle with kitchen twine. Add the tomatoes, oregano leaves, and the herb stem bundle to the pot and bring to a gentle simmer. After 10 to 15 minutes, break up the sauce with a whisk until it has reached your desired texture (personally, I like it rustic, but well whisked). Cook, uncovered, until the liquid has reduced by about three-quarters, 2 to 3 hours. Remove the pot from heat and stir in the chopped basil leaves right before serving.

make the garlic bread

When ready to serve the stew, preheat the oven to 325°F (160°C/Gas 3).

In a bowl, toss the bread with the melted butter, Parmigiano, garlic, and salt and pepper to taste and mix thoroughly to combine. Spread the mixture out on a baking sheet and bake until the bread is just crunchy on the edges, 12 to 15 minutes.

to serve

Spoon the hot tomato stew into bowls and follow with the warm garlic bread. Top with mounds of burrata and kimchi, then garnish with basil leaves, and finish with a drizzle of olive oil.

treviso, chèvre, mushroom bacon, pine nut & beet molasses

serves 4

6 heads treviso radicchio, outer and
 brown leaves removed
extra-virgin olive oil
kosher salt
juice of 2 lemons
flaky sea salt
¼ cup (60 ml) Pine Nut Pudding
 (page 301)
2 tablespoons chopped toasted pine nuts
1 cup (240 ml) fresh goat cheese, at room
 temperature for about 1 hour
¼ cup (60 ml) Beet Molasses (page 266)
1 cup (115 g) Mushroom Bacon (page 292)

This recipe is exciting to me because a lot of extreme flavors—bitter, smoky, sweet, tart—are pitted against one another but then meet in the middle and keep the dish balanced.

directions

Halve 4 of the heads of radicchio lengthwise through the root. Break down the remaining radicchio into individual leaves. Rinse the radicchio halves and leaves under cold running water, pulling back the leaves on the halved heads to dislodge any trapped dirt. Dry the radicchio on paper towels.

Heat an outdoor gas or charcoal grill (barbecue) to medium heat. Drizzle the radicchio halves with olive oil and season with kosher salt. Grill the radicchio, cut-side down, until it is lightly charred, about 3 minutes. Remove from the heat and season with lemon juice and flaky sea salt to taste.

Dress the radicchio leaves to taste with olive oil, kosher salt, and lemon juice.

To serve, spread a swipe of pine nut pudding across each of 4 plates. Sprinkle the pine nuts over the plates, allowing some to anchor into the pudding and others to go astray. Plate a dollop of goat cheese near the center and season with flaky sea salt and a touch of olive oil. Evenly divide the grilled radicchio halves and raw leaves across the plates and spoon some beet molasses onto each. Finish with mushroom bacon.

spring vegetable & sunflower panzanella

Panzanella is usually more of a summer bread salad in central Italy, but this version was actually inspired by a *rughrød* (rye bread) toast that I had on the menu at Esters—the wine bar I helped open with Kathryn Coker in Santa Monica in Los Angeles.

serves 4

kosher salt
½ pound (225 g) shucked peas (from about 1 pound of whole pea pods)
1 pound (455 g) sunflower loaf (or any good, dense rye bread), lightly toasted and cut into ½-inch (1.25 cm) cubes
4 persian cucumbers, thinly sliced
16 stalks pencil-thin asparagus, cut into 1-inch (2.5 cm) lengths
1 tablespoon chopped fresh dill
2 tablespoons extra-virgin olive oil
1 tablespoon red wine vinegar
1 tablespoon sunflower seeds
1 teaspoon minced shallot
freshly ground black pepper
¼ cup (60 ml) Labneh (page 281) or greek yogurt
2 ounces (60 g) sunflower sprouts

directions

Bring a pot of salted water to a boil over high heat. Prepare an ice bath in a bowl. Add the peas to the boiling water and blanch until just tender, about 2 minutes. Transfer the peas to the ice bath until cool. Drain on paper towels until dry.

In a bowl, combine the bread with the peas, cucumbers, asparagus, and dill. Dress with the olive oil, vinegar, sunflower seeds, and shallot. Season to taste with salt and pepper.

To serve, divide the salad across 4 bowls. Top each with a dollop of labneh and a sprinkling of sunflower sprouts. Dust the labneh with a pinch of black pepper.

white yams, garlic butter, celery & dukkah

A surprise hit at Rustic Canyon, this recipe highlights Japanese sweet potatoes, but I like calling them white yams. Practically overnight, this dish became one of just a few that I could not take off the menu. And it continues to support my theory that garlic butter makes everything taste better.

serves 4

dukkah
1 tablespoon coarsely chopped toasted hazelnuts
2 tablespoons white sesame seeds
¼ teaspoon ground coriander
½ teaspoon ground cumin
¼ teaspoon flaky sea salt
¼ teaspoon kosher salt

white yams
2 pounds (910 g) japanese sweet potatoes or garnet sweet potatoes
4 cups (about1 liter) grapeseed oil, for frying
3 tablespoons (45 g) unsalted butter
2 teaspoons chopped garlic, germ removed
kosher salt
2 tablespoons thinly sliced scallions (spring onions)
finely grated zest and juice of 1 lemon

to serve
4 tablespoons Mayonnaise (page 268)
2 celery stalks, from the heart, thinly sliced
4 tablespoons Pickled Red Onion (page 306)

make the dukkah | Mix together the hazelnuts, sesame seeds, coriander, cumin, and both salts until combined.

make the white yams | Place the yams in a steamer basket. Fill a large pot with 2 inches (5 cm) water and bring to a simmer over medium-high heat. Reduce to medium, place the steamer basket in the pot, cover, and steam until the sweet potatoes are completely soft, 30 to 40 minutes. Transfer the potatoes to a cutting (chopping) board and carefully, as not to burn yourself, cut them, skin-on, into roughly 1-inch (2.5 cm) chunks.

In a pot or a deep cast-iron skillet, heat the oil until it registers 350°F (180°C) on a deep-frying thermometer.

Meanwhile, in a small pan, combine the butter, garlic, and a pinch of salt and heat over low heat until butter is just melted. Remove from the heat and set aside.

Working in batches if necessary, carefully lower the sweet potatoes into the hot oil and fry until golden, 3 to 4 minutes. Transfer to a cooling rack or plate lined with paper towel, season immediately with salt, and transfer the potatoes to a bowl.

Add the garlic butter, scallions, and lemon zest and juice to the potatoes and toss to coat. Season to taste with salt.

to serve | Divide the sweet potatoes across 4 plates and drizzle some mayonnaise on top. Arrange the celery and pickled onions over the potatoes, and sprinkle with some dukkah.

ratatouille, zucchini bread & basil

This is essentially tomatoes cooked down with other vegetables until they become one. You don't even need to cut them into perfect little dice, as everything will eventually break down and get mashed up a bit. I also call ratatouille "snacks for days" because its leftovers are great to pull out of the fridge and use as a topping on pretty much anything.

serves 6 to 8

ratatouille
4 pounds (1.8 kg) red tomatoes, cored
½ pound (225 g) eggplant (aubergine), cut into 1-inch (2.5 cm) chunks
1 tablespoon plus 2 teaspoons kosher salt, plus more as needed
½ pound (225 g) red onions, cut into 1-inch (2.5 cm) chunks
½ pound (225 g) zucchini (courgette) or any summer squash, cut into 1-inch (2.5 cm) pieces
½ pound (225 g) red bell peppers, cut into 1-inch (2.5 cm) pieces
½ cup (120 ml) extra-virgin olive oil
1 bunch of basil, leaves picked and stems reserved
4 tablespoons grated garlic (germ removed)

zucchini bread
1 cup (240 ml) extra-virgin olive oil, plus more for greasing the pan
3¼ cups (400 g) all-purpose (plain) flour
1½ cups (300 g) granulated sugar
1 tablespoon kosher salt
1 teaspoon baking soda (bicarbonate of soda)
1 teaspoon baking powder
3 packed cups (255 g) grated zucchini (courgette)
3 large eggs, lightly beaten

to serve
¼ cup (60 ml) Pesto (page 270)
1 pound (455 g) burrata cheese (optional)

make the ratatouille

To roast the tomatoes, follow the cooking method in Tomato Sauce (page 315). Set aside. Leave the oven on but reduce the temperature to 350°F (180°C/Gas 4).

In a bowl, toss the eggplant with 2 teaspoons of the salt and set aside for about 30 minutes. Press on the eggplant to drain out any moisture, and then spread on paper towels to dry.

In a bowl, combine the eggplant, onions, zucchini, bell peppers, olive oil, and 1 tablespoon of the salt. Place the vegetables in a large heavy pot, transfer to the oven, and roast, stirring every 10 minutes, until the vegetables are browned and tender, about 30 minutes. Leave the oven on but reduce the temperature to 325°F (160°C/Gas 3) for the zucchini bread (see below).

In the meantime, tie the basil stems into a bundle with kitchen twine.

Remove the pot from the oven and add the cooked peeled tomatoes, garlic, and basil stems. Place the pot on the stove over low heat, cover, and cook, stirring occasionally, until most of the liquid has evaporated, 4 to 6 hours.

Remove from the heat. Set aside 20 of the basil leaves for garnish. Cut the remaining leaves into a chiffonade and add to the ratatouille. If making the ratatouille ahead, reheat before serving. →

make the zucchini bread

While the ratatouille is cooking on the stovetop, make the zucchini bread. Grease a 16 x 4-inch (40 x 10 cm) loaf pan with olive oil.

In one bowl, whisk together the flour, sugar, salt, baking soda, and baking powder. In another bowl, mix together the zucchini, 1 cup (240 ml) olive oil, and eggs until combined. Add the wet ingredients to the dry ones, and mix together until you have a cohesive batter.

Pour the batter into the loaf pan and cover it with foil. Bake until a cake tester inserted in the center comes out clean, 45 to 60 minutes.

Let sit for 5 minutes in the pan, then carefully remove from the pan and cool on a rack. Inverted, it should slide out easily on its own, but if not, try using a knife to loosen around the edges.

to serve

Cut the zucchini bread into slices about 1 inch (2.5 cm) thick and toast until slightly crisped up. Tear the reserved basil leaves.

Ladle some ratatouille into a bowl and place some zucchini bread next to it. Garnish with pesto, torn basil leaves and, should you desire it, some burrata.

the larder

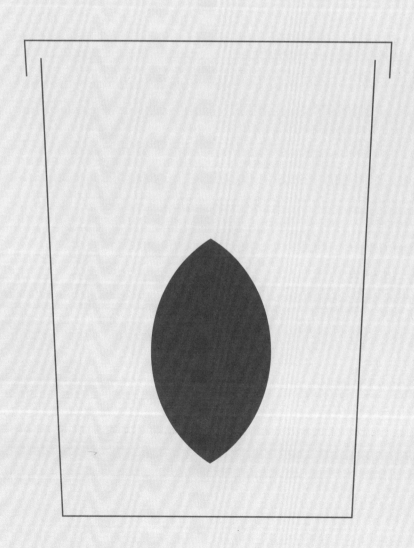

Building a larder from scratch may be the most important thing you ever do in your kitchen.

When I started working at Manresa, the kitchen team was already fairly experienced. Chef Kinch would let us work on a lot of personal cooking projects, hoping that our experiments might eventually wind up on the menu. I was ordering ingredients just for my own experiments, messing around with them, and trying to accomplish something new and different. But really, I was just trying to impress Kinch. Whenever I did manage to impress him, my heart bounced with pride.

So when I took over Rustic Canyon I wanted to bring that same process to my own kitchen. It didn't take long, though, before I realized that everything was off track. Nobody had the necessary experience. Cooks were just throwing ingredients together and seeing what would stick. It was, basically, young kids working on elaborate, conceptualized dishes and directing their focus on the wrong things.

So I scrapped it. We got back to basics. We started making sauerkraut, our own pickles, and mustard. Then we started making cheese, and suddenly we had whey lying around. What could we do with whey?

The team wasn't ready to be creative yet. Instead, I was teaching them how to put together building blocks, and cultivate a repertoire so that the next time they got the opportunity to be creative, they would be ready. There's just no substitute for knowing how to make a really good mayo. It's not about learning a recipe—it's about learning how to taste. Making good mayonnaise requires you to understand the balance of fat, salt, lemon, garlic, and mustard. You will identify flavors better. You will acquire context.

Ultimately, the most basic goal in building your larder is to turn your kitchen into a grocery store. Rather than just grabbing a package of fresh ricotta from the supermarket, you can now use ricotta that you've made yourself. Does it taste better than the finest ricotta money can buy? Perhaps. But it is better anyway, *because* you made it. There is now narrative and personal appreciation built into your food. As it turns out, work tastes good sometimes.

In the end, creating your larder is not about some theoretical idea of a "better" meal, but to make the hours you spend in the kitchen *more* efficient rather than less. When you have the luxury of free time—say on a lazy Sunday afternoon—you can work on some of the slower, more meditative cooking processes. When you have the freedom to spend your energy on things like Calabrian Chili Butter (page 277), Shallot Confit (page 313), and Labneh (page 281), it will pay you back on all those nights when you're just hungry, and too damned tired to build slow, meticulous flavor. You don't need to chop raw garlic when you already have a container of the stuff confited (page 312). A quick weeknight dinner tastes a whole lot better when you can pull homemade Preserved Lemons (page 207) and Miso Bagna Cauda (page 269) right out of the refrigerator. You invest in flavor when you have the time so that you can reap the benefits when you do not.

blends
& salts

andy's shichimi

makes ⅓ cup (80 ml)

peels of 6 oranges

2 ounces (60 g) or a handful of sea
  moss (*ogonori*)

2 tablespoons calabrian chili seeds

1 tablespoon Homemade Salt
  (page 263)

1 tablespoon granulated sugar

This is my sous-chef Andy Doubrava's version of the
classic Japanese spice mixture, *shichimi*. It is great even
on something as simple as a bowl of rice, or anything that
could use a nice floral, spiced kick.

Place the orange peels, sea moss, and chili seeds on separate dehydrator trays and
dehydrate at 135°F (57°C) for about 3 hours until fully dry.

Using a mortar and pestle, separately grind the orange peels, sea moss, and chili seeds,
and sea moss until they are coarse but not powdered. Measure out 2 tablespoons each
of ground sea moss and chili seeds and 1 tablespoon of orange peels into a small bowl
and combine with the salt and sugar until well mixed. Transfer to an airtight container
and store for a few months in a dry place (though after a few months the ground chili
seeds will start to lose some of their potency).

You can store any excess dehydrated, mortared orange peels, sea moss, and chili seeds
separately, covered in an airtight container at room temperature, for up to 3 months.
They could be used to season rice, roasted potatoes, or anything you like.

bbq spice

makes ½ cup (120 ml)

2 tablespoons smoked paprika
  (pimenton)

1½ tablespoons brown mustard
  seeds

2 teaspoons dried Mexican oregano

1 teaspoon cumin seeds

1 teaspoon fennel seeds

1 teaspoon black peppercorns

½ teaspoon chili flakes

3 whole cloves

3 tablespoons light brown sugar

2 tablespoons kosher salt

I love this seasoning tossed with freshly fried potato chips
(crisps). You can also use it to make BBQ Nuts (page 299).
It works really well in a compound butter too, melted over
beans with some charred tomato.

In a medium sauté pan, combine the paprika, mustard seeds, oregano, cumin seeds,
fennel seeds, peppercorns, chili flakes, and cloves and toast over medium heat, stirring
occasionally, until fragrant, 3 to 4 minutes. Transfer to a plate and set aside to cool to
room temperature. Process in a spice grinder until finely ground. Toss with the brown
sugar and salt until combined. Transfer to an airtight container and store at room
temperature for up to 2 months. If you find that it has lost a lot of its fragrance, you
should probably make a new batch.

chili salt

makes 1 cup (240 ml)

1 cup (95 g) calabrian chili pepper seeds and ribs, from oil-packed calabrian chilies

½ cup (65 g) kosher salt

NOTE This is a also great way to use all of the ribs and seeds from making Calabrian Chili Butter (page 277).

This salt blend is made from the innards of Calabrian chili peppers. It's a bit spicy, and is about having a good red chili flavor without being overpowering. This versatile seasoning is great on things like roasted potatoes or a sunny-side-up egg. You could even sprinkle it over some yogurt dip and eat it with, say, kohlrabi batons.

Spread the chili seeds and ribs on a dehydrator tray and dehydrate at 135°F (57°C) for 24 hours. They just need to be dry enough to grind well. Transfer to a mortar and pestle and grind the chili to a fine powder. Toss with the salt until combined. Transfer to a jar, cover, and store at room temperature. Chili salt will keep indefinitely, but if it starts to lose its heat over time, you should probably make a new batch.

curry spice

makes ¾ cup (180 ml)

¼ cup (24 g) madras curry powder

3 tablespoons ground turmeric

2 tablespoons fennel seeds

2 tablespoons cumin seeds

1 tablespoon brown mustard seeds

1 tablespoon black peppercorns

1 teaspoon chili flakes

1 teaspoon ground mace

½ teaspoon whole cloves

This recipe is adapted from the spice blend used for the Vadouvan Butter (page 280). It's great on things like Curry Cashews (page 299) or popcorn. Of course, you could also use it in any way you'd normally use a curry spice blend.

In a wide sauté pan, combine the curry powder, turmeric, fennel seeds, cumin seeds, mustard seeds, peppercorns, chili flakes, mace, and cloves and toast over medium heat, stirring, until fragrant, 3 to 4 minutes. Transfer the spice mix to a spice grinder and process until very finely ground. Transfer the curry to an airtight container and store at room temperature for up to 2 months. When the blend loses its fragrance, you should make a new batch.

fox spice

makes ⅓ cup (80 ml)

2½ tablespoons black peppercorns
2 tablespoons ground mace
1 tablespoon plus 1 teaspoon ground
  cinnamon
1 tablespoon coriander seeds
1 teaspoon whole cloves

This started out as my custom charcuterie blend at Manresa. Even after I had left, they would still label the container Fox Spice with a copyright symbol. But I actually just slightly tweaked Paul Bertolli's charcuterie blend from his amazing book, *Cooking by Hand*. While it's great in the Carrot Crumble (page 290), it would be delicious in a shrimp boil as well.

In a wide sauté pan, combine the peppercorns, mace, cinnamon, coriander seeds, and cloves and toast over medium heat, stirring, until fragrant, 3 to 4 minutes. Transfer the spices to a spice grinder and process until very finely ground. Transfer the spice blend to an airtight container and store at room temperature for up to 2 months. When the blend loses its fragrance, make a new batch.

homemade salt

makes about 3 cups (710 ml)

5 gallons (19 liters) seawater (good,
  clean seawater only)

There's something really exciting and elemental about making salt. But it is time consuming, so when I do make it, I only use it as a fancy finishing salt.

While you're working on the recipe, you may think that the process isn't working. The water will reduce down to almost nothing, and then all of a sudden you've got a bunch of salt. [Many thanks to Gabe Loeb for bringing back my first 5-gallon bucket of seawater from 5 miles off the coast of Big Sur.]

To start, you'll want to strain the water several times through cheesecloth to remove any sediment. Next, pour the water into a large pot. Bring it up to just below a simmer (180°F/82°C). Basically, try to keep it at this temperature for as long as you possibly can. (Don't allow it to come up to a full simmer. Just keep an eye on it and adjust the flame as needed.)

As it reduces down, you can transfer it to progressively smaller pots. You might not even get it all done on the same day, in which case you can turn off the heat while you sleep and then turn it back on in the morning.

Once the water reduces to the last few cups (finally!), you will think I'm playing a trick on you—no way this is going to make salt.

And then all of a sudden . . . salt! It depends on the water you use, but mine usually yields 3 to 4 cups (700 to 950 ml) of fine sea salt.

Transfer the salt to trays lined with cloth towels to cool off. If it clumps, you can flake it with a fork. Finally, transfer it to a container and keep indefinitely.

NOTE Keep in mind that you're making your own salt, so don't rush the process. Let it be gradual. Yes, it will take a long time—possibly multiple days in fact—but you're making your own salt, which is really cool.

condiments

1 teaspoon kosher salt

5 garlic cloves, germ removed

2 large egg yolks (see Note)

1 cup (240 ml) olive oil (preferably in a squeeze bottle)

a small dish of tepid water (if needed)

aioli

This is the fancy stuff. It is excellent with fries or Patatas Bravas (page 219). I skip the oft-used lemon or mustard in my version, creating a versatile, thick aioli. This recipe will keep in the fridge for a day or two, but will spoil faster than mayo because it isn't made with lemon juice (which "cooks" the raw egg a bit).

True aioli, as it is made in Provence, is a romantic sauce, and begs to be made with a mortar and pestle rather than a food processor. You can use a food processor if you want, just know that someone's French grandmother is rolling over in her grave.

Start by grinding the salt and garlic in a mortar and pestle. Salt is abrasive and will help break the garlic down.

Start working the yolks in with the garlic and salt. Once they are well combined, start with a few droplets of olive oil. Aioli is delicate stuff and cannot be rushed. Keep working the sauce, adding a few drops at a time. As you get further along in the process you can begin adding a little bit more olive oil each time—just don't go too crazy. Once you're about halfway through, you can switch to a whisk in your mortar if you like.

Keep going until all of the olive oil is used up. It should look like custard when it is finished, able to form in thick dollops that do not run. It does not need to hold stiff peaks, but should still hold shape and have a luxurious mouthfeel. It is too thick if it will be bouncy like a panna cotta with too much gelatin. If it is getting too thick or pasty, add a drop or two of tepid water (and only a drop or two because too much water will kill the mousse-like consistency you're looking for).

NOTE I find that egg yolks oxidize quickly, so leave the eggs whole until you're ready to use them. And once you crack open and separate the eggs, get to work immediately.

1 quart (1 liter) red beet juice, finely
   strained
1 cup (200 g) granulated sugar
½ cup (120 ml) rice vinegar
2 teaspoons kosher salt

NOTE   Beet molasses takes around
4 hours of mostly inactive cooking
time on the stove. You can halve this
recipe if you'd like, but since it takes
so long to make and lasts almost
indefinitely, you may as well just
make a lot of it.

beet molasses

We call this "Molly" at Rustic Canyon. But basically, this is
just a byproduct of making Beet Soil (page 293). It's a good
thing to have on hand in place of things like pomegranate
molasses or a reduced balsamico. It's also great as a cassis
replacement in a Kir Royale.

In a wide, heavy-bottomed pot, combine the beet juice, sugar, vinegar, and salt and bring
to a slow simmer over medium heat. Cook, maintaining a bare simmer, until the liquid is
reduced by 75 to 80 percent of its original volume, about 4 hours. As the liquid reduces,
brush down the inside of the pot with a pastry brush.

To test for doneness, drizzle a little of the molasses on a plate and let it cool. It should
have the consistency of aged balsamic vinegar. Once the molasses is ready, strain it
through a fine-mesh sieve and allow it to come down to room temperature. Cover and
refrigerate for up to 3 months.

---

makes 1½ cups (350 ml)

1 cup plus 2 tablespoons (225 g)
   granulated sugar
8 ounces (225 g) pitted kalamata
   olives, processed to a fine paste
   (or store-bought black olive paste
   at room temperature, with excess
   oil drained off)

black olive caramel

This is a preserved, sweet, squeezable condiment. When
I worked at Manresa, they would make these black olive
madeleines with it. Those madeleines were one of my
favorite foods in the world until I finally went overboard
and got sick of them.

Now I love to use black olive caramel in dishes like the
Chilled Asparagus, Saffron, Olive & Fennel Pollen (page 63),
and the Chickpea Panisse, Celery, Olive & Manchego
(page 110).

In a stainless steel sauté pan, combine the sugar and 2 tablespoons water. Set the pan
over medium-high heat and let the mixture begin to caramelize. It will take on the
texture of wet sand, but you really don't want to stir it. Don't worry if the sugar starts
to crystallize, as you can just purée the caramel at the end should it seize. If you notice
certain areas not really caramelizing, you can tilt the pan a bit. But really, just leave it
alone and look for an amber caramel color. It shouldn't be reducing or getting too dark.
All in all, it should take 3 to 5 minutes.

Remove the pan from the heat and carefully add the olive paste—it will probably
splatter a bit. While it sizzles, shake the pan in a circular motion to make sure it is well
incorporated, otherwise it will start to start getting dark around the edges as it cooks.
Let the caramel cool to room temperature and then purée it in a blender until smooth.
(You can skip this step if you like, but blending makes for a nicely unified sauce.)
Refrigerate in an airtight container for up to 2 months.

brittany's pepper jam

makes 5 cups (1.2 liters)

5 cups (1 kg) granulated sugar

1 pound 10 ounces (740 g) red bell
  peppers, roughly chopped

1½ cups (355 ml) apple cider vinegar

3½ ounces (100 g) jalapeño peppers,
  seeded

¼ cup (60 ml) fresh lime juice

1 teaspoon kosher salt

2 teaspoons powdered apple pectin

This is the pepper jam as made by Rustic Canyon's chef de cuisine, Brittany Cassidy. She started making it for our homemade (I hate the word "housemade") cotechino on a buttermilk biscuit, but now we use it on a lot of dishes at the restaurant, because it's pretty much good on everything. I liked the recipe so much that I stole it for this book and didn't even credit her for it.

In a food processor, combine the sugar, bell peppers, vinegar, jalapeños, lime juice, and salt and pulse until you have a coarse paste. Depending on the size of your food processor, you may need to do this in batches. Transfer the paste to a stainless steel pot and bring to a boil over medium-high heat. Reduce the heat and simmer gently for about 8 minutes, stirring occasionally. Remove the pot from the heat and fold in the pectin.

Transfer the pepper jam to jars, let cool to room temperature, and refrigerate until chilled through. Store, refrigerated, for up to 3 months.

carrot purée

makes 1 cup (240 ml)

2 pounds (910 g) carrots

6 tablespoons grapeseed oil

1 tablespoon kosher salt, plus more
  as needed

When raw ingredients are salted, it helps extract the water from them. By breaking down the carrots first, it increases the surface area and expedites the process even more. As a result, it's possible to make a carrot purée with no extra water added, highlighting the pure flavor of carrot and nothing else. Serve as a side dish, or as a component of a larger dish, such as the Carrot Juice Cavatelli, Tops Salsa & Spiced Pulp Crumble (page 103).

Peel the carrots (the peels can be reserved for Vegetable Stock, page 312) and then cut the carrots into rough 1-inch (2.5 cm) cubes. These do not have to be perfect, as they will all eventually be puréed.

In a bowl, toss the carrots with 2 tablespoons of the grapeseed oil and the salt and set aside for about 10 minutes. Transfer the carrots to a food processor and blend until broken up.

Transfer the mixture to a saucepot or large sauté pan. Set the pan over medium-low heat, cover, and cook, undisturbed, for 40 to 45 minutes. You'll know it's ready when you can smear it with a spoon. (If you take it off the heat too early, you will find the texture of the purée to be somewhat grainy after you purée it.) Transfer the mixture to a blender and blend on low speed, then gradually increase to high speed while slowly drizzling in the remaining 4 tablespoons grapeseed oil. Blend the purée to the consistency of mayonnaise. Season to taste with salt; it should have a pure carrot flavor. Store in an airtight container refrigerated for up to 3 days.

2½ pounds (1 kg) fresh figs,
stemmed and quartered

a generous 1 cup (260 ml) riesling
wine

¼ cup (50 g) granulated sugar

½ cup (60 g) finely chopped,
charred red bell pepper skins
(from Roasted Peppers, page 309)

1 teaspoon kosher salt

fig, pepper skin & riesling jam

This jam utilizes the charred roasted pepper skins from
making Roasted Peppers and Pepper Tears (page 309),
which impart a smoky flavor to this jam. The end product
tastes like a grilled fig jam, despite the figs not being
grilled. It is great in the Creamed Corn, Fig Jam & Dried
Vanilla Pod (page 173). It's also delicious alongside cheeses.

In a large saucepot, combine the figs, riesling, sugar, pepper skins, and salt. Cook over
medium heat, uncovered, stirring occasionally, until the wine is cooked out and the figs
are very soft, 25 to 30 minutes.

Run the jam through a food mill, then transfer to a baking sheet or any flat surface. Cool
to room temperature, then transfer to an airtight container. Refrigerate for at least 2
hours and up to 2 weeks.

makes 1½ cups (350 ml)

2 large egg yolks (see Note)

1 teaspoon kosher salt

juice of 1 lemon, plus more as
needed

2 garlic cloves, germ removed

¼ cup (60 ml) dijon mustard

1½ cups (360 ml) grapeseed oil

mayonnaise

Mayonnaise, to me, is *the* mother sauce. I don't understand
why hollandaise is listed as a mother sauce; I use
mayonnaise way more often than I do hollandaise. Also,
homemade mayonnaise is so far superior to the store-
bought kind that it should not even be open for discussion.
This mayo is intended to be aggressively flavored—
mustardy, lemony, garlicky, salty, creamy, and tart.

Drop the egg yolks, salt, and lemon juice into a food processor and pulse it to combine.
(Now, how much juice comes out of a lemon can obviously vary, but you can tell if
you're in the right ballpark based on the consistency of the result. So feel free to be
conservative at first, and if it is too thick you can add more lemon juice at the end.) Add
the garlic and mustard and pulse to combine thoroughly; I've noticed that if the mustard
isn't well incorporated, the oil will never fully emulsify. With the processor running,
pour in the grapeseed oil in a thin stream. You are looking for a consistency that will
hold its shape when spooned onto something. Transfer to an airtight container and
refrigerate for up to 5 days.

NOTE I find that egg yolks oxidize
quickly, so leave the eggs whole
until you're ready to use them. And
once you crack open and separate
the eggs, get to work immediately.

miso bagna cauda

makes 2½ cups (600 ml)

2 lemons, seeded and diced

2 cups (480 ml) extra-virgin olive oil

a scant 5.3 ounces (150 g) miso paste (I prefer red miso but any type will do)

about 3 heads (100 g) garlic, peeled, germ removed, and finely grated

½ teaspoon chili flakes

kosher salt, as needed

Bagna cauda (literally, "hot bath" in Italian) is typically made from olive oil, garlic, lemon, and anchovy, and is served as a dip for raw or cooked vegetables. My version uses miso to replace the anchovy and I really love how much this even looks like real bagna cauda. It's just a great thing to have in your fridge. You can use it as a condiment on all sorts of things: I really like it on scrambled eggs, poached potatoes, or even as a way to dress greens.

Fill a medium saucepot with about 2 inches (5 cm) water (enough water so it doesn't evaporate out during cooking, but not so much that it touches the bowl that will be set over it). Bring the water to a simmer.

Place the diced, seeded lemons in a metal bowl (that will sit snugly over the saucepot) and add the olive oil, miso paste, garlic, and chili flakes. Stir to combine, cover the bowl with plastic wrap (clingfilm), and set it over the pot of gently simmering water.

Allow the mixture to cook in your double boiler for about 45 minutes—the result will be a combined but broken sauce. Remove from the heat and let the sauce come to room temperature. Taste it for salt, but it should be plenty salty from the miso paste. Transfer to a jar, cover, and refrigerate for at least 1 week (and up to 2 months if the solids stay fully covered by oil). Serve at room temperature.

salsa verde

makes ¾ cup (180 ml)

½ cup (25 grams) chopped carrot tops

½ cup (120 ml) extra-virgin olive oil

2 garlic cloves, germ removed, finely chopped

2 tablespoons pickled vegetable brine or lemon juice

finely grated zest of 2 lemons

I like this salsa on everything—be it fish, a grilled piece of meat, or roasted vegetables. Thanks to the brine, this salsa is similar to chimichurri, and like with Pesto (page 270), you can swap the carrot tops for whatever herbaceous greens you have on hand: celery leaves, parsley leaves and stems, and so on. Additionally, this is a great way to use pickle brine, but if you don't have any, feel free to use the juice of the lemons you've zested.

In a bowl, combine the carrot tops, olive oil, garlic, pickle brine (withhold this ingredient if not using the salsa right away), and lemon zest and whisk thoroughly until combined. Use immediately or cover and refrigerate for up to 3 days. If storing to use later, don't add the brine (or lemon juice) until right before serving. The sauce may separate a bit, so just give it a quick whisk again before using.

1 ounce (30 g) pine nuts, toasted
  until deep golden brown

½ ounce (15 g) grated garlic (germ
  removed)

½ teaspoon kosher salt

2 cups packed (115 g) basil leaves
  (stems reserved for other things,
  such as tying in a sachet and using
  it to flavor a sauce or soup)

½ cup (120 ml) extra-virgin olive oil

pesto

This is a recipe for basil pesto, but it can also function as a starting point. You can use a wide variety of different greens you have on hand: carrot tops, arugula (rocket), mustard greens, celery leaves, nettles, borage, parsley—the possibilities are seemingly endless.

I don't like to use cheese in my pesto, because it doesn't need it, and also tends to lend a broken, grainy texture. Plus, you can always add cheese to the dish itself.

A quick note on blanching: Some people prefer to blanch and shock basil in an ice bath prior to making pesto in order to give it a bright green color. In choosing flavor over color, I prefer it raw. If you are using heartier greens, however, like nettles, borage, or broccoli rabe (rapini), you will want to blanch and shock them.

Can you purée this with a food processor? Of course. But if you're feeling especially romantic, I recommend the use of a mortar and pestle.

mortar and pestle method

Grind the pine nuts, garlic, and salt. Once you have the beginnings of a paste, add the basil. After working it for a minute or so, slowly drizzle in the olive oil and continue pounding until you have a rough, textured sauce. Use right away or refrigerate for up to 3 days. If storing, cover with a layer of olive oil to prevent discoloration.

food processor method

Add all of the ingredients except the olive oil to the food processor and pulse until the ingredients have begun to break down. Slowly drizzle in the olive oil, continuing to pulse until you have a rough, textured sauce. Be careful not to over-purée into a fine paste.

Pesto is best when fresh, but will hold in the fridge in an airtight container for 3 days if necessary.

sea moss tapenade

This is a good recipe for all those people who always say, "I've got tons of sea moss, but what should I do with it?" I personally find that black olive tapenade can be overpowering, whereas this will bring some of those familiar flavors, without overwhelming whatever it is that you are accompanying it with.

makes ½ cup (120 ml)

¼ cup (45 g) fresh sea moss (*ogonori*)

½ cup (120 ml) olive oil

¼ cup (60 ml) oil from Garlic Confit (page 312)

Finely grated zest and juice of 1 lemon

3 tablespoons grated parmigiano-reggiano cheese

2 tablespoons brined capers, drained and roughly chopped

1 garlic clove, germ removed, finely grated

kosher salt, as needed

Prepare an ice bath in a medium bowl 0. Bring a medium pot of unsalted water to a boil and blanch the sea moss for 10 seconds. It cooks very quickly. Immediately transfer the moss to the ice bath and let cool. Remove the moss from the ice bath and gently squeeze out as much of the water as you can, being careful not to bruise the moss. Lay the moss on towels (can be cloth or paper) and allow to dry until the moss is no longer waterlogged, about 30 minutes.

Transfer the moss to a food processor and blend into a fine, crumbly texture. Transfer the crumbled moss to a medium bowl and mix with the olive oil, garlic confit oil, lemon zest and juice, parmigiano, capers, and garlic. Taste and season with salt if needed, as there is likely a good bit of salt in it from the cheese. Transfer to an airtight container and refrigerate for up to 5 days.

romesco

Romesco sauce is basically ketchup of Spain. It is great with Patatas Bravas, (page 219), roasted sunchokes (Jerusalem artichokes), fried eggs with roasted scallions (spring onions), and Potato Beignets (page 214). It's really quite versatile, and I find that it pairs nicely with Aioli (page 265).

makes 3 cups (710 ml)

guajillo paste

4 ounces (115 g) dried guajillo chilies, stemmed and seeded

romesco

2 ounces (60 g) blanched almonds, toasted

2 ounces (60 g) blanched hazelnuts, toasted

8 ounces (225 g) Roasted Peppers (page 309)

8 ounces (228 g) canned whole tomatoes, drained

½ cup (120 ml) extra-virgin olive oil, plus more for storing

2 tablespoons minced garlic (germ removed)

2 tablespoons sherry vinegar

1 tablespoon smoked paprika (pimenton)

1 tablespoon kosher salt, plus more as needed

NOTE The guajillo chili paste can be made hours, or even days, in advance. Just give yourself time to soak the chilies for at least an hour.

make the guajillo paste

Soak the chilies in warm water for 1 to 2 hours, until they soften. Transfer the chilies to a blender along with ¾ cup (180 ml) of the soaking water and blend on low speed at first, gradually raising it to high speed, until smooth. Transfer to an airtight container, cover, and refrigerate for up to 4 weeks.

make the romesco

In a food processor, pulse the almonds and hazelnuts enough to get a nice chop—we're not looking for nut butter, but a breadcrumb-like consistency. Transfer the nuts to a large bowl.

Add the peeled peppers and tomatoes to the food processor and pulse to incorporate. Add the mixture to the bowl with the nuts, then fold in the guajillo paste, olive oil, garlic, vinegar, and paprika. Season with 1 tablespoon of kosher salt, plus more to taste if needed. The final result should be a rough, textured sauce. Transfer the romesco to an airtight container, cover with a layer of olive oil, and refrigerate for up to 3 weeks.

squash seed gremolata

makes 1½ cups (360 ml)

1 cup (100 g) seeds, from butternut, kabocha, or similar squash
¼ cup (60 ml) extra-virgin olive oil
a handful of chopped flat-leaf parsley
finely grated zest of 2 lemons
1 teaspoon kosher salt

Gremolata is a classic condiment of parsley, garlic, and lemon zest—but this version gets a nice nutty kick from the roasted squash seeds. It's also a great way to use leftover seeds from dishes like Butternut Squash & Ricotta Mousse, Spiced Bread (page 228). Gremolata is also delicious on things like eggs with Romesco (page 271), or lamb with squash and brown butter.

Preheat the oven to 300°F (150°C/Gas 2).

Using your fingers, try to remove as much of the squash guts from the seeds as you can, but don't worry—they'll dry, turn brittle, and fall away partway through roasting. Spread the seeds on a baking sheet and toast the seeds, tossing them halfway through, until golden and brittle, 25 to 30 minutes. Let them cool slightly, then transfer the seeds to a cutting (chopping) board and chop until they have a coarse, breadcrumb-like texture.

Combine the seeds with the olive oil, parsley, lemon zest, and salt. Use immediately refrigerate in an airtight container for up to 2 days.

whole-grain mustard

makes 2½ quarts (2.4 liters)

6 cups (1.4 liters) white wine vinegar
2 cups (385 g) brown mustard seeds
2 cups (385 g) yellow mustard seeds
1 tablespoon kosher salt
½ cup (110 g) light brown sugar
½ cup (120 ml) beer (something not bitter)

The texture of whole-grain mustard is unique—almost similar to caviar. It can serve as a base for honey mustard, be added to vinaigrettes, or tossed with potato salad. I also like to utilize it as an accompaniment to charcuterie.

You can cut this recipe in half if you'd like, but as mustard essentially lasts forever, I like to make a lot of it.

In a nonreactive container, combine the vinegar, both types of mustard seeds, and the salt. Cover tightly with a few layers of cheesecloth and secure in place with a rubber band or string. Set the container aside, away from direct sunlight, for 3 days. (This rather light fermentation will give your mustard a little extra zing.)

In a saucepot, melt the brown sugar into the beer over low heat. Working in batches, add the beer mixture and mustard seed mixture to a food processor and pulse gently to combine. The mustard should be a cohesive mixture, with some grains broken up and others left whole. Transfer to a nonreactive container, stir to combine, cover, and refrigerate for up to 6 months.

blue cheese dressing

makes 2 cups (480 ml)

1 cup (190 g) crumbled blue cheese

⅓ cup (80 ml) apple cider vinegar

¼ cup (60 ml) Crème Fraîche (page 278)

¼ cup (60 ml) Mayonnaise (page 268)

¼ cup (60 ml) buttermilk

1 garlic clove, germ removed, grated

kosher salt

I think blue cheese dressing gets a bad rap, but it is so, so good. I will take any salad with it. While I think that it is impossible to make a good ranch dressing at home (some things just need disodium phosphate and MSG, I guess), that is not the case with blue cheese dressing. The trick is using as high quality of a blue cheese as you can get your hands on. I love blue cheese dressing with pine nuts and bitter greens. Try it with radicchio, apples, nuts, and pancetta lardons; or just use it for dipping grapes.

This one is really easy. Are you ready?

Combine the blue cheese, vinegar, crème fraîche, mayonnaise, buttermilk, garlic, and salt to taste in a large bowl. Using a hand blender (or a whisk), blend until fully combined. See? Wasn't that easy?

lemon vinaigrette à la minute

3 parts extra-virgin olive oil to 1 part fresh lemon juice

kosher salt (optional)

freshly cracked black pepper (optional)

Some restaurants have pantries full of vinegars, but I stick to the basic ones: red wine, white wine, distilled white, sherry, rice vinegar. That's because I prefer lemon on everything: vegetables, fish, steak, beef tongue. I think that lemon makes food taste even more like itself, while vinegar makes it taste like vinegar.

So here's the thing—I don't think you need a detailed recipe for lemon vinaigrette. Sure, you can have very specific quantities of ingredients, emulsify them in a blender, and then store it in the fridge all week.

But do you know what I like a lot more? For me, lemon vinaigrette is about taking olive oil and lemon wedges, and using them to dress things just at the very moment that you need them. I like to cut my lemons into 4 wedges (you can extract more juice from quarters than halves) and then remove the seeds and pith.

As for the dressing itself, all that matters is the ratio.

Keep in mind though that this is a guide, rather than an exact recipe. So really, do it to taste, but you'll find that if you put in about three times as much olive oil as you do lemon juice, that it will work out quite well.

Season it with salt perhaps, and even some fresh cracked black pepper if you like.

makes 2 cups (480 ml)

½ cup (120 ml) red wine vinegar

3 tablespoons dijon mustard

1 teaspoon kosher salt

1 teaspoon freshly cracked black
  pepper

1½ cups (360 ml) extra-virgin
  olive oil

red wine–mustard vinaigrette

This is my workhorse salad vinaigrette. Romaine lettuce or arugula
(rocket) with croutons, shaved Parmesan, and this vinaigrette
make, to me, a perfect salad. If I could only pick one dressing,
it would be this. Actually, it would be the Blue Cheese Dressing
(page 273). But if I could pick two, I would also pick this one.

In a bowl, whisk together the vinegar, mustard, salt, and pepper until combined and
the salt has dissolved. While still whisking, slowly pour in the olive oil and continue to
whisk to emulsify. Use right away or transfer to a nonreactive container and refrigerate
for up to 1 month. (If you're keeping this dressing for longer than a month, you should
probably be eating more salad.)

makes about 1⅓ cups (315 ml)

4 cups (1.4 kg) sweet yellow corn
  kernels (from about 3 ears of corn)

kosher salt

2 tablespoons cornstarch
  (cornflour), if necessary

yellow corn pudding

The yield depends on how much juice you get from the
corn, but the juice you start off with will be the same as the
final yield.

Here is a pretty brief recipe; it's one of my favorites. This
pudding requires sweet, yellow corn, as the sugars in the
corn are converted to starch, which is what naturally
thickens the pudding. It is possible that the pudding just
won't thicken (as there might not be enough starch), so be
prepared to adjust with a cornstarch (cornflour) slurry. If
you have to resort to cornstarch, know that you're only
adding what should have been there anyway.

Juice the corn in a juicer (reserve the pulp for Corn Pulp Crackling, page 290). Strain
the juice through a fine-mesh sieve into a large sauté pan.

Set up an ice bath in a large bowl. Set the pan of juice over medium-high heat and whisk
constantly—don't let the flames come up the sides of the pot and scorch the juice. As the
juice heats up it will begin to thicken. Once the juice is creamy and has the viscosity of
mayonnaise, remove it from the heat and season to taste with salt.

If the corn juices don't thicken up (every once in a while, corn won't have enough starch
in it for this to work properly), simply whisk together the cornstarch and 2 tablespoons
water, adding more if needed, until you have a syrup-like consistency. Whisk some of
the slurry into the hot corn juice, a small amount at a time (you likely won't need it all),
and keep cooking until it reaches your desired thickness.

Transfer the thickened juices to a medium bowl and set it in the ice bath. Whisk until
completely cooled and then taste again and adjust seasoning if necessary.

Once the pudding has cooled, cover it with plastic wrap (clingfilm) pressed directly
against the surface of the pudding (this is to prevent a skin from forming).

Serve the pudding at room temperature or chilled; the warmer it is, the looser it'll be. If
making ahead of time, refrigerate for up to 3 days. Whisk vigorously just before serving.

NOTE You can juice the corn a day
ahead if necessary, but be aware
that the starches will sink to the
bottom of the container, so you'll
have to whisk to reincorporate.
Keep in mind that the juice will not
smell as good after a day or so, but
that's normal.

dairy

2 tablespoons olive oil

1 cup (400 g) finely chopped garlic

1 cup (400 g) finely chopped shallots

1 cup (240 g) oil-packed calabrian
    chili peppers, seeded and ribs
    removed; finely chopped (see Note)

kosher salt

1 pound (455 g) unsalted butter, at
    room temperature

2 tablespoons chopped flat-leaf
    parsley leaves

2 tablespoons fresh oregano leaves

½ tablespoon yellow mustard
    powder

½ tablespoon smoked paprika

finely grated zest and juice of 1
    lemon

NOTE   Reserve the seeds and
trimmings from the calabrian chili
peppers to make Chili Salt (page 262).

calabrian chili butter

I like this compound butter on toast, tossed in with roasted vegetables, tossed with hot pasta, or as a finishing touch for tomato sauce. If you're cooking chickpeas, you can just throw it in at the end to add a lot of complexity really quickly. Should you be inclined toward such things, it pairs rather well with a pan-roasted steak, or squid.

In a large sauté pan, warm the olive oil over medium heat. Add the garlic, shallots, and chilies to the pan and cook until just fragrant, stirring occasionally, about 3 minutes. There should be no color on the vegetables. Season to taste with salt. Remove from the heat and let cool completely.

In a food processor, combine the butter, parsley, oregano, mustard powder, and paprika and blend until completely combined and whipped. Transfer the spiced butter to a bowl, add the cooled chili mixture, and mix until thoroughly combined. (You can also skip the food processor and just do it all by hand with a whisk—so long as you're really diligent and don't have any clumps of pure butter.)

At this point, you're pretty much good to go. Store the chili butter in 1-cup (240 ml) deli containers if possible. It will last up to 2 weeks, refrigerated. It also freezes quite well, and will last up to 2 months when frozen.

1 pound (455 g) cold unsalted butter,
cut into 1-inch (2.5 cm) cubes

brown butter

Brown butter is a great thing to have around, and keeps for
a fairly long time. So there's no need to make it fresh every
time you want some.

Place the butter in a saucepan large enough to let the butter foam up to 4 times its
original volume. Set the pan over medium heat and let the butter melt and break.
You will notice the milk solids beginning to caramelize as the butter clarifies. Stir
occasionally to prevent any solids from burning on the bottom. If using a gas burner,
be careful not to let the flames come up too far on the sides of the pot, as the butter
will scorch.

Cook the butter until it turns foamy and has a nutty aroma, and the solids turn dark
brown. Remove from the heat, transfer to a dry, heatproof container (such as a bowl or
another pan) and cool to room temperature. Once cooled, transfer to airtight containers.
I suggest using multiple 1-cup (240 ml) containers rather than one large one, unless you
plan on using it all in one sitting. Be sure to stir the butter solids as you go, to evenly
distribute into each batch that you are storing. Brown butter will keep, refrigerated, for
3 months.

makes 2 cups (480 ml)

2 cups (480 ml) heavy (double)
cream
3 tablespoons buttermilk or crème
fraîche

crème fraîche

This is basically a fancy term for sour cream (as proven
by the fancy accent over the first "e"). It has a higher fat
content (and is also less sour) than American sour cream,
and can be used to make salad dressing (like Blue Cheese
Dressing, page 273) or dolloped on top of something as
basic as a baked potato. It has dessert applications, too,
such as whipping it with cream (adding crème fraîche to
whipped cream stabilizes it and prevents the whipped
cream from "weeping").

As a fun bonus, once you've made your own crème fraîche,
you can use it as a starter (in place of the buttermilk in this
recipe) when you want to make more.

In a nonreactive container, combine the cream and buttermilk and cover with
plastic wrap (clingfilm). Poke a few tiny holes in the plastic wrap and let sit at room
temperature for 24 to 36 hours, or until nicely thickened.

Carefully skim off the very top layer and discard. Whisk the remaining crème fraîche
to incorporate, cover, and refrigerate for up to 2 weeks.

horsey goat

makes about ½ cup (120 ml)

8 ounces (225 g) soft fresh goat
cheese, at room temperature
2 tablespoons heavy (double) cream
2 ounces (60 g) prepared
horseradish
kosher salt

This is essentially goat cheese combined with prepared horseradish. It could be served with Potato Tostones (page 210) as a sort of chip-and-dip, or Poor Man's Lox (page 243) and would be great on something like a cold lamb sandwich.

Using a silicone spatula, gently fold together the goat cheese, cream, and horseradish until thoroughly combined. Season to taste with salt. Cover and refrigerate for up to 1 week.

fresh ricotta & whey

makes 1½ pounds (680 g) ricotta
and 6 cups (1.5 liters) whey

2 quarts (about 2 liters) whole milk
2 cups (480 ml) buttermilk
1 cup (240 ml) heavy (double) cream
2 tablespoons kosher salt

It is very important to use the highest quality dairy products possible. This has only four ingredients, and one of them is salt, so the result will only be as good as the ingredients you're putting in.

As for the type of dairy, I suppose you could use the milk of whatever creatures you have on hand, but I prefer cow or goat.

In a stainless steel pot, combine all of the ingredients and set over medium heat. As it heats up, stir the bottom occasionally to avoid sticking or burning.

Eventually, the mixture will come up to a very slight simmer and the mixture will break—allowing the curds to begin separating from the whey. Reduce the heat to low and allow the curds and whey to keep cooking and separating. Continue to gently stir the bottom from time to time. The goal is to prevent burning or sticking without agitating the process. Gradually, in 20 to 30 minutes, curds will begin to form on the surface.

After 30 to 45 minutes, you will notice that the liquid has lost its sheen and has gone from glossy to matte. The curds should have formed and be floating on the top like pillowy clouds of creamy goodness.

Remove the pot from heat and cool down both: the cheese and whey. I prefer to let the ricotta cool down in the whey so that it doesn't dry out. At the restaurant, I line a perforated hotel pan with cheesecloth and then set it inside of another hotel pan. Then, when it is cooled down to room temperature, I can gently remove the perforated pan, and allow the cooled whey to drain out. Otherwise, line a sieve with cheesecloth so that there is overhang. Then, just follow that same process – allowing it to cool in the liquid before you remove the sieve and drain the curds.

Let the ricotta drain (ideally overnight) in the refrigerator. This makes for a dense ricotta, which I prefer for cooking, as you have more control over its consistency and can add liquid back into it if needed. Transfer the ricotta and the whey to separate airtight containers and refrigerate for up 2 to 3 days.

1 pound (454 g) unsalted butter

10 ounces (285 g) shallots, thinly
    sliced

4 garlic cloves, germ removed,
    thinly sliced

2 teaspoons madras curry powder

2 teaspoons ground turmeric

1 teaspoon fennel seeds

1 teaspoon cumin seeds

1 teaspoon kosher salt

1 teaspoon black cardamom seeds

1 teaspoon brown mustard seeds

1 teaspoon black peppercorns

¼ teaspoon chili flakes

¼ teaspoon ground mace

⅛ teaspoon whole cloves

1 (2-inch/5 cm) thumb of fresh
    ginger, peeled and thinly sliced

peel of 1 orange, pith removed

vadouvan butter

This butter will be one of the best smelling things you will ever make in your kitchen. I was first introduced to vadouvan curry by Ludo Lefebvre (chef/owner of Trois Mec in Los Angeles), when he came to Manresa for a guest chef dinner. One of the dishes he made was lobster with vadouvan curry blend. I'd never even heard of vadouvan, but I fell for it—and Ludo—immediately. The spice blend is, essentially, a French colonial version of masala.

I incorporated this butter as a key component in one of my most popular dishes at Ubuntu: Cauliflower in a Cast-Iron Pot (page 106). It is also really nice spooned over a wedge of roasted winter squash.

While this recipe yields a large batch, the butter lasts for a long time in the fridge—and even longer if frozen. As preparing this butter can be a bit time consuming, I recommend making a big batch.

Make sure that you're using a pot that's at least twice the size of the contents you're putting into it. When butter browns, it will foam and double in size—and nobody wants to clean butter foam from their stove.

Place all of the butter in the bottom of the pot. Sprinkle the shallots, garlic, curry powder, turmeric, fennel seeds, cumin seeds, salt, cardamom seeds, mustard seeds, peppercorns, chili flakes, mace, cloves, ginger, and orange peel on top of the butter (this way the butter will melt before the spices hit a hot surface and start toasting). Set the pot over medium heat and cook the butter slowly, for about 3 hours. You don't want any of these ingredients to heat or brown too quickly, as you want slow-developing, layered, nutty flavor. Do not burn your butter—or you'll be very sad—and be sure to keep an eye on it. Stir it occasionally so the shallots, garlic, and milk solids will not stick, allowing it to simmer without ever reaching a rolling boil.

You will know that the butter is done when the shallots and garlic look almost candied— not crunchy, but translucent, glossy, golden, and jammy. The butter should be colored with turmeric and curry but with the nutty flavor of browned butter.

Remove from the heat and allow it to cool for a few minutes. Blend well with a hand blender until smooth and fully incorporated before moving it into airtight containers to store (butter hates oxygen); I prefer to use plastic deli containers. Allow the butter to fully cool before you put the lids on, as trapped heat will turn the butter rancid. If using deli containers, press down as to force out as much air as possible. If not, try to use containers that will fill all the way to the top. Refrigerate for up to 4 weeks or freeze for up to 6 months.

makes just under 2 pounds (850 g)

Fresh Ricotta (page 279)
3 tablespoons Whey (page 279)

whipped ricotta

While unwhipped ricotta is great as a base ingredient for cooking (it could also be used like queso fresco on a taco, or simply sprinkled over pasta), whipped ricotta is rich and luxurious.

In a food processor, blend one-third of the ricotta and the whey and transfer it to a bowl Fold in the remaining ricotta. Use immediately or cover and refrigerate. This keeps for as long as the ricotta itself keeps—2 to 3 days from when it was originally made.

makes 8 cups (almost 2 liters) yogurt and 3 to 4 cups (700 to 950 ml) labneh

8 cups (about 2 liters) whole milk
½ cup (120 ml) thick full-fat yogurt

yogurt and labneh

Yogurt is great. We all love yogurt.

Labneh, meanwhile, is Turkish strained yogurt and is ideal as a dip for crudités when seasoned with olive oil, salt, and pepper. Labneh works best as a condiment (if you want to cook with yogurt, use regular yogurt instead) and like almost all edible things in the world, it is very good when spread on some kind of bread.

In a stainless steel pot, add the milk and insert an instant-read thermometer. Warm the milk over medium heat, stirring occasionally to avoid scorching, until is reaches 180°F (82°C).

Remove the milk from the heat and let it cool down to 115°F (46°C). Gently whisk in the yogurt and then strain it into a stainless steel 4-quart (4-liter) container. Cover tightly with plastic wrap (clingfilm) and set aside at room temperature for 24 hours. Transfer the mixture to the refrigerator and leave overnight. The next day, skim off just the very top layer from the surface and discard.

If you are keeping the yogurt as is, pack it into smaller jars or containers and refrigerate, covered, for up to 2 weeks. If you want to make labneh, follow the directions below.

to turn your yogurt into labneh

In the restaurant, I line a perforated 4-inch-deep (10 cm) half hotel pan (about 10 x 12 inches/25 x 30 cm) with 3 layers of cheesecloth and then set it over a nonperforated, 6-inch-deep (15 cm) half hotel pan. That way I can set the yogurt in the perforated, cheesecloth-lined hotel pan, and it can drain into the deeper hotel pan to catch all of the whey. If you have hotel pans at home, that would be ideal. If not, you can use any largish sieve that will fit over of a bowl or pot and line the sieve with 3 layers of cheesecloth. Cover, refrigerate, and drain the yogurt for 24 hours. Discard the liquid and store the labneh, covered, in the refrigerator for up to 1 week.

NOTE   Give yourself 36 hours to make the yogurt. Then you can follow the steps to make labneh (which requires an additional 24 hours of inactive cooking time).

dough

makes 1 loaf

350 g (2¾ cups) all-purpose (plain)
  flour
350 g (2¾ cups) bread flour (strong
  white flour)
7 large eggs
100 g (½ cup) granulated sugar
100 ml (a scant ½ cup) whole milk
10 g (2 teaspoon) active dry (fast-
  action) yeast
15 g (2 tablespoons) kosher salt, plus
  more as needed
600 g (1 pound 5 ounces) cold
  unsalted butter, diced, plus
  more for greasing the pan,
  work surfaces, and plastic wrap
  (clingfilm)

deanie's brioche

The amount of butter is what makes this brioche really stand out. Since it is so decadent, I often use it as a fill-in for meat in a vegetarian dish. I think that where a lot of vegetarian food falls short is the assumption that it has to be "healthy," so everyone just winds up eating tofu (which is actually not all that healthy) with brown rice. I like serving this with mushrooms, or grilled frisée with a fried egg and sunchokes (Jerusalem artichokes). You can also take just about any condiment from this section of the book, spread it on brioche, and be pretty happy.

Brioche will hold for up to a week under refrigeration, if chilled first and then covered tightly in plastic wrap (clingfilm). I recommend making a few loaves at a time and freezing the extra for later. The fat content helps brioche to hold up better in the long run than regular bread. Shout-out to my ex-wife, and celebrated Ubuntu pastry chef Deanie Hickox, for letting me use this recipe.

In a stand mixer fitted with a dough hook, combine both of the flours, 6 of the eggs, the sugar, milk, yeast, and salt. With the mixer on low speed, knead the ingredients for about 5 minutes, or until all of the flour is wet. (Warning: Brioche dough is very sticky and wet. You will have the urge to add more flour in the mix or on your work surface to prevent it from sticking, but please do not. Otherwise, it will become dense and dry.)

Stop the motor and scrape the dough hook. Return the mixer to low speed and add the butter, 3.5 ounces (100 g) at a time, mixing well and pausing the motor to scrape the dough hook and the bottom of the bowl after each butter addition. (Scraping is very important to prevent lumps from forming. This process will probably take 10 to 15 minutes in total.)

When all of the butter has been mixed in, knead the dough for another 10 minutes, stopping to scrape the sides and bottom of the bowl every 3 to 4 minutes. The dough should be smooth and cohesive.

Transfer the dough to a large buttered bowl and cover loosely with plastic wrap (clingfilm). Place the dough in a warm area until it doubles in size, about 2 hours. Punch down the dough, and transfer to a lightly buttered work surface—the butter will help to keep it from sticking too much.

Shape the dough into a 16 x 4-inch (40 x 10 cm) rectangle. Set the dough with a long side facing you and roll up the dough like you are rolling a jelly roll (Swiss roll). Transfer the shaped brioche into the buttered Pullman loaf pan, seam-side down.

At this point, you have two options for proofing the dough (letting it rise):

Option 1: After placing the dough in the pan, wrap loosely with greased plastic wrap and refrigerate for 8 hours, letting the dough rise slowly for the third time—this will enhance and deepen the flavor. Let the dough come to room temperature and proof for another 2 to 4 hours, until the dough has risen to the edge of the loaf pan.

NOTE Depending on the method you use, proofing (rising) could take 5½ to 6 hours, or 14 to 16 hours. Also, for baking in general, the metric units are much more precise and accurate than the volume measures we're so used to in the United States. So, for best results, I highly recommend following the measurements for grams and milliliters.

Option 2: Loosely cover the dough with greased plastic wrap and proof at room temperature for 1½ to 2 hours, until the dough has reached the edge of the pan.

Preheat the oven to 350°F (180°C/Gas 4).

In a small bowl, whisk the remaining egg with 1 tablespoon water and a pinch of salt. Gently brush the top of the brioche with the egg wash and bake until the internal temperature on an instant-read thermometer is between 180° and 190°F (82° and 87°C), about 30 minutes.

Let the brioche cool in the pan on a cooling rack for 15 minutes. Remove the loaf from the pan (it should come out easily) and cool completely on the rack. If the brioche sticks to the bottom of the pan, carefully run a small knife between the bread and the pan to loosen it up. Cool completely before slicing—or at least try.

panisse

Panisse is, essentially, cooked chickpea (gram) flour batter that can be cut into French-fry (chip) shapes—or really, whatever shapes you want—once it cools and sets. Once deep-fried, they're good on their own, or dipped into any number of the condiments in this larder section: Aioli (page 265), Labneh (page 281), Romesco (page 271), and the like. You can also serve the fries on a cucumber salad with yogurt to make for a heartier course. Fun fact: In 2002, *Aspen Magazine* called this the best appetizer in that city.

Lightly grease a 13 x 9½ x 1½-inch (33 x 24 x 4 cm) pan with olive oil.

In a medium saucepan, whisk together the flour, cornmeal, salt, garlic, and olive oil with 4 cups (950 ml) cool water. Set the saucepan over medium-high heat and gently whisk the batter as it cooks (to allow even cooking). The batter is ready when it starts to pull away from the sides of the pan, 5 to 8 minutes. Remove from the heat, stir in the parsley, and adjust seasoning if needed.

Add the panisse batter to the greased pan, spreading it evenly with an offset (angled) spatula. Cover the panisse with parchment paper and place another 13 x 9½-inch (33 x 24) pan on top. Place 1 to 2 pounds (450 to 900 g) of weight in the pan and refrigerate for at least 8 hours, or overnight. (Chilled and set panisse will keep for 2 to 3 days in the refrigerator, covered.)

When ready to fry, fill a deep pot with at least 6 inches (15 cm) of oil (as a rule, never fill your frying vessel more than halfway with oil, and make sure that the pot is fully dry before adding the oil to prevent splattering). Heat the oil until it registers 375°F (190°C) on a deep-frying thermometer.

Remove the panisse from the refrigerator and carefully upend the panisse onto a cutting (chopping) board. Remove and discard the parchment and cut the panisse into desired shapes—I like planks, as in the Chickpea Panisse, Celery, Olive & Manchego (page 110).

Fry the panisse—in batches if necessary—until they are golden and quite crisp, 3 to 4 minutes. Fish them out with a spider (skimmer) and set onto wire racks or plates lined with paper towels. Season immediately with salt and serve right away.

---

serves 8

205 g (1¼ cups) chickpea (gram) flour

65 g (½ cup) fine cornmeal

1½ tablespoons kosher salt, plus more as needed

1 tablespoon grated garlic (germ removed)

1 tablespoon extra-virgin olive oil, plus more for greasing

¼ cup (20 g) chopped flat-leaf parsley

2 to 3 quarts canola (rapeseed) or grapeseed oil, for deep-frying

NOTE Plan a day ahead before making this recipe.

makes 1 loaf

795 g (6⅓ cups) all-purpose (plain) flour or bread (strong) flour, plus more for dusting

240 ml (1 cup) whole (full-fat) milk

2 generous tablespoons granulated sugar

30 g (2 tablespoons) unsalted butter, at room temperature

2 tablespoons plus 1 teaspoon kosher salt, plus a pinch for egg wash

1 tablespoon active dry (fast-action) yeast

grapeseed oil, for greasing

1 large egg

NOTE Plan on around 3 hours of total proofing time before baking the pain de mie.

pain de mie

Pain de mie is basically a fancy white bread, but with its sturdy structure, it will hold ingredients really well without bending or wilting. This makes it especially useful with dishes like Grilled Cheese Sandwich (page 9) and Avocado Toast (page 55)

In a stand mixer fitted with the dough hook, combine the flour, milk, sugar, butter, salt, and yeast with 1 cup (240 ml) room-temperature water. Knead the dough on low speed for about 15 minutes, or until the dough has a somewhat smooth surface (it doesn't have to be perfect, because nothing is). You can also knead the dough by hand if you'd like; it will probably take around 20 minutes.

Transfer the dough to a large oiled bowl or container, then cover with plastic wrap (clingfilm) and leave it in a warm area of your kitchen to proof until it has doubled in size, about 1 hour.

Punch down the dough, transfer it to a lightly floured work surface, and stretch it into a rectangle 16 x 4 inches (40 x 10 cm). Set the rectangle with a long side facing you and roll it up like you are rolling a jelly (Swiss) roll. Oil a Pullman loaf pan, then place the dough inside, seam-side down. Cover loosely with plastic wrap and proof in a warm area until the dough is about ½ inch (1.3 cm) past the edge of the pan, about 1 hour. While proofing, preheat the oven to 350°F (180°C/Gas 4).

In a small bowl, whisk together the egg, 1 tablespoon of water, and a pinch of salt. Gently brush the top of the loaf with the egg wash. Transfer the pan to the oven and bake until the internal temperature is 180° to 190°F (82° to 87°C) on an instant read thermometer, 30 to 40 minutes.

Let the bread cool in the pan on a wire rack for 10 minutes. Remove the bread from the pan and cool completely on the rack. (If the bread is sticking on the bottom of the pan, carefully run a small knife between the bread and the pan to loosen it.)

Let cool completely before slicing.

Pain de mie for 1 week if wrapped tightly in plastic and kept under refrigeration, or 2 to 3 days wrapped at room temperature.

300 ml (1¼ cups) water (heated to
   110°F/43°C), plus more as needed

120 ml (½ cup) plus 3 tablespoons
   olive oil, plus more as needed, and
   for greasing

3 tablespoons honey

540 g (4⅓ cups) all-purpose (plain)
   flour, plus more as needed

2½ teaspoons kosher salt

½ teaspoon active dry (fast-action)
   yeast

flaky sea salt, such as maldon

freshly cracked black pepper

fresh rosemary leaves

NOTE   Focaccia is best the day
it is made. You can freeze the
leftovers and use them for croutons
or Breadcrumbs (page 290). Give
yourself plenty of time for this, as
the dough will have to proof (rise)
for an hour or two before it is baked.

jun's focaccia

Focaccia is an olive oil–rich, salty, and fairly easy-to-make
bread. The main thing with focaccia is to remember that
it loves olive oil; don't be afraid to go heavy with it. It's
great for sandwiches, dipping in olive oil and balsamic,
or with mozzarella.

In a stand mixer fitted with the dough hook, combine the warm water, 3 tablespoons of
the olive oil, and the honey. Add the flour (this creates a barrier to keep the yeast from
hitting water right away). Then add the salt and yeast and knead the dough on medium
speed for 10 to 15 minutes. You're looking for dough with a nice sheen and tacky, but not
sticky, consistency; it should pull away neatly from the bowl. During the kneading, if
you find that the dough is overly dry, add a touch more water. If it is too wet, add a little
bit more flour.

Turn out the dough ball onto a lightly floured surface and roll it with your hands into a
smooth, even ball.

Lightly coat a large bowl with olive oil and place the dough inside. Cover the bowl with
plastic wrap (clingfilm) and set it aside to proof at room temperature (70° to 80°F/21° to
27°C) for 1 to 2 hours, or until the dough ball roughly doubles in size.

Preheat the oven to 400°F (200°C/Gas 6).

Punch down the dough and divide it into 6 portions of 5 ounces (140 g) each. Lightly
flour your work surface. Working with one dough piece at a time (keep the other
pieces lightly covered with plastic wrap to prevent them from drying out.), roll it into a
smooth, even ball. Pinch the bottom of the ball to seal it closed, being careful not to trap
any big air pockets while rolling it. The texture of the dough should be smooth when
rolled. Set the balls onto an 18 x 13-inch (46 x 33 cm) baking sheet coated with olive
oil. Cover with plastic wrap and proof for another 20 minutes—the balls will increase
slightly in size and become much more workable.

Set each dough ball onto a lightly oiled surface and using the tips of your fingers, shape
the dough into rounds, while creating a dimpled pattern on top. (Those dimples will
trap the oil and other condiments when you serve it.) As you shape the dough, it will get
slightly wider in diameter, but don't worry about trying to spread it out thin. Once you
have a round shape with good dimples, you're ready to go.

Pour the remaining ½ cup olive oil into an 18 x 13-inch (46 x 33 cm) rimmed baking
sheet. Place the shaped focaccias on top and season with flaky salt, pepper, and
rosemary leaves.

If your oven isn't large enough to fit all 6 breads at the same time, divide everything in
half and bake in two batches.

Bake for about 5 minutes, then rotate the pan front to back and bake until the focaccias
are light golden on the top and bottom, another 3 minutes. If making in advance, you can
warm them again in the oven at 350°F (180°C/Gas 4) for about 2 minutes.

dried

green tops of leeks, spring onions (salad onions), scallions (spring onions), or green garlic

onion top ash

This is a great way to use the tough, green tops of spring onions (salad onions), leeks, and the like, which can be a bit bitter and fibrous. Basically, you just char and grind them. The result is a smoky, slightly bitter onion flavor that gives a nice counterpoint and complexity to dishes that have not been charred. Great with roasted onions, potatoes, tomatoes, and eggs, this black powder also looks great on a finished dish.

Rather than give specific quantities for this recipe, I'm just going to explain the technique—make as much as you'd like with whatever tops you have on hand, so long as they fit in a single layer on your baking sheet. The ash keeps for a really long time.

Preheat the oven to 450°F (235°C/Gas 8). Do not use convection (fan-assisted), or the fan will blow the onion greens all over the place.

Place the greens on a baking sheet and roast until the greens are completely brittle, blackened, and crumbly, about 30 minutes. Remove from the oven and set aside to cool.

Roughly chop or break them up by hand, then, using a spice grinder, pulverize to a fine powder. Store airtight indefinitely.

makes about 2 cups (240 g)

1 pound (455 g) crusty white bread
  (such as boule, baguette, or
  ciabatta), cut into slices ½ inch
  (1.25 cm) thick
1 teaspoon extra-virgin olive oil, plus
  more for brushing
3 garlic cloves, germ removed,
  finely grated

breadcrumbs

At all of the restaurants I've ever worked at, I made breadcrumbs.
We just toasted the bread, ground it up, and called it breadcrumbs.
Sometimes it was too powdery, and one day on my long drive into
work, I realized that we should be paying more attention to
breadcrumbs. So I came up with this method.

Preheat the oven to 300°F (150°C/Gas 2).

Brush the bread slices on both sides with olive oil and toast in the oven on a rack until
crisp, 20 to 30 minutes. Remove the bread from the oven, let cool for 1 minute, then
break up the pieces by hand and transfer them to a mortar and pestle in batches and
grind until you have coarse crumbs—not too powdery. Store at room temperature in
airtight containers for up to a month.

Right before using the batch of breadcrumbs, I like to season them with the grated
garlic and 1 teaspoon olive oil.

makes about 3/4 cup (100 g)

2 cups (480 g) carrot pulp (from 3
  pounds/1.3 kg orange carrots that
  have been juiced)
2 teaspoons granulated sugar
1½ teaspoons Fox Spice (page 263)
1 teaspoon kosher salt
2 tablespoons extra-virgin olive oil

carrot crumble

Another dehydrated pulp (like beet soil), carrot crumble can
basically function as a carrot-based breadcrumb. It is especially
delicious sprinkled over dishes like the Carrot Juice Cavatelli,
Tops Salsa & Spiced Pulp Crumble (page 103), but also works well
sprinkled over any carrot preparation.

Spread the pulp evenly on a dehydrator tray and dehydrate at 125° to 135°F (52° to 57°C)
for at least 8 hours, or until completely dry. You should get about ¾ cup (53 g)
of dehydrated pulp.

Transfer the pulp to a mortar and pestle and grind until you have the rustic texture of a
fine breadcrumb. (A food processor will turn your breadcrumbs into more of a uniform
powder.) Transfer to a bowl and add the sugar, spice, and salt and stir together.

Store in an airtight container indefinitely at room temperature. Stir in the olive oil
until combined.

cured egg yolk

makes 12 yolks

1 pound (455 g) kosher salt
1 pound (455 g) granulated sugar
12 large egg yolks

This cured egg yolk functions as a great vegetarian replacement for the salty, briny taste of bottarga (cured fish roe). It is excellent grated over things like pasta, Caesar salad, or steak tartare. Try to find the freshest eggs from your local farmers market—with rich, orange yolks—and give the yolks six full days to cure.

Combine the salt and sugar in a large bowl. Transfer three-fifths of the cure to an 18 x 13-inch (46 x 33 cm) rimmed baking sheet.

Using the pointy end of a whole egg, dig 12 evenly spaced divots in the cure, being careful not to burrow so deeply that you are exposing the bottom of the pan (you are going to be filling the divots with egg yolks and the yolks need to be entirely surrounded by the cure).

Place each yolk in its own divot. Using the remaining cure, cover each yolk so they are completely encased.

Cover the sheet with plastic wrap (clingfilm) and refrigerate for 2 days.

Remove the plastic wrap, flip the egg yolks over, and then cover again with the cure. By this point, the yolks should be quite sturdy and shouldn't break easily, making the flipping quite easy. Cover again with plastic wrap and refrigerate for 2 more days.

After curing the egg yolks for 4 days (total), remove the yolks from the cure and rinse them under a gentle stream of room-temperature running water. At this point, there is still an outer membrane, which you may not be able to see—but I swear it's there. While running the yolks under water, carefully remove and discard that membrane, then set the yolks aside on paper towels.

Pat dry the yolks thoroughly (don't worry about handling them, as they should be sturdy, and even if they become misshapen, you can usually reshape them into their original form).

Lay the egg yolks on a dehydrator tray (not on a pan or dehydrator sheet as you want as much air circulation as possible) and dehydrate at 135°F (57°C) for 2 days until fully dried.

Wrap each yolk individually in paper towels and refrigerate for up to 1 month. (They may well last longer than a month, but they're so damn tasty that I've never waited long enough to find out.)

dried pickle powder

makes about ¼ cup (60 ml)

1 pound (455 g) Dill Pickle slices
(page 304), made with kirby
cucumbers

This powder can be sprinkled over things like Kohlrabi Kraut, Dill Spaetzle, Poached Egg & Pickle Powder (page 142) or potato chips. I also like it as a garnish for a Bloody Mary.

Arrange the pickle slices on dehydrator trays and dehydrate at 135°F (57°C) for 24 hours. Allow them to cool for 2 hours, and then break them up with your hands or coarsely chop them. Add them to your spice grinder, and then grind into a fine powder. Store in an airtight container at room temperature for up to 3 months.

corn pulp crackling

When you juice corn (as for Yellow Corn Pudding, page 274), the solids can be set aside and dehydrated to make corn pulp crackling. After that, it can be crumbled over polenta topped with ricotta; treated like an amaretti cookie and crumbled into pasta dishes or lasagna; or served with vanilla ice cream, figs, and good balsamic vinegar. You can also just eat it.

Since this is an ingredient based on scraps, it makes more sense to offer general guidelines rather than a specific recipe.

After you juice corn, spread the pulp evenly on a dehydrator tray and dehydrate at 135°F (57°C) for 18 to 24 hours, or until it is totally dried and brittle.

If you are not going to serve this right away, you're better off leaving it unseasoned, as it will hold indefinitely. After a day or two of being left out, it should probably go back in the dehydrator for an hour or two before seasoning.

When you're ready to eat corn pulp crackling, break the dehydrated pulp into little clusters, then toss with some salt, sugar, cayenne, and a just enough olive oil to bind it. The final texture reminds me of wafers.

mushroom bacon

This preparation does a really great job of mimicking the salty, smoky, crispy properties of pork bacon.

makes about 4 ounces (115 g)

2 quarts (about 2 liters) canola (rapeseed) or grapeseed oil, for frying
1 pound (450 g) king trumpet mushrooms, thinly sliced lengthwise on a mandoline
maple sugar
mesquite smoked salt

Fill a deep pot with at least 6 inches (15 cm) oil (as a rule, never fill your frying vessel more than halfway with oil, and make sure that the pot is fully dry before adding the oil to prevent splattering). Heat the oil until it registers 275°F (135°C) on a deep-frying thermometer.

Working in batches, fry the mushroom slices, being careful not to let the oil temperature drop too much between batches, until they are golden brown in color and are no longer bubbling, 4 to 5 minutes. (If they're still bubbling, it means they still have water content that is cooking out.)

Using a spider/skimmer, transfer the cooked mushrooms to a bowl and immediately season to taste with maple sugar and smoked salt.

As with most fried things, the bacon is best when quite fresh, but will hold in an airtight container at room temperature for a day.

beet soil

makes about 1½ cups (255 g)

3.5 ounces (95 g) shelled pistachios, toasted

4 ounces (115 g) dehydrated red beet pulp (dehydrated at 135°F/57°C) for 12 hours or overnight)

2 ounces (60 g) granulated sugar

½ teaspoon kosher salt

5 tablespoons extra-virgin olive oil

These dehydrated beet solids can be ground in a food processor, but I prefer the texture you get from a mortar and pestle. The addition of olive oil changes the color from reddish maroon to a brown, and the green bits of pulverized pistachio make it really look like soil. In addition to the Beets & Berries (page 81), beet soil is also great sprinkled over ice cream that's been drizzled with Beet Molasses (page 266).

Grind the toasted pistachios in a mortar and pestle until it looks somewhat like dirt with bits of minerals mixed in. The result should not be a uniform powder, but, rather, chunks of various sizes. Set aside.

Place the beet pulp in a mortar and pestle or grind in a food processor (a blender will make it much too fine) and process until it is fairly broken down. There should not be any big pieces of beet pulp. A lot of the pulp will turn into a powder, which is fine.

Transfer the pulp to a bowl and fold in the ground pistachios, sugar, and salt. Using your hands (wear gloves so as not to stain your hands), mix the ingredients thoroughly. (You want to use your hands to make sure that there are no clumps, which would throw off the ratio.) Slowly, and in stages, gradually add the olive oil and work it into the mixture. Use less than you need to start, as you can always add more, but removing it is difficult. Work it into your palms and between your fingers. You want it to crumble without getting clumpy; it should be the texture of healthy soil. The color will change from purple burgundy to a dark color of dirt. Keep agitating it with your fingers, so that the oil is evenly dispersed. You need to add enough oil so that the beet soil is not powdery and tastes luxurious, sweet, and nutty. Just don't add too much oil, which will give you a texture like wet sand. (If you do add too much oil, lay the soil between layers of paper towels to absorb the excess oil. Repeat the process until enough of the excess oil has been absorbed, but try to avoid this, as it is a long and annoying process.) Store in an airtight container at room temperature for up to 1 month.

garlic powder

makes about ½ cup (72 g)

2 cups (200 g) sliced garlic cloves, germ intact

Yes, you can easily buy this seasoning, but there is something about edible powder made in a giant industrial factory that makes me decidedly uncomfortable. Also: if you buy really good garlic, guess what? It makes really good garlic powder.

Arrange the garlic in a single layer on a dehydrator tray and dehydrate at 135°F (57°C) for 48 hours, until completely dry. Grind in batches in your spice grinder until you have a fine powder. Store in an airtight container at room temperature for up to 3 months.

fermented

12 heads of garlic

black garlic

Black garlic became one of the "in" ingredients of the early 2000s. At first, it was only available at Asian markets, but after that it got a lot more popular—and expensive. The black color is striking, and it is a unique ingredient that tastes a lot like Worcestershire sauce.

Black garlic pairs well with asparagus (as in the Asparagus Vichyssoise, Black Garlic Mustard & Potato, page 64). You can also serve the peeled cloves whole, or as a purée (see below). It also works great in a stir-fry, where it almost acts like a fermented bean paste. If you plan on making it yourself, keep in mind that it takes about two weeks to fully ferment.

Place the garlic heads in a rice cooker. Turn the heat setting to "warm" and leave the rice cooker on for 12 to 14 days. Be sure to open the rice cooker every day for about 15 minutes to let out any accumulated steam.

When fully fermented, the garlic should be black all the way through. Let it cool down on a baking sheet until it reaches room temperature. Transfer to an airtight container and store in a cool, dry place—or refrigerated—for up to 6 months.

makes ¾ cup (180 ml)

1 cup (175 g) Black Garlic (page 295), peeled

2 teaspoons extra-virgin olive oil

black garlic purée

This is nice way of opening up the black garlic flavor and turning it into a condiment. On its own, it can be served with things like roasted potatoes, but you can also add whatever additional flavors to it that you'd like, to make things like Black Garlic Mustard (page 296), or Black Garlic Aioli (page 59).

In a blender, combine the garlic, olive oil, and 1 tablespoon water and purée until completely smooth. Store in an airtight container in the refrigerator for up to 1 month.

¼ cup (60 ml) Black Garlic Purée
  (page 295)
¼ cup (60 ml) Whole-Grain Mustard
  (page 272)
2 tablespoons apple cider vinegar
kosher salt

black garlic mustard

I really like the pungent, acidic flavor that this brings to a dish, like with the Asparagus Vichyssoise, Black Garlic Mustard & Potato (page 64). But you could also use it on, say, a salad of cucumbers and shallots, for example.

In a bowl, whisk together the garlic purée, mustard, and vinegar until combined. Season to taste with salt. Store in an airtight container in the refrigerator for up to 1 month.

makes 3 cups (710 ml)

2 tablespoons glutinous rice powder
2 cups (200 g) *gochugaru* (Korean
  chili powder)
1 white onion, cut into 8 wedges
1 apple, peeled, cored, and roughly
  chopped
2-inch (5 cm) thumb of fresh ginger,
  peeled
3 garlic cloves, germ removed
3 tablespoons granulated sugar
2 tablespoons kosher salt
1 pound (455 g) ramp tops, washed

ramp kimchi

Ramps have a short season in the spring, so we stock up on ramp bulbs and pickle them. The result produces a lot of ramp greens, which have a tendency to deteriorate quickly, bruising and turning to mush. We use some of the tops for a mushroom barley stew, and then make kimchi with the rest. That way, we stop the time on them.

Ramp kimchi is great with an omelet or frittata, in a lettuce wrap with mushrooms, or with boiled potatoes and parsley. It's also great alongside sliced mushrooms that have been dredged in rice flour, fried until crispy, and tossed with cilantro (coriander) and lime juice. Right now I really love it as a garnish for Pappa al Pomodoro (page 247).

This recipe is adapted from one of my cooks, Jihee Kim. When I asked if we could try making it without fish sauce, I thought she was going to stab me. I'm glad she humored me though.

Ramp kimchi ferments for three to seven days—the longer it ferments, the funkier it gets.

You can also substitute any hearty green leaves for the ramps: kale, napa (Chinese) cabbage, collard greens, radish tops, and the like. I even did this with basil leaves once.

In a small pan, whisk together the rice powder and 2 cups (475 ml) water. Place the pan over medium heat and continue to whisk until mixture forms a paste, 3 to 5 minutes. Remove from the heat and cool to room temperature.

In a food processor, combine the *gochugaru*, onion, apple, ginger, garlic, sugar, and salt and process to a coarse paste. Transfer the paste to a large bowl. Add the cooled rice mixture to the paste and mix to combine thoroughly.

Put all of the ramp leaves in the bowl and mix until the leaves are thoroughly coated with the paste. Transfer the ramp leaves to mason jars or deli containers and tightly seal. Let the kimchi stand at room temperature, away from direct light, for 3 to 5 days, and up to 1 week. The ideal conditions would be something of a cellar-like environment. Open the containers once a day for 5 minutes to release any built-up CO_2. As it ferments, the kimchi will develop a stronger tang. Once the kimchi is fermented to your liking, move the containers to the fridge where they will hold for several months.

sauerkraut, rutabaga, or kohlrabi kraut

**makes 6 cups (1.5 liters) sauerkraut
or 4 cups (1 liter) rutabaga (swede)
or kohlrabi kraut**

5 pounds (2.25 kg) savoy cabbage,
    rutabaga (swede), or kohlrabi
3 ounces (85 g) fine sea salt

Kraut can be made with everything from cabbage to rutabaga (swede) or kohlrabi. I have not had good luck making a turnip kraut, because the texture tends to get a bit mushy. While cabbage kraut takes two to four weeks, rutabaga and kolhrabi kraut can be ready in as little as four to five days. You can use any of these krauts in pretty much the same way you would use traditional sauerkraut.

Cooked, kraut will retain some of its crunch but you can also eat it as is. While cabbage kraut can be sort of squeaky when you eat it raw, that does not happen with rutabaga or kohlrabi kraut. (For the record, I hate vegetables that squeak when I chew them.)

You can also make a combined rutabaga-kohlrabi kraut if you like.

If using cabbage, remove the outer leaves (reserve for other uses, like stuffed cabbage). Cut the cabbage into thin chiffonade. If using rutabaga or kohlrabi, cut them into matchsticks.

Place the vegetables in a large container and massage them thoroughly with the salt. Let them sit, uncovered, at room temperature for about 1 hour. Transfer to mason jars or deli containers, tightly seal, and set aside at room temperature.

The salt should make the vegetables release juices. If, after 12 hours, the vegetables are not completely submerged in liquid, you will have to add a salt-water solution—1 tablespoon of fine sea salt for every 1 cup (240 ml) water—until they are fully submerged.

Allow the kraut to ferment at room temperature, opening the jars once a day for 5 minutes to release the CO_2. The cabbage kraut will take somewhere between 2 and 4 weeks, depending on how tangy you like it. The rutabaga and kohlrabi kraut, meanwhile, will take anywhere from 4 days to 2 weeks.

Once the kraut has reached the desired amount of tang, transfer it to the fridge, where it will keep for up to 4 months.

NOTE   Cabbage leaves break down much more than root vegetables, hence the difference in yields.

nuts

bbq nuts

makes 2 cups (480 ml)

2 cups (240 g) raw peanuts
2 tablespoons extra-virgin olive oil
½ cup (55 g) BBQ Spice (page 261)

I love snacking on these nuts. They're heavily coated with spices—like a dry rub on BBQ. As with most good BBQ, it should be a little bit messy to eat.

Preheat the oven to 300°F (150°C/Gas 2).

Spread the peanuts on a baking sheet and roast, tossing them occasionally, until they are golden all the way through but not burned or bitter, about 20 minutes. (I prefer a more gradual toasting process, as it builds more consistent, even flavor.) Let the nuts cool to room temperature.

Toss the cooled peanuts with the olive oil until coated. Add the spice and toss to thoroughly coat. Eat immediately or store in an airtight container for up to 1 week at room temperature. As they settle or dry out, you may need to re-toss them and add a few drops of olive oil to help the seasoning adhere.

curry cashews

makes 3 cups (710 ml)

1 pound (455 g) raw cashews
1 to 2 tablespoons extra-virgin olive
   oil, plus more as needed
2 tablespoons granulated sugar
1 tablespoon Curry Spice (page 262)
½ tablespoon kosher salt

These cashews are great for snacking on their own, but I also love them on Bananas, Créme Fraîche, Honey & Curry Cashews (page 68).

Preheat the oven to 300°F (150°C/Gas 2).

Spread the cashews on a baking sheet and roast the nuts, tossing occasionally, until they are golden all the way through and not burned or bitter, about 20 minutes. Let the nuts cool to room temperature.

Toss the cooled cashews in a bowl with just enough olive oil to coat. Finish them up by tossing with the sugar, curry spice, and salt. Eat immediately or store in an airtight container for up to 1 week at room temperature. As they settle or dry out, you may need to re-toss them and add a few drops of olive oil to help the seasoning adhere.

frosted nuts

makes 3 cups (710 ml)

3 large egg whites

¾ cup (150 g) granulated sugar

2 teaspoons kosher salt, plus more
as needed

1 pound (455 g) raw nuts, such
as walnuts, almonds, pecans,
hazelnuts

This snack is inspired by the childhood joy of reaching with your hands into a box of Kellog's Frosted Flakes (Frosties) cereal. If you manage not to eat the entire batch right away, out of hand, you could also toss some into a salad for added crunch and sweetness, or use them in the Spiced Butternut Squash & Ricotta Mousse, Spiced Bread (page 228).

Preheat the oven to 300°F (150°C/Gas 2). Line an 18 x 13-inch (46 x 33 cm) baking sheet with a silicone baking mat (if you don't have a silicone mat, I would rather go straight onto the pan than use parchment, as the nuts will tend to stick to and rip the parchment).

In a large bowl, lightly whisk the egg whites (don't aerate, just make sure they are combined). Add the sugar and salt and whisk until the mixture is smooth.

Add the nuts, folding thoroughly until they are completely coated. Pour the mixture out onto the lined baking sheet. Pour in any remaining egg white liquid over the nuts and spread the nuts so that they fit in the pan in a single layer.

Roast the nuts, stirring every 5 minutes, until coated and dry—but not sticky, about 30 minutes. As they roast you will see the liquid beginning to thicken. Remove the pan from the oven and give everything a final stir. Taste and adjust the seasoning as desired.

Let the nuts cool in the pan to room temperature, then taste again and adjust seasoning if needed. Break the nuts up and store in an airtight container at room temperature for up to 1 week.

lavender almonds

makes 6 cups (1.4 liters)

2 pounds (910 g) Marcona almonds

¾ cup (150 g) granulated sugar

⅓ cup (80 ml) extra-virgin olive oil,
plus more as needed

1½ tablespoons ground dried food-
grade lavender

1 tablespoon plus 1 teaspoon
kosher salt

We grew a lot of lavender at Ubuntu and I was looking for ways to use it in the kitchen. Lavender kind of looks like rosemary, so this was my way to riff on that. The almonds are perfect for snacking, and also work well as an accompaniment to a cheese plate.

These nuts are also one of the most popular things I've ever created, but I'm especially partial to them as they led me directly to meeting my wife.

Preheat the oven to 300°F (150°C/Gas 2).

Spread the almonds on a baking sheet and roast, tossing them occasionally, until they are golden brown all the way through and not burned or bitter, about 20 minutes. Set the baking sheet aside and let the almonds cool completely.

Transfer the nuts to a big bowl and add the sugar, oil, lavender, and salt. Toss to make sure all the ingredients are evenly distributed throughout. Eat immediately or store in an airtight container for up to 1 week at room temperature. As they settle or dry out, you may need to re-toss them and add a few drops of olive oil to help the seasoning adhere.

3 ounces (85 g) raw pine nuts

½ cup (120 ml) whole (full fat) milk
  or soy milk

½ teaspoon kosher salt, plus more
  as needed

2 tablespoons extra-virgin olive oil

pine nut pudding

Pine nuts are one of the few nuts that will purée into something so smooth that it won't need to be strained. I use this pudding on our Brassicas a la Catalan (page 91). While pine nuts can be roasted a little darker than most nuts, try not to burn them, because they're expensive.

Preheat an oven to 300°F (150°C/Gas 2).

Spread the pine nuts in a baking sheet and roast, stirring occasionally, until intense golden brown in color and aromatic, about 20 minutes.

Meanwhile, in a pot with a metal bowl fitted snugly on top, bring a few inches of water to a simmer over low heat.

Transfer the toasted pine nuts to the bowl and add the milk and salt. Wrap the top of the bowl tightly with plastic wrap (clingfilm) and let the mixture steep over the simmering water for about 30 minutes.

Transfer the nut-milk mixture to a blender and start to purée. With the blender motor running, slowly pour in the olive oil in a steady stream. The pudding should have a mousse-like consistency; if it seems too stiff, add more olive oil. Taste and adjust seasoning, if needed.

Pour the pudding into a bowl and place plastic wrap directly over the surface. If the plastic does not have direct contact, the pudding will form a skin, which you don't want in a smooth purée like this. Set the pudding aside to cool to room temperature, then transfer to an airtight container and refrigerate for up to 3 to 5 days.

pickled

makes 3 cups (710 ml)

1 pound (455 g) green garlic or whole ramp bulbs

1 cup (240 ml) white wine vinegar

1 cup (200 g) granulated sugar

2½ tablespoons kosher salt

2 teaspoons yellow mustard seeds

1 teaspoon ground coriander

1 teaspoon freshly cracked black pepper

NOTE If you opt for using thinner early-season ramp bulbs, I prefer to pickle them whole, trimming just under where the greens begin. If they are larger, late-season ramps, you can thinly slice them, as I do with green garlic.

pickled green garlic/pickled ramps

Milder and more herbaceous than regular garlic, green garlic or ramps (when the latter are in season) are especially good picked and served with roasted or fried potatoes. It's also a tremendous addition to giblet gravy, potato salad, roasted mushrooms, or on grilled bread with some burrata. You might have noticed, but I like rather a lot of things on grilled bread with burrata.

for garlic

Trim any discolored tops from the garlic and thinly slice the bulbs.

for ramps

Cut off the greens and reserve for Ramp Kimchi (page 296). Leave the bulbs whole, but trim off the "beards."

Place the garlic/ramps in a heatproof nonreactive container.

In a saucepan, combine the vinegar, 1 cup (240 ml) water, the sugar, salt, mustard seeds, coriander, and pepper and bring to a simmer over medium-high heat. Remove the pickling solution from the heat and pour it over the garlic/ramps. Allow the garlic/ramps to cool to room temperature, cover, and refrigerate. The garlic/ramps are ready to eat after 3 days and will keep for up to 4 months refrigerated.

makes eight 1-quart (1 liter) jars

5 pounds (2.25 kg) kirby (pickling)
cucumbers (for slices) or mexican
sour gherkins (for small whole
pickles)

2 white onions, julienned

¼ cup (25 g) sliced garlic (germ
removed)

a handful of chopped fresh dill

2 quarts (about 2 liters) distilled
white vinegar

¼ cup (35 g) kosher salt

½ cup (100 g) granulated sugar

¼ cup (50 g) yellow mustard seeds

2 tablespoons freshly cracked black
pepper

NOTE   You can halve this recipe if
you like, but if I'm making pickles,
I'd rather make a big batch and have
them around for a while.

If you're making sliced pickles and
are in a rush, you can skip the ice
step, but it will give the pickles less
crunch. The ice step adds a few
hours of inactive cooking time.

dill pickles

Mexican sour gherkins have a relatively short season, so
you should get your hands on as many as you possibly can,
and pickle them. If you're lucky, they'll last you the whole
year. (Do not bother using these for something like a
relish—gherkins are precious little jewels that should not
be wasted.) When you don't have gherkins, use sliced Kirby
(pickling) cucumbers. Those are much more common and
also good.

for sliced pickles

Cut the Kirby cucumbers on a mandoline into slices ¼ inch (6 mm) thick. In a large
bowl, toss the slices with the salt until combined. Cover them with 3 to 4 quarts (3 to 4
liters) of ice (just enough to completely cover) and let sit for 3 hours. It will be mostly
melted by the end.

Drain the liquid and transfer the cucumbers to a nonreactive 12-quart (12-liter)
container (this could be a mixing bowl or even a large pot). Add the onions, garlic, and
dill and toss to combine.

In a large pot, combine the vinegar, 1 quart (950 ml) water, the sugar, mustard seeds,
and black pepper and bring to a simmer over medium-high heat. Once the sugar
has dissolved, pour the mixture over the cucumbers and let everything cool to room
temperature. Transfer the pickles and their pickling liquid to airtight containers, and
refrigerate for up to 3 months.

for whole gherkins

In a large nonreactive container, combine the Mexican sour gherkins, onions, garlic,
and dill, and toss to combine. Set aside.

Meanwhile, in a large pot, combine the vinegar, 1 quart (about 1 liter) water, the salt,
sugar, mustard seeds, and black pepper and bring to a simmer over medium-high heat.

Once the salt and sugar have dissolved, pour the mixture over the cucumbers and let
everything cool to room temperature. Transfer the pickles and their pickling liquid,
to jars, seal, and refrigerate. The pickles will keep for up to 4 months, refrigerated.

green tomato preserves

makes 4 cups (about 1 liter)

5 pounds (2.25 kg) green tomatoes, cored and chopped into ½-inch (1.25 cm) pieces

2 cups (440 g) dark brown sugar

2 cups (260 g) chopped red onion (½-inch/1 cm pieces)

2 cups (300 g) golden raisins (sultanas)

2 cups (475 ml) apple cider vinegar

2 tablespoons yellow mustard seeds

1 tablespoon fennel seeds

2 teaspoons chili flakes

2 teaspoons kosher salt

½ teaspoon ground allspice

6 cinnamon sticks (3 inches/7.5 cm long)

This sweet-tart condiment is great as a garnish on a cheese plate, an accoutrement to a Grilled Cheese Sandwich (page 9), with a crock of baked ricotta, or simply spooned on top of some bread. It prominently features in the Fried Green Tomatoes, Burrata & Green Tomato Preserves (page 244).

In a heavy-bottomed pot, combine the tomatoes, brown sugar, onion, raisins, vinegar, mustard seeds, fennel seeds, chili flakes, salt, allspice, and cinnamon sticks. Bring to a simmer over medium heat, stirring occasionally. Let the jam simmer, uncovered, until the mixture turns syrupy, 2 to 3 hours. Be careful not to overcook, or the jam will seize up like rock sugar. Remove from the heat and ladle into a storing container, or run the jam through a food mill if you want a smoother consistency. (If you are using a food mill, be sure to remove the cinnamon sticks prior to milling.) The preserves will keep for up to 1 month in an airtight container under refrigeration. Serve the jam either at room temperature or chilled.

mushroom conserva

makes 2 cups (480 ml)

1½ pounds (680 g) cremini (chestnut) mushrooms

1 teaspoon kosher salt

½ cup (120 ml) extra-virgin olive oil

½ cup (120 ml) brine from Pickled Green Garlic or Pickled Ramps (page 00) or white wine vinegar

1 tablespoon chopped fresh rosemary

A delicious, tart mushroom condiment that tastes good on basically everything. I like it in the Mushroom Conserva, Ricotta & Gochugaru (page 159); on toast with a poached egg; or even tossed with soba noodles.

In a bowl of water, quickly wash the mushrooms, agitating them with your hands and letting the dirt fall off. Drain the mushrooms and let them dry on towels for at least 15 minutes.

Transfer the mushrooms to a bowl, toss with the salt and let sit for 30 minutes (this will help pull the moisture out of the mushrooms once they start cooking).

In a medium saucepot, heat 2 tablespoons of the olive oil over medium heat. Add the mushrooms and cook until the mushrooms release liquid and it evaporates, 5 to 10 minutes.

Add the remaining 6 tablespoons olive oil, the brine, and rosemary. Bring to a boil, remove from the heat, cover, and let the mushrooms steep in the liquid for 20 minutes.

Transfer the conserva to a food processor and pulse it gently until a chunky, coarse paste forms.

Cool the conserva to room temperature, ladle into airtight containers, and refrigerate for up to 1 week.

makes a 1-pint (490 ml) jar

3 ounces (85 g) nasturtium pods
   (see Note)
4 sprigs fresh thyme
4 sprigs fresh tarragon
2 fresh bay leaves
1 clove garlic, smashed with the side
   of a knife
¾ cup (180 ml) white wine vinegar
3 tablespoons raw cane sugar
2 tablespoons kosher salt

NOTE   When choosing nasturtium
pods, what you want, ideally, are
the ones that grow together in
clusters, rather than the stand-alone
variety. The clustered ones are often
more tender, while the stand-alone
ones tend to not soften up. In my
experience, the best nasturtium
pods are not perfectly round, but
rather more oval.

nasturtium capers

The pods from these beautiful, edible flowers are
wonderful when brined like capers, but with a unique,
mustardy, spicy flavor.

Rinse and dry the nasturtium pods on towels. Pack the herbs, garlic, and nasturtium
pods into a 1-pint (475 ml) mason jar.

In a pot, combine the vinegar, 1 cup (240 ml) water, the sugar, and salt and bring to
a simmer. Remove the liquid from the heat and add it to the jar. Seal, cool to room
temperature, and store in the refrigerator for at least 1 month and up to 6 months.

makes 8 cups (about 2 liters)

3 pounds (1.4 kg) red onions,
   julienned or cut into half moons
3 cups (710 ml) white wine vinegar
3 cups (600 g) granulated sugar
2 tablespoons kosher salt

pickled red onion

Like quick-pickled peppers (page 307), these bright and
beautiful pickled onions are ready to eat right away. I like
them paired with cilantro (coriander), whether chopped
into a cucumber salad or served over grilled chicken.

Even after I've eaten all of the pickled onions, I like to save
the brine. Instead of throwing it away, use it in place of
regular vinegar for things like salad dressing. Just know
that it's a little sweeter and milder than straight vinegar, so
you may need to add a little bit of regular vinegar to the
dressing as well. Again, I hate throwing things away, so why
not try to find another use for the brine?

Tightly pack the onions into a heatproof nonreactive containers.

In a pot, combine the vinegar, 3 cups (710 ml) water, the sugar, and salt and bring to a
simmer over medium-high heat. Once the solids are completely dissolved, remove the
pot from the heat and immediately pour the liquid over the onions.

Cool the onions to room temperature, then cover and refrigerate for up to 3 months.

½ cup (65 g) kosher salt
¼ cup (50 g) granulated sugar
6 Meyer or regular lemons

preserved lemon

Preserved lemon is a quick way to add briny lemon flavor to a dish. A little bit goes a long way. Try adding some julienned rind on top of sliced cucumbers, or stirred into hummus. It is also great in Gold Beets, Nectarine, Hazelnut & Oregano (page 77).

In a bowl, combine the salt and sugar. Wash and thoroughly dry the lemons. Cut off just the very ends on both sides.

Set a lemon on its end and quarter it by making two vertical cuts almost to the other end, but leaving the lemon intact. (You want the salt and sugar to be able to penetrate the lemon, while keeping the 4 quarters wholly attached.)

Add the lemons to the bowl with the salt and sugar. Wearing latex gloves, massage the cure all over the outside and into the cuts of the lemons. Transfer the lemons, as well as any extra salt and sugar to a sterilized jar (sterilize in boiling water for 1 minute).

Seal the jar and leave at room temperature for about 1 month. Over time, the lemons will start to submerge in their own liquid. If they do not fully submerge after 3 days, you can add additional lemon juice to cover. Also, though rare, it is possible that they will turn moldy. If this happens, discard the lemons and try again.

Once the lemons are tender, refrigerate and store for up to 6 months.

To use, rinse the lemons in cool water and remove any seeds. Some people only use the rinds, but I find that the flesh works well, too.

makes 3 cups (710 ml)

1 pound (450 g) sweet peppers, seeded and sliced into rings
1 cup (240 ml) rice vinegar
½ cup (100 g) granulated sugar
2 tablespoons kosher salt
3 cloves garlic, germ intact, sliced

quick-pickled peppers

This pickle is ready to eat almost immediately. Like onions, they soften up easily and take on the flavors of the rice vinegar, sugar, and garlic. These peppers are good tossed with braised kale, chopped into potato salad, or served alongside roasted squash or scrambled eggs. You can use any type of pepper you like. Jalapeños work great if you want to make a spicy pickle.

Tightly pack the peppers and sliced garlic into heatproof nonreactive containers.

In a saucepan, combine the vinegar, ¾ cup (180 ml) water, the sugar, and salt and bring to a simmer over medium-high heat. Once the solids are completely dissolved, remove the pan from the heat and immediately pour the liquid over the peppers.

Cool the peppers to room temperature, then cover and refrigerate for up to 3 months.

NOTE   I always slice the peppers (or halve them if they're baby peppers), because if left whole, the flavors won't fully penetrate as quickly.

stocks, sauces & confits

makes 2½ pounds (1 kg) roasted peppers and about 1 cup (240 ml) pepper tears

5 pounds (2.25 kg) red bell peppers

roasted peppers and pepper tears

Pepper tears are the natural, fairly viscous juices that leach from roasted peppers. The pepper tears are thicker than just water, and taste strongly of the peppers, but with some smoke from the charring process. I use these in a lot of ways: as an element in different layered sauces, as a broth for a brassica salad, and as a component in red-eye gravy.

Some people like to use oil before they char the peppers, but I do not, so that the pepper tears have a purer flavor. Do not peel the peppers under running water, or it will drastically dilute their flavor (while also making it impossible to collect all of the tears).

Char the peppers over an open flame—on a grill (barbecue) or directly over the gas burner on your stove—until they are blackened all over, using tongs to move them around.

Transfer the peppers to a bowl and cover with plastic wrap (clingfilm)—the steam will make the peppers easier to peel when cool.

Once the peppers are cool enough to handle, carefully peel, stem, and seed the peppers over a bowl, being careful to reserve all of the juices ("tears"). Discard the stems and seeds (and reserve the charred skins for Fig, Pepper Skin and Riesling Jam, page 268). Use immediately or refrigerate (in separate airtight containers) for up to 1 week.

corn cob stock

makes 2 quarts (about 2 liters)

8 corn cobs, cut into thirds
1 teaspoon kosher salt

This is a fast, flavorful stock that uses up leftover corn cobs, which can then be used in soups, chowders, and as the only liquid in my Vegan 4x Corn Polenta (page 117).

This recipe easily scales up or down—though don't add too much salt, as you can always add more later. Certain recipes in this book that call for the stock reduce it down, thus the small quantity of salt used in this base recipe.

In a medium stockpot, combine the cobs, salt, and 2 quarts (about 2 liters) water. Bring to a bare simmer over medium-high heat, then reduce the heat to low. Cover and keep just below a simmer for 1 hour 30 minutes.

Strain the stock through a fine-mesh sieve into airtight containers (discard the corn cobs). Refrigerate for up to 4 days or freeze for up to 3 months.

caramelized onion stock

makes 10 cups (2.4 liters)

5 pounds (2.25 kg) white onions, trimmed and peeled
1 tablespoon kosher salt

This stock is mostly hands off, as long as you don't care about your oven being occupied for two to three days. But this ultra-slow process of onion caramelization makes for an incredibly rich and complex flavor that simply can't be attained with a faster cooking method. It is an excellent base for French Onion Soup (page 180). It can also be used to glaze vegetables, or moonlight as cooking liquid for grains like farro, barley, or rice.

I recommend making this in the colder months, as it will help heat your house. If you do this in the hotter months, you'll wind up being really hot, or spending extra money on air conditioning.

Preheat the oven to 200°F (95°C). Place the onions in a large pot or a hotel pan along with the salt and add 10 cups (2.4 liters) water. Cover tightly with a lid or foil (a loose seal will result in evaporation) and set it in the oven for 2 to 3 days—until you have a flavorful stock with a deep brown color.

Strain the stock, pressing all the liquid out of the onions, and cool it to room temperature. Transfer to airtight containers and refrigerate for up to 10 days or freeze for up to 3 months.

mushroom stock

makes about 5 cups (1.2 liters)

5 pounds (2.25 kg) cremini
(chestnut) mushrooms, cleaned
and dried
1 tablespoon kosher salt
1 tablespoon grapeseed oil
4 garlic cloves, germ intact
4 celery stalks
1 medium white onion, chopped into
1-inch (2.5 cm) pieces
12 stems thyme
3 bay leaves

This stock works well as a base for my red-eye gravy (page 237) or mushroom Bordelaise (page 163); or as a component in Porcini Mushrooms en Papillote, Fondue of the Peels & Egg (page 166). One of my favorite tricks is to reduce mushroom stock, then cook fresh mushrooms in it, glazing as you go. The result is something that tastes hypernatural: a mushroom infused with the condensed flavor of itself (see King Trumpet Mushrooms, Potato Purée, Puntarelle & Bordelaise, page 163).

Preheat the oven to 350°F (180°C/Gas 4). Line a baking sheet with parchment paper.

In a bowl, toss the mushrooms with the salt and oil. Arrange on the lined baking sheet and roast until the mushrooms take on a nice color, about 20 minutes. Remove the mushrooms from the oven and transfer to a stockpot.

Add the garlic, celery, onion, thyme, bay leaves, and 6 cups (1.4 liters) water to the stockpot. Bring the liquid to a light simmer over medium heat. Simmer for 1 hour 30 minutes—anything longer will just be reducing without extracting any additional flavor. Strain the stock into a heatproof airtight container, and refrigerate for up to 10 days or freeze for up to 3 months.

pea shell stock

makes 1 quart (about 1 liter)

1 pound (455 g) shucked pea pods
(from about 2 pounds of whole
pods)
2 sprigs fresh spearmint
1 garlic clove, smashed, germ
removed
1 shallot, sliced

This is a gently cooked stock, made with pea pods, garlic, and mint. It's terrific in Asparagus Vichyssoise, Black Garlic Mustard & Potato (page 64); Smoked Split Pea Shell & Carrot Soup (page 200); and Peas, White Chocolate & Macadamia (page 193).

Wrap the pea pods, mint sprigs, garlic, and shallot in cheesecloth, then tie it up with twine into a bundle.

In a pot, combine 1 quart (about 1 liter) water and the sachet. Set the pot over low heat, but don't let the stock bubble or the drab color of the pods will start to bleed into the stock—you want to steep the sachet to create a clear broth.

After 2 hours, remove the sachet, allow it to drain back into the pot for a moment, then discard. Transfer the stock to an airtight container, cover, and refrigerate for up to 2 days or freeze for up to 2 months.

vegetable stock

makes about 2 quarts (2 liters)

2 cups (475 ml) white wine

3 carrots, washed thoroughly,
   roughly chopped

3 celery stalks, roughly chopped

2 white onions, roughly chopped

1 fennel bulb, roughly chopped

12 sprigs fresh thyme

3 bay leaves

1 tablespoon coriander seeds

1 tablespoon kosher salt

This is something of an all-purpose stock. You don't necessarily have to use these precise ingredients, and can use pretty much whatever you have on hand. To me, the main things to think about are flavor and color—you want this stock to be as clear as possible and have a neutral flavor. Avoid ingredients like onion skins, cabbage scraps, or any vegetable that might overpower your stock, like turnips or radishes.

In a stockpot, bring the white wine to a boil over medium-high heat. Let it boil for about 1 minute to cook out the alcohol. Add 3 quarts (2.8 liters) water, the carrots, celery, onions, fennel, thyme, bay leaves, coriander seeds, and salt. Bring to a boil, reduce the heat to low, and simmer gently, uncovered, for 1 hour 30 minutes (at which point, as with Mushroom Stock on page 311, you will have extracted all the flavor, so further simmering will just be reducing the liquid). Strain the stock (discard the solids) and cool it to room temperature. Ladle into airtight containers, cover, and refrigerate for up to 1 week.

garlic confit

makes 2 cups (480 ml)

1 pound (455 g) whole garlic cloves,
   peeled

4 sprigs thyme

1 teaspoon kosher salt

1 cup (240 ml) extra-virgin olive oil

1 cup (240 ml) grapeseed oil

Confiting is the process of slowly cooking something while it is submerged in fat. Duck confit is probably the most famous version of this method, and it is cooked in duck fat. Garlic confit is not cooked in garlic fat, because to my knowledge, garlic fat does not exist.

Confited ingredients are incredibly useful to keep in your larder. They add deep, slowly developed flavors to any dish, even if you don't have the time to slow-cook something. At Ubuntu, we'd often wind up with too many greens, so we would blanch and purée them with some of the confited garlic and its oil. The purée would look bright, fresh, and green, while also tasting of deep, slow cooking.

Preheat the oven to 250°F (120°C/Gas ½).

Place the garlic cloves in a pot or a baking dish with a lid. Add the thyme and salt and pour over the olive and grapeseed oils. Cover and transfer to the oven. Bake until the cloves are spreadable but not falling apart, 2 to 3 hours.

Let the garlic cool to room temperature. Store airtight in the refrigerator for up to 1 month.

garlic confit purée

makes 1½ cups (360 ml)

1 cup (240 ml) Garlic Confit (page 312)
1½ tablespoons apple cider vinegar
½ teaspoon kosher salt

Here is yet another of the many great things you can do with garlic confit. This purée has a garlicky, roasted flavor that functions as an excellent condiment for all sorts of things, like tomato salad or roast chicken.

In a blender, combine the garlic confit, vinegar, ½ cup (120 ml) water, and the salt and purée until smooth. Store in an airtight container in the refrigerator for up to 1 week.

shallot confit

makes 4 cups (about 1 liter)

1 pound (455 g) shallots, peeled
1½ cups (360 ml) grapeseed oil, plus more as needed
1 teaspoon kosher salt
2 fresh bay leaves

Shallot confit, because it is slightly sweeter and more neutral than Garlic Confit (page 312), is a bit more versatile. Garlic likes to show off—if you eat garlic, you're aware of its presence, whereas shallots are more subtle, and will enhance a dish without having to brag about it.

Preheat the oven to 250°F (120°C/Gas ½).

In a pan or baking dish, combine the shallots, oil, salt, and bay leaves—adding additional oil if the shallots are not fully submerged. Cover the dish and transfer to the oven. Bake until the shallots are spreadable but not falling apart, 3 to 4 hours.

Let cool to room temperature. Store in an airtight container in the refrigerator for up to 1 month.

makes 4 cups (about 1 liter)

8 ounces (225 g) finely diced fennel
bulb

2 cups (220 g) finely diced white
onions

1 cup (135 g) raw pine nuts

1 cup (240 ml) extra-virgin olive oil

1 teaspoon kosher salt, plus more as
needed

2 pounds (910 g) strawberries

cracked black pepper

NOTE Set aside around 6 hours to
cook this sofrito.

strawberry sofrito

This idea came about from my time at Manresa, where they
would make a strawberry gazpacho, replacing tomatoes
with strawberries. Eventually I discovered that if you cook
onions, pine nuts, fennel, and strawberries for a long time,
it will taste like short rib. This is great in dishes like Corn
Polenta, Curds, Whey & Strawberry Sofrito (page 113) and
Pane Frattau: Fennel, Strawberry Sofrito, Carta da Musica
& Egg (page 135). If you have old Focaccia (page 286) lying
around, you could use this sofrito to make crispy little
margherita pizzas. Strawberry sofrito also pairs well with
braised meats or just about any preparation of pork.

In a wide, heavy-bottomed pot, combine the fennel, onion, pine nuts, olive oil, and salt
and cook over low heat, stirring occasionally, until everything has a nice golden-brown
color, 2 to 3 hours. (The goal here is to slowly caramelize the fennel and onion evenly,
while also slow-toasting the pine nuts. You should really take your time here and not
rush it.)

Meanwhile, wash the strawberries. I like to submerge them in a bowl of water, agitating
them with my hands and letting all of the grime fall to the bottom.

Gently lift the strawberries from the water with your hands and let them dry on tea
towels. Once dry, hull the berries. Place them in a bowl and give them a rough crush
with your hands, like an Italian grandmother making tomato sauce.

Add the strawberries and any resulting juices to the pot of caramelized fennel, onion,
and pine nuts. Continue to cook over low heat until the sofrito is dark, jammy, and
savory, another 3 hours.

Season with additional salt if needed, then season to taste with pepper. (I like this
with a strong dose of black pepper.) Let cool to room temperature. Store airtight in the
refrigerator for up to 1 week.

makes 6 cups (1.4 liters)

5 pounds (2.25 kg) red tomatoes
  (I frequently use momotaro
  tomatoes, but any will do), cored
10 cloves Garlic Confit (page 311)
¼ cup (60 ml) oil from Garlic Confit
  (page 311)
40 sprigs thyme, tied with twine
¼ cup (20 g) chopped rosemary
kosher salt
freshly ground black pepper

tomato sauce

This will be your base tomato sauce for everything from lasagna to pasta with basil and olive oil. If fresh tomatoes are out of season, you can substitute good canned tomatoes (simply skip the part where you score, roast, and peel them).

Preheat the oven to 400°F (200°C/Gas 6). Line an 18 x 13-inch (46 x 33 cm) baking sheet with foil.

Place the tomatoes, cored-side down, on the baking sheet. Carve a little "x" into the top-facing side of the tomatoes, then roast them in the oven until you can easily and gently peel off the tomato skins with a pair of tweezers or a bird's beak knife, 12 to 15 minutes.

Transfer the tomatoes to a large pot. Add the garlic confit and oil, thyme, rosemary, and salt and pepper to taste. Bring to a gentle simmer over medium heat and, as it cooks, break up the sauce with a whisk. Continue to simmer the sauce, uncovered, until is reduced by about three-quarters of the original volume, about 2 hours. Remove the bundle of thyme sprigs and discard. Let cool to room temperature. Store in an airtight container in the refrigerator for up to 1 week.

index

Phaidon Press Limited
Regent's Wharf
All Saints Street
London N1 9PA

Phaidon Press Inc.
65 Bleecker Street
New York, NY 10012

phaidon.com

First published 2017
Reprinted 2017 (three times), 2018, 2019
© 2017 Phaidon Press Limited

ISBN 978 07148 7390 9

A CIP catalogue record for this book is
available from the British Library and the
Library of Congress.

Commissioning Editor: Emily Takoudes
Project Editor: Olga Massov
Production Controller: Nerissa Vales
Photography: Rick Poon
Design: Sanchez/Lacasta, project
 management by María Aguilera
Artwork: Ana Rita Teodoro

Printed in China

jeremy fox acknowledgments

I would like to acknowledge the following
people...

noah galuten: for being the mvp. I was
really pushing for the title Noah 2: The
Cookbook, but maybe next time. also,
noah thinks acknowledging him here is
unnecessary.

rick poon: for devoting so much time, skill,
and love to these photos.

emily takoudes: for believing in this book,
even before I did.

olga massov: for catching all my mistakes,
all the while convincing me I wasn't doing
a horrible job.

emilia terragni: for giving me this
opportunity way back in 2010.
better late than never.

josh loeb & zoe nathan: for providing
the home I needed.

brittany cassidy, andy doubrava & jun
tan: for keeping it all together at the
restaurants so I could focus on this book.
without the confidence y'all gave me,
I could not have done this.

kristyne starling: for making sure I made
it to the shrink for all of my appointments.

rachael & birdie: the loves and the ladies
in my life. without you two, none of this
would be possible.

-

The publisher would like to thank the
following people: Evelyn Battaglia,
João Mota, and Kate Slate.

Milk is always whole.
Cream is always heavy (double).
Eggs are always large (US)/medium (UK).
Herbs, unless indicated otherwise,
are always fresh, and parsley is always
 flat-leaf.
Butter is always unsalted.
Kosher salt is Diamond Crystal
(UK, please use coarse salt in its place).

Cooking and preparation times are for
guidance only, as individual ovens vary.
If using a fan (convection) oven, follow
the manufacturer's instructions concerning
oven temperatures.

Some of the recipes require advanced
techniques, specialist equipment,
and professional experience to achieve
good results.

To test whether your deep-frying oil is hot
enough, add a cube of stale bread. If it
browns in 30 seconds, the temperature
is [350–375°F/ 180–190°C], about right
for most frying. Exercise a high level of
caution when following recipes involving any
potentially hazardous activity, including the
use of high temperature and open flames.
In particular, when deep-frying, add the
food carefully to avoid splashing, wear long
sleeves, and never leave the pan unattended.

Some recipes include raw or very lightly
cooked eggs. These should be avoided
particularly by the elderly, infants,
pregnant women, convalescents, and
anyone with an impaired immune system.

Both metric and imperial measures are
used in this book. Follow one set of
measurements throughout, not a mixture,
as they are not interchangeable.

All spoon measurements are level.

When no quantity is specified, for
example of oils, salts, and herbs used
for finishing dishes, quantities are
discretionary and flexible.

Exercise caution when making fermente
products, ensuring all equipment is
spotlessly clean, and seek expert advic
if in any doubt.

All herbs, shoots, flowers, and leaves
should be picked fresh from a clean
source. Exercise caution when forag
for ingredients; any foraged ingredie
should only be eaten if an expert ha
deemed them safe to eat. Mushro
should be wiped clean.